RISKING
EVERYTHING

A solitary African American woman braves
hostile white onlookers to approach the Leflore
County courthouse in Greenwood, Mississippi.

RISKING EVERYTHING

A Freedom Summer Reader

Edited by **Michael Edmonds**

Wisconsin Historical Society Press

Published by the Wisconsin Historical Society Press
Publishers since 1855

Publication of this book was made possible in part by a grant from the Alice E. Smith fellowship fund.

The Wisconsin Historical Society is a not-for-profit state agency and all royalties from sales of *Risking Everything* will go toward further digitization of the Society's civil rights manuscripts.

wisconsinhistory.org

Photographs identified with WHi or WHS are from the Society's collections; address requests to reproduce these photos to the Visual Materials Archivist at the Wisconsin Historical Society, 816 State Street, Madison, WI 53706.

Cover photos: Greenwood, Mississippi, and Leflore County courthouse (top and bottom left), photographed by Ted Polumbaum, used by permission of the Newseum; Democratic National Convention 1964 and Greenwood Freedom Day, July 16, 1964 (bottom center and right), unidentified photographers; images from the archives of the Mississippi Freedom Democratic Party.

Previous page: unidentified photgrapher; image from the archives of the Mississippi Freedom Democratic Party.

The illustration credits are continued on page 230, which constitutes a continuation of this copyright page.

Printed in Canada
Designed by Diana Boger

18 17 16 15 14   1 2 3 4 5

Library of Congress Cataloging-in-Publication Data
Risking everything : a Freedom Summer reader / edited by Michael Edmonds.
      pages cm
  Includes bibliographical references and index.
     ISBN 978-0-87020-678-8 (paperback : alkaline paper)—ISBN 978-0-87020-679-5 (ebook)
1. Mississippi Freedom Project—Archives. 2. African Americans—Civil rights—Mississippi—History—20th century—Sources. 3. Civil rights movements—Mississippi—History—20th century—Sources. 4. African American civil rights workers—Mississippi—Biography. 5. Civil rights workers—Mississippi—Biography. 6. Mississippi—Race relations—History—20th century—Sources. 7. Wisconsin Historical Society—Archives. I. Edmonds, Michael, 1952–
  E185.93.M6R57 2014
  323.1196'0730762—dc23
    2014002221

∞ The paper used in this publication meets the minimum requirements of the American National Standard for Information Sciences—Permanence of Paper for Printed Library Materials, ANSI Z39.48-1992.

This volume is dedicated
to the thousands of brave citizens
who risked everything to create an America
that lived up to their dreams.

CONTENTS

1 BEFORE FREEDOM SUMMER

2 DEBATES, PREPARATIONS, TRAINING

3 OPPOSITION AND VIOLENCE

Supporters of the Mississippi Freedom Democratic Party protest on the Atlantic City boardwalk outside of the Democratic National Convention in August 1964. Their signs show images of murdered Freedom Summer workers James Chaney (left) and Andrew Goodman (right).

INTRODUCTION

Mississippi is the stronghold of the whole vicious system of segregation. If we can crack Mississippi, we will likely be able to crack the system in the rest of the country.[1]

—*SNCC chairman John Lewis, July 1964*

A delightful young man walked into my office recently and asked to volunteer. He'd just finished high school in a comfortable suburb and seemed eager, good-natured, and competent. I assigned him to digitizing civil rights manuscripts and suggested he begin by watching the Freedom Summer episode of the PBS documentary *Eyes on the Prize*.

An hour later he was back in my office, stunned.

"I had no idea it was like that," he said, despite having spent more than a decade in well-funded public schools.

Like most Americans today, he'd acquired what Bob Moses once called a children's book understanding of the civil rights movement. According to this sanitized version, a few charismatic leaders organized huge demonstrations that pressured Washington to change the laws. After that, black people didn't have to sit at the back of the bus. Everything was fine. We even elected a black president.

This book tries to rectify that oversimplification.

If you're under fifty, you can't remember when the government deliberately sponsored racism and enforced segregation. But until the mid-1960s, laws in many states separated black citizens from whites in neighborhoods, workplaces, churches, schools, stores, restaurants, and other public places. Government and business leaders made sure that the African Americans had the dirtiest jobs, lowest wages, poorest services, worst health care, and hardest lives.

---

1   Atwater, James. "If We Can Crack Mississippi." *Saturday Evening Post* (July 25, 1964): 19.

In Mississippi in 1960, 42 percent of citizens were black. Most of them lived in poverty, indebted to white banks or plantation owners. From the governor's office to the pulpit, in the classroom and the media, virtually every authority figure insisted that black people were dangerously inferior to whites and had to be kept in submission. After decades of this indoctrination, most whites believed in the necessity of segregation. Most blacks, constrained inwardly by the ceaseless message that they were second-class citizens and checked outwardly by institutional racism, limited their hopes and dreams. Those who dared to challenge the system were routinely fired from their jobs, evicted from their homes, beaten, jailed, tortured, and even murdered.

When the federal government in Washington passed laws prohibiting segregation, Southern states fought them all the way to the Supreme Court. When the court upheld the laws, local police simply ignored them. Federal officials did little or nothing to protect civil rights on the streets of the South, claiming that law enforcement was a matter for local authorities. Most Northerners, when they thought about segregation at all, viewed it as a Southern problem that didn't concern them.

By 1963, civil rights leaders had concluded that direct action would not succeed in Mississippi. Over the previous decade, courageous local NAACP leaders had tried to fight segregation in isolated cities and towns. Several, like Lamar Smith, Herbert Lee, and Medgar Evers, had paid for it with their lives. Nonviolent sit-ins and demonstrations that worked elsewhere had been met in Mississippi with firebombings, beatings, and assassinations. Leaders of the Student Nonviolent Coordinating Committee (SNCC) concluded that the entire power structure had to be overturned, and the ballot box was the best way to do it. If black residents could vote, they would choose mayors, sheriffs, city councils, and school boards that served rather than oppressed them. To test this assumption, they organized an unofficial "Freedom Vote" during the gubernatorial election of November 1963. More than 80,000 black Mississippians braved intimidation and harassment to cast symbolic ballots.

A mock election was one thing; real political power was something else. "Sure," a white Southerner told a visitor, "I reckon it's all right for a nigger to vote if he wants to and it don't harm nothing, but what if they all begun to vote here! We'd be swamped. You put yourself in <u>our</u> place and you'll see why we got to keep <u>them</u> in their places."[2]

---

2   Quoted in *Barnard Bulletin*, March 16, 1964; clipping in Robert and Vicki Gabriner papers, 1964–1966 (SC 1203) at the Wisconsin Historical Society.

For decades Mississippi authorities used literacy tests, poll taxes, economic reprisals, and terror to keep African Americans from voting. In 1963, more than 90 percent of the state's eligible black residents could not vote. Even in counties where blacks were a majority of the population, just a handful were registered to vote. In some counties, no African Americans were registered at all.

After much discussion and debate during the winter of 1963–64, SNCC decided to organize a large-scale voter registration drive the following summer, using hundreds of Northern volunteers. Other civil rights groups joined in, and leaders began planning the Mississippi Summer Project, as it was called at the time.

Enrolling new voters was a principal goal of the 1964 Freedom Summer project. Its leaders knew, however, that it wouldn't succeed. Most black residents would be too intimidated to try to register, and most of those who did try would be turned away at county courthouses. But by documenting this illegal treatment, organizers expected to gather massive amounts of evidence for federal lawsuits. And if they could ignite a grassroots voter registration movement, they might replace generations of fear and apathy with newfound pride and hope.

Another goal of the project was to start "Freedom Schools" that would encourage young people to think critically about their lives and overcome white-supremacist indoctrination. A third was to open community centers where medical help, child care, and other basic services denied to poverty-stricken black neighborhoods could be provided.

Perhaps the most ambitious goal of Freedom Summer was to create a new political party, the Mississippi Freedom Democratic Party. Leaders hoped that tens of thousands of the state's African Americans would join the MFDP and vote in another parallel "Freedom Election" in November 1964. They also planned to challenge the state's segregationist representatives to the Democratic National Convention in Atlantic City in August 1964 and contest Mississippi's incumbent white congressmen in January 1965. Both legal challenges would argue that the all-white Mississippi delegations should be denied seats because 42 percent of the electorate had not been allowed to participate.

Bob Moses and Dave Dennis ran the 1964 Freedom Summer project. They'd fought for voter rights and desegregation with SNCC and CORE (the Congress of Racial Equality) since the beginning of the decade. They'd been beaten, shot at, and jailed, and were well respected in African American communities.

On paper, Freedom Summer staff worked for the Council of Federated Organizations (COFO), an umbrella group including not just SNCC and CORE but also the National Association for the Advancement of Colored People (NAACP) and Martin Luther King's Southern Christian Leadership Conference (SCLC). In practice, SNCC provided about 80 percent of the people and resources for Freedom Summer, CORE contributed about 20 percent, and the other two partners mainly watched from the sidelines.

About 120 SNCC and CORE veterans were paid ten dollars a week to run offices in thirty-three cities and towns (see map, page xviii). Roughly one thousand college students, mostly white Northerners, volunteered to come to Mississippi and work with them. Also volunteering that summer were 254 clergy, 169 attorneys, and 50 doctors and nurses. More than sixty thousand black Mississippians attended mass meetings, picketed, and voted in the Freedom Election that fall. Several hundred of them risked their lives by letting Northern volunteers live in their homes for the summer.

During the spring of 1964, SNCC recruiters visited campuses around the nation enlisting volunteers. Other staff lined up places for them to live and offices for them to work in. A curriculum team prepared Freedom School materials, and a legal team marshaled defense attorneys. Political staff laid the groundwork for the MFDP.

From June 15 to 28, 1964, the National Council of Churches sponsored two week-long training sessions for volunteers at Western College for Women in Oxford, Ohio. Recruits were given background on Mississippi life, shown methods of nonviolent resistance, counseled on personal safety and security, and instructed how to teach in Freedom Schools or canvass voters door to door. Then they packed into cars and buses, drove all night, and spread out across Mississippi.

Mississippi's leaders had followed the planning for Freedom Summer in the press and banded together to defeat it. During the spring, the state police nearly doubled in size, legislators passed new laws prohibiting picketing and leafleting, and local police acquired new weapons. The city of Jackson even bought a tank. Businessmen joined together in white "Citizens' Councils" to coordinate economic reprisals against African American supporters of the summer project. Ku Klux Klan membership skyrocketed as the group prepared to wage war on "uppity" blacks and "invading" outside agitators.

These opponents attacked Freedom Summer workers as soon as they arrived. Three CORE workers—James Chaney, Mickey Schwerner, and Andrew Goodman—were killed on June 21, 1964, the project's first day.

Greenwood, Mississippi, police drag away an unidentified African American woman who resists nonviolently.

Over the course of the summer, there were at least six murders, twenty-nine shootings, fifty firebombings, more than sixty beatings, and over four hundred arrests of nonviolent civil rights workers. The violence sobered but did not deter the project's staff and volunteers.

A convention to form the Mississippi Freedom Democratic Party was held in Jackson on April 26, and the MFDP sent sixty-eight delegates to the Democratic National Convention in August. After an emotional appeal to the party's Credentials Committee that was broadcast on national television, the MFDP delegates were spurned by national party leaders and denied the right to attend the convention. In the fall elections three months later, Freedom Voters outnumbered regular Democratic Party voters everywhere the two faced off. But their legal challenge to white incumbents was rejected in Washington, and white supremacists took Mississippi's seats in Congress.

By the fall of 1964, the organizers of Freedom Summer were exhausted and demoralized. Only one goal of Freedom Summer seemed to have been reached: more than forty Freedom Schools had opened in twenty communities, and nearly 3,000 students took classes from 175 teachers. But leaders of the summer project had failed to achieve their short-term objectives, six of their friends were dead, hundreds of others had been hurt, and segregation was still as deeply entrenched in Mississippi as ever.

Many of the Freedom Summer organizers lost faith in nonviolence and mainstream politics. After enduring brutality from the Klan, harassment by police, foot-dragging by federal officials, and betrayal by white liberals, many of the Freedom Summer organizers decided that black Americans had to seize their rights themselves, by any means necessary. Over the next two years, SNCC would eject its white members, remove the word "nonviolent" from its name, and become a major force in the Black Power movement.

But Freedom Summer had actually accomplished more than its leaders could appreciate at the time. It had awakened sleeping giants. First, tens of thousands of Mississippi's black residents had transcended their fears, joined together, and stood up to their oppressors. They would no longer be cowed into submission. And across the rest of the nation, media coverage of racist savagery had appalled mainstream Americans.

Millions had watched on television when Fannie Lou Hamer detailed her torture by police and then asked, with tears streaming down her face, "Is this America, the land of the free and the home of the brave?" They contacted their elected representatives and, after media coverage of even more brutality in Selma, Alabama, the next year, Congress passed the 1965 Voting Rights Act. The system, as SNCC chairman John Lewis hoped, had been cracked.

The 1965 Voting Rights Act gave federal registrars the power to enter local courthouses and register voters wherever rights were being denied. Within six weeks of its passage, more than forty thousand new black voters had registered in Mississippi. Within eighteen months, more than half of eligible African Americans in the South had joined the voting rolls. Soon, hundreds were elected to local offices such as mayor, school board, and sheriff.

After Freedom Summer, many SNCC and CORE staff went on to important careers in public service. John Lewis was elected to the US Congress, where he still serves. Julian Bond won several terms in the Georgia legislature before heading the NAACP. Marion Barry became mayor of the nation's capital. SNCC's Mary King ran the Peace Corps and VISTA. Other staff became influential professors, attorneys, and civil servants.

Many Northern volunteers went on to lead or contribute to the antiwar, draft resistance, women's liberation, farm workers' rights, and gay rights movements. Voter registration worker Mario Savio started the Berkeley Free Speech Movement. Casey Hayden and Mary King's 1964 SNCC paper, "The Position of Women in the Movement," helped spark second-wave feminism. Freedom School teacher Chude Allen organized early women's liberation groups in New York and San Francisco. Elizabeth Sutherland ("Betita") Martinez became a leading Chicana feminist. Barney Frank, who had worked in the COFO office in Jackson, became one of the nation's first openly gay legislators. Many others devoted their careers to legal or social services for the poor and disadvantaged.

As the decades passed, however, the true history of Freedom Summer was lost. The 1988 film *Mississippi Burning* taught millions of viewers that the FBI was the summer's hero and local black residents were just minor characters. Julian Bond joked that most Americans seemed to reduce the civil rights movement to "Rosa [Parks] sat down, Martin [Luther King] stood up, and the white kids came down and saved the day."[3]

The truth was utterly different. The struggle in the Deep South was never about where people sat on a bus. It was about the brutal exploitation of one half of the population by the other half. To overturn that system, thousands of African Americans across the South had to question everything they'd been taught, conquer their fears, and put their bodies in front of shotguns and firebombs.

For many of them that transformation began when young CORE or SNCC workers arrived in town and risked their lives to teach voter registration classes or start a Freedom School. The catalyst for this revolutionary shift in people's beliefs, desires, and values was not huge national organizations holding marches or arguing court cases but rather, in Bob Moses's words, "a few people willing to risk everything."[4]

In this book you'll hear those people's voices, read their letters, eavesdrop on their meetings, shudder at their fears, and admire their courage. No punches are pulled. Sensitive readers should be prepared to encounter offensive racism, graphic violence, and other disturbing content. Louis Lomax's account of the murders of three volunteers, for example, with its gruesome conclusion, may not be suitable for young readers. All of the documents are from collections in the archives of the Wisconsin Historical Society.

The selection of documents goes beyond the standard, frequently cited sources to feature equally powerful little-known ones. The ratio of male and female authors reflects that of Freedom Summer participants and most chapters represent local residents, paid staff, and volunteers. The Afterword explains where the documents came from, and how they came to be in a collection in the Midwest.

If you're a student, consider that many of the people speaking from these pages were barely out of their teens when they risked everything to overturn injustice. And if you're under fifty and learned that the civil rights movement was mainly about big names and bus seats, you'll appreciate the comprehensive grassroots change that transformed Mississippi and the nation in 1964.

---

3   Quoted in Hogan, Wesley. *Many Minds, One Heart: SNCC's Dream for a New America* (Chapel Hill: University of North Carolina Press, 2007): 226.

4   Obituary of Mendy Samstein, *New York Times*, January 25, 2007.

Map of Office Locations during Freedom Summer

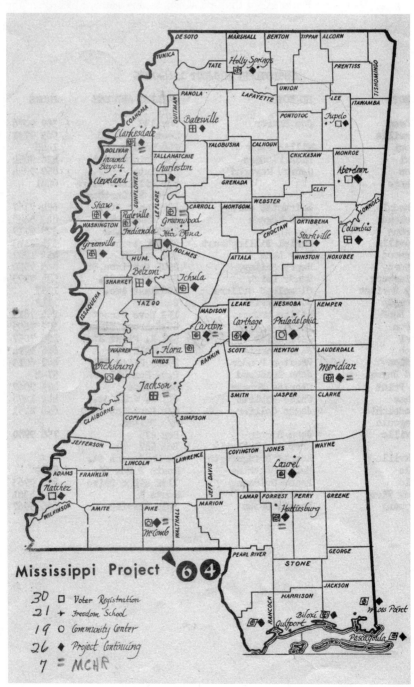

Abbreviations

COFO   Council of Federated Organizations

CORE   Congress of Racial Equality

DNC   Democratic National Convention

JFK   President John F. Kennedy

KKK   Ku Klux Klan

LBJ   President Lyndon B. Johnson

MFDP   Mississippi Freedom Democratic Party

NAACP   National Association for the Advancement of Colored People

NCC   National Council of Churches

SCLC   Southern Christian Leadership Council

SNCC   Student Nonviolent Coordinating Committee

WATS   Wide Area Telephone Service

A man and a woman pick cotton on a Mississippi plantation in 1964. At the time, two-thirds of black Mississippians worked as field hands or maids.

1
BEFORE FREEDOM SUMMER

Segregated Mississippi has been compared to feudal Europe, Nazi Germany, and the Soviet Union, all societies in which a privileged elite controlled everyone else through laws, money, media, and violence. Overturning segregation required confronting those forces not only in the courts and at the ballot box, but also inside the hearts and minds of millions of people.

It's hard for Americans who never experienced segregation to imagine it. This chapter opens with Jerry DeMuth's 1964 "A Guide to Mississippi," written to explain that world to outsiders. (With the passage of time, nearly all of us are outsiders today.) The next article, M. W. Newman's "Rugged, Ragged 'Snick,'" describes the young people who composed the shock troops of the civil rights movement. The people Newman depicts will appear frequently throughout the book.

The next piece, a short legal deposition by Fannie Lou Hamer, recounts in her own words what happened when black Mississippians resisted the status quo by protesting segregation or trying to register to vote. The final two documents, a short press biography of SNCC's Bob Moses and rough, unsigned notes for a biography of CORE's Dave Dennis, shed light on the two people who coordinated the work of 1,500 staff and volunteers during Freedom Summer.

"A Guide to Mississippi," Spring 1964

> *Freelance journalist Jerry DeMuth wrote many articles about the movement in the mid-1960s while volunteering with the American Friends Service Committee and working for SNCC. His articles appeared in* The Nation, The New Republic, *and other national magazines. This essay has never before been published.*

"The only real and truly white state left in this nation is ours," Mississippi Governor Paul B. Johnson exclaimed last December [1963], one month after his election.

And indeed it is. Every bit of energy in the state—except for an alliance of civil rights groups in Jackson called COFO (Council of Federated Organizations)—is devoted to not only keeping Mississippi a "white state," but to strengthening the forces of segregation and white supremacy.

Because of this, Mississippi is a unique entity, a "sovereign state" which tries to ignore the rest of the country, but does not refuse benefits from Washington. An area which has the same phases of life as the other 49 states, but which has twisted them into something that Mississippians in power may relish, but would make others reel back in abhorrence. One idea weaves through everything: white-only.

Other states have churches, maybe even a few with odd philosophies. But only one philosophy is prevalent in Mississippi churches: segregation.

Early last year, John Satterfield, a Yazoo City attorney who was lay leader of the Mississippi delegation to the General Conference of the Methodist Church in Pittsburgh, declared, "We can support the church as long as the segregated system is maintained."

Speaking before the same group, Dr. Medford Evans warned, "The Methodist Church has drifted into an extremely dangerous devotion to racial integration and nuclear disarmament. Integrationists are victims of an emotional disorder and live in a world of fantasy." In his world, Evans serves as co-ordinator of the John Birch Society, secretary of the States' Rights Party of Louisiana, consultant to the White Citizens' Council, and a member of the Citizens' Council in at least seven states, and father of M. Stanton Evans, editor of the *Indianapolis News*.

The group Satterfield and Evans were appearing before was the Mississippi Association of Methodist Ministers and Laymen. MAMML was "organized in 1951 as an unofficial group of Methodists," it says of itself, "whose aim is to rid the churches of socialistic-Marxist material in its literature and publications and to maintain segregation."

The president of MAMML is Garner M. Lester, who also keeps busy as a watchdog over Mississippi's way of life as chairman of the public affairs committee of the Jackson Citizens' Council and as a member of the advisory board of Mississippi's largest bank. Secretary-treasurer of the Methodist group is John R. Wright, who is also chairman of the membership and finance committee of the Jackson Citizens' Council and a colonel for Gov. Paul Johnson.

When 28 Methodist ministers, all native Mississippians, said they were opposed to segregation because "Jesus Christ teaches that all men are brothers," MAMML, ever watchful for such unchristian moves, said their statement does not accurately reflect the wishes of the majority of Mississippi's Methodists. MAMML also declared that integration was "a crime against God."

More recently, MAMML attacked a religious group for "giving aid and comfort to race-mixers in the Methodist Church."

Since MAMML's conception, close to a hundred seminary-trained Methodist ministers have been driven from the state because of their views.

But the Baptists aren't pure either. Last April, Rev. Paul Jackson, speaking before the American Council of Churches convening in Jackson, explained, "The Southern Baptist Convention is past the point of no return on its drift toward liberalism."

Mississippi Baptists will obviously have no part of such liberalism. In fact, last year in annual session, the Mississippi Baptist Convention refused to endorse a resolution which reaffirmed "our intelligent good will toward all men" and which called upon Christians to pray "that we may live consistent with Christian citizenship."

The non-recognition by Mississippi of churches outside the state was further exemplified when, last spring, an interracial group of seven ministers from out of the state were arrested when they tried to worship at a Methodist Church in Jackson. The ministers were charged with disturbing public worship and trespassing on church property.

When all hope is lost, as happened last spring with a group of Episcopalians, Mississippians can always start their own church. Paul J. Brannan, senior warden of the group said they would have "no affiliation with the National or World Council of Churches, will use the King James translation of the Bible and the [Episcopal] Book of Common Prayer, and will repudiate current trends of the Episcopal clergy toward socialism and integration of the races."

Besides being spiritually committed to segregation, Mississippians must also be mentally committed to it—which means they must have the right education; and no education is better than the wrong education. The "wrong education" is what the United States Supreme Court demanded in 1954, and Mississippi reacted by abolishing its compulsory school attendance law and making it mandatory that schools be closed rather than integrated. The state also passed a law providing for a fine or a jail sentence for any white person attending a school also attended by Negroes and passed another law calling on all elected officials to preserve segregation.

James Meredith is the only real stain on the state's lily-white schools. But Mississippi officials certainly tried to keep him out of Ole Miss. A month before the bloody riot, state senator E. K. Collins stood in the upper house and proclaimed, "We must win this fight regardless of the cost in time, effort, money and in human lives."

And the cost even included human lives. But only in Mississippi will Americans learn that it was the federal marshals who shot and killed that French newsman so that Europe wouldn't find out the truth about what was going on in Mississippi.

But if one knew about Negroes what Mississippians know, one might not want to go to school with them either.

According to Gov. Paul Johnson, African Negroes "sit around sharpening their teeth on rocks to tear human flesh."

And a Mississippi newspaper recently told its readers that Africans "have just quit eating one another and have just started wearing clothes."

Early this year state senator Corbett Patridge explained, "It is not necessary to prejudge a Negro or for him to prejudge a white man. We both know that each exists and that we each have a line of thought. Mine is to work and build for the future. His is to work and enjoy the fruits of his labor and to make every Saturday night Christmas eve."

This is why former Gov. Ross Barnett said that segregation is needed "to avoid mongrelization and to maintain the purity and the integrity of both races."

So that no one disrupts the stability of this segregated society, the state carefully selects textbooks to use in public schools. But still these don't tell the right story—outsiders just don't seem to be able to do anything right—so the Citizens' Council prepared its own readers. The reader for third and fourth grades explained:

> God wanted the white people to live alone. And he wanted colored people to live alone. The white men built America for you. White people built America so they could make the rules. George Washington was a brave and honest white man. The white men cut away big forests. The white man has always been kind to the Negro. We do not believe that God wants us to live together. Negro people like to live by themselves. Negroes use their own bathrooms. They do not use white people's bathrooms. The Negro has his own part of town to live in. This is called our Southern Way of Life. Do you know that some people want the Negroes to live with white people? These people want us to be unhappy. They say we must go to school together. They say we must swim together and use the bathroom together. God has made us different. And God knows best. Did you know that our country will grow weak if we mix the races? White men worked hard to build our country. We want to keep it strong and free.

And from the fifth and sixth grade reader:

> The Southern white man has always helped the Negro whenever he could. Southerners were always their best friends. The South went to war to prevent the races from race-mixing. If God had wanted all men to be one color and to be alike, He would not have made the different races. One of the main lessons in the Old Testament of the Bible is that your race should be kept pure. God made different races and put them in different lands. He was satisfied with pure races so man should keep the races pure and be satisfied. BIRDS DO NOT MIX. CHICKENS DO NOT MIX. A friend had 100 white chickens and 100 reds. All the white chickens got to one side of the house, and all the red chickens got on the other side of the house. You probably feel the same way these chickens did whenever you are with people of a different race. God meant it to be that way.

But some Mississippians do not even want segregated Negroes. Last January [1964], Earnest Watson wrote in an editorial in the *Jackson Times*, "If the Negro wants to leave the South, that would be the best thing the South could have; then it would become a white man's paradise."

The Negroes that the state has the greatest desire to see leave are the "uppity" ones; if there's one thing the state doesn't want, it's "uppity" Negroes, or "uppity" whites for that matter.

"Over 98 percent of Mississippi's population are native born Americans with less than 2 percent being foreign born," the Area Development Department of Mississippi Power and Light Co. proudly explains. "These people are free thinkers and not easily steered to the 'left.' You will find no radical or 'ism' groups in the state."

The management of a new factory in Natchez observed: "They all seem to have the right attitude and are willing to learn and work with management 100 percent. They are 'All American' and this, I think, helps a lot."

However, some workers still get "un-American" ideas and try to form unions. But true Mississippians know how to handle them. For example, in August of last year, four days before an NLRB [National Labor Relations Board] election, a plant put up posters showing a Negro woman saying to a white woman: "Mr. Kennedy and the union man says we'uns must work with you'uns." The union lost the election.

Thus the Mississippi Agriculture and Industrial Board could report, "In the few elections held during the 1950–58 period, the union won relatively fewer elections and got relatively fewer votes than in elections held in other areas."

The state and local communities will go to any steps to bring industry to the state, even give them tax-free land, with a structure already built upon it. Bonds are then floated for the land and building. In one instance, a company bought the bonds themselves and made a profit.

A section of land along the Gulf Coast had been given to Mississippi by the federal government for the purpose of building schools on the property. But Mississippi is never one to be told what to do by the federal government, so in 1961 the Mississippi legislature and then Mississippi voters approved two constitutional amendments. The first changed the status of the land, the second exempted oil refineries from taxation. Standard Oil then built a refinery on the land.

Mississippi taxes its citizens, not its industries. Still, the Mississippi Agriculture and Industrial Board believes, "Mississippi has an enviable record for maintaining good government and paying for it through a fair and equitable tax system ably administered."

Mississippi gets over fifty percent of its revenue from the state sales tax of 3 percent. Towns levy an additional 0.5 to 1 percent. A drivers license costs $2 a year [$15 in 2014 dollars] and may be raised. Car owners have to pay an annual motor vehicle inspection charge plus ad valorem taxes, privilege taxes and municipal taxes, in addition to the cost of car tags which is figured on the basis of the car's value and engine size. Car tags for a new, medium-priced car cost about $80 [$594 in 2014 dollars]. And each time the driver purchases a gallon of gas, he pays 7 cents state tax and 1 cent sales tax in addition to 4 cents federal tax. [A 1964 penny is 7.73 cents in 2014.]

The state is also considering more unique ways of taxing its citizens. Last April, Rep. John Hough of Sunflower County introduced a bill to place a 10 percent tax on soft drinks and a 20 percent tax on soft drink syrup sales.

Another source of income for the state is a black market liquor tax which is collected by a governmental department. Sen. Ellis Bodron of Vicksburg explains, "The legislature has refused to legalize whiskey and the people have refused to permit enforcement of the prohibition laws."

As a result, liquor is more common than beer which is only legal in some counties. Along the Gulf Coast beer is illegal, but stores, bars, restaurants all sell liquor openly.

An attempt to legalize liquor last spring failed. And the chance for legalization in the future is slim. When the wets can have their whiskey and the drys can have their prohibition laws, why should anyone want to change things?

A large percentage of additional funds comes from the federal government. For example, in the first nine months of 1963, Mississippi received from the federal government close to $200 million [$1.48 billion in 2014 dollars] for military and defense purposes alone.

Nevertheless, Mississippi feels it could live independent of the rest of the country, or live as part of an independent South. As Earnest Watson wrote in the *Jackson Times* last January: "If the remainder of the Nation wants to secede from the South, that also would be a windfall, whereby the South would rise to the occasion, put in its own factories, spend its money in the South, and become an economic paradise."

One federal program the state still participates in to some extent is urban renewal, but there's a reason.

Early in the year there was a discussion in the House on the pros and cons of urban renewal. Those opposed, claimed the program would further integration. Those supporting it claimed it could be used to maintain segregation.

"As freakish as it may sound," Mayor George Howell of Aberdeen explained, "we are using urban renewal to maintain segregation."

Senator J. P. Dean said his town, Corinth, would use urban renewal funds to relocate 82 Negro families "who live within a block of our white high school. We can move them near the Negro school and solve a potentially serious situation."

Enough said. Though the House passed a bill outlawing participation in urban renewal programs, it exempted Aberdeen, Corinth and two other towns who knew how to do things the Mississippi way.

Meanwhile in McComb, officials were devising their own "urban renewal" program. They began an attempt to de-annex a Negro section of the city.

If this and other political debates sound one-sided, it must be remembered that there is no opposition party in Mississippi.

Senator [James] Eastland [chairman of the US Senate Judiciary Committee] has admitted that he is "proud of the one-party system, because that one-party system was used to defeat the carpetbaggers and scalawags one hundred years ago and it still serves its purpose perfectly."

The Mississippi House of Representatives made this opinion formal in August, 1963, when they passed a resolution declaring: "We are unalterably opposed to the formation of a two-party system in Mississippi because of the division of the white qualified electors and the inherent danger of the minority block becoming the balance of power."

More honestly, a policeman in Ruleville told a campaign worker for a Negro candidate in early 1964, "We don't have no nigger politics in Ruleville."

Paul B. Johnson clearly explained the dangers. "The birth of a two-party system in the state," he warned, "would divide the conservative white vote. Then Mississippi would have to reap the whirlwind harvest of racial discord, more socialism, more taxes, more Negro participation in government and more integration."

Johnson and Carroll Gartin, candidate for lieutenant governor, issued a joint statement in October, 1963, detailing the situation Mississippi found itself in:

"Mississippi stands today as the only state in the American union whose public institutions are totally and completely segregated. The backbone of white control and constitutional, conservative government in our state has been and is the one party system. Under this system Mississippi has been able thus far to preserve our customs, traditions, and particular way of life here in the South.

"The creation and maintenance of a so-called two party system in Mississippi is the most deadly peril facing our people since Reconstruction. The end of the one party system in our state would foretell the abandonment of Mississippi's noble fight for the rights of the states, the integrity of its races, and constitutional government."

Mississippi Democrats go all out to destroy Republicans, and the means may be verbal . . . or legal . . . or illegal. Last March someone broke into the office of Stanford E. Morse [Jr.], Republican candidate for lieutenant governor in the 1963 general election. Only one thing was stolen from the office: a drawer containing records of persons who contributed to his campaign.

Official Paul Johnson campaign literature further explains the Mississippi political picture:

"To have Mississippi Democratic nominees and Republican nominees running for every public office every four years would constitute an unnecessary nuisance and would bring to Mississippi the same political evils and dangers that now beset such states as Illinois, New York, Michigan, Pennsylvania and California. . . . Mississippi has no need for a two party system that would divide our people and stretch our political campaigning over many additional months and resulting expense, confusion and disunity. . . . Both the National Republican Party and the National Democratic Party are the dedicated enemies of the people of Mississippi. . . . Both parties threaten our Mississippi traditions, institutions and segregated way of life. . . . The Mississippi Democratic party is not subservient to any national party. It has its own statement of principles and these are in direct conflict with the position of both national parties. . . . We do not have to belong to and participate in an integrated national party, which tolerates in its ranks radical leftists like Governor Nelson Rockefeller and Senator Jacob Javits of New York and 'Black Monday' Earl Warren, in order to cast Mississippi's electoral votes for a true conservative."

In 1960, all 8 unpledged Mississippi Democratic electors cast their votes for Sen. Harry F. Byrd of Virginia. [John F. Kennedy was the official nominee.]

In 1962 a resolution was entered in the [state] Senate titled, "A concurrent resolution declaring and recording the contempt of the Mississippi legislature for the Kennedy administration and its puppet courts; calling upon its sister states to join in ridding this once great nation of the Kennedy family dynasty and accompanying evils; and for related purposes."

More simply in 1963 the Magnolia State Quartet sang Paul Johnson's campaign song:

"Up there on the wide Potomac,
Kennedy Democrats done gone mad,
But so help me, I believe,
The GOP is just as bad."

The one party system continues to exist because Mississippi carefully controls those who vote.

Since 1954, voter applicants have been required by law to read, write and interpret any section of the state constitution.

"The amendment is intended solely to limit Negro registration," admitted Robert B. Patterson, executive secretary of the Association of Citizens' Councils.

Since 1960, applicants have been required to be of good moral character and to have their names and addresses published in a local paper for two weeks.

"This is not aimed at keeping white people from voting, no matter how morally corrupt they may be," explained the *Jackson State-Times*. "It is an ill-disguised attempt to keep qualified Negroes from voting."

The Association of Citizens' Councils reported how these laws came about. "Although this same amendment failed to pass in 1952, it passed by a tremendous majority (in 1954) when the people of Mississippi, through the Citizens' Councils, were informed of the necessity and reason for the passage of this amendment."

The legislature thought of other voting restrictions, too. Dr. James Silver, professor of history at the University of Mississippi, has written: "The House unanimously called for a constitutional amendment barring from voting persons guilty of vagrancy, perjury, and child desertion, and concurred in the addition of adultery, fornication, larceny, gambling, and crimes committed with a deadly weapon. A still further addition of habitual drunkenness was defeated when a member suggested that it 'might even get some of us.' There was some objection, also, to the inclusion of adultery."

Last February in Madison County, over three hundred Negroes stood in line at the court house over a two-day period to take the registration test. Registrar L. F. Campbell only processed seven of them, although he has registered as many as 49 whites in one day. In the county, 97 percent of the whites are registered but only slightly more than 1 percent of the Negroes. Besides registrar Campbell and the state's laws acting as deterrents, there also is a red, blue and grey sticker on Campbell's office door. It bears the Confederate flag and the message, "Support Your Citizens' Council."

Other times the deterrent hasn't been as sophisticated.

Three years ago, Herbert Lee, a Negro active in voter registration activities, was shot to death by a member of the state legislature—also a member of the Citizens' Council. "Justifiable homicide" a coroner's jury called it. Early this year, a Negro witness to the killing [Louis Allen] was also murdered.

Back in 1955, a Negro, Lamar Smith, was urging other Negroes to vote in a gubernatorial election. He was shot to death on the Brookhaven courthouse lawn. A grand jury refused to indict the three men who were charged with the slaying.

In Rankin County, February of last year, the sheriff and two deputies assaulted in the court house three Negroes who were applying to register, driving the three out before they could even finish the form.

As Mississippi political leaders explain, Mississippi Negroes aren't interested in voting.

The Citizens' Council is but one organization in Mississippi, a highly organized state, but it is the one that controls the state. The council was started in Indianola in July 1954 when 14 citizens met, organized by Robert B. Patterson, a plantation manager in Greenwood. [The US Supreme Court had handed down its *Brown v. Board of Education* school desegregation decision on May 17.]

Within six weeks, the council was operating in 17 counties. By the end of the year, there were councils in over 100 cities in the state. Today, most leading businessmen are leading council members and about one-third of the counties have at least one representative who is a council member.

It is no wonder then that Hodding Carter, Pulitzer Prize winning editor of the Greenville, Miss., *Delta Democrat-Times*, could write that the "legislature represents probably the lowest common denominator of any political assembly in the United States."

Working closely with the council is the official State Sovereignty Commission, established [in 1956] to "do and perform any and all acts and things deemed necessary and proper to protect the sovereignty of the

State of Mississippi and her sister states from encroachment thereon by the federal government or any branch, department, or agency thereof."

The commission was voted $250,000 [$2.143 million in 2014 dollars] to start its work.

Among the acts it deems necessary is to support the Citizens' Council. By last spring it had given $174,000 [$1.314 million in 2014 dollars] to the Citizens' Council Forum, a weekly program carried by some 400 radio and television stations.

Erle Johnston, director of the Commission, has said that the Commission has sent one million letters to citizens "about the dangers of the civil rights bill." The commission has also given some $300,000 [$2.265 million in 2014 dollars] to the Coordinating Committee for Fundamental American Freedoms, the anti-civil rights bill lobby [founded in 1963], and pays the $25,000 a year salary [$214,250 in 2014 dollars] of the lobby's legal advisor, [Yazoo City attorney] John Satterfield.

The State Sovereignty Commission has also mailed a manual to all law enforcement officers in the state, outlining laws under which civil rights workers can be arrested.

The size and strength of the Citizens' Council has eclipsed other racist groups within the state, but other groups still exist.

Last spring, the Ku Klux Klan claimed 91,003 members in the state. The Klan's greatest strength is in the southwest corner of the state where it operates openly as the White Knights of the Ku Klux Klan—"Dedicated to maintain and extend the dignity, heritage and rights of the White Race of America." Here, in the early months of the year, eight Negroes were killed, numerous others were beaten, Negro businesses were bombed, and dozens of crosses were burned.

But cross-burnings recently became standard fare throughout the state. "A regular Friday night affair," according to the *Jackson Clarion-Ledger*.

Also powerful in southwest Mississippi is the Association for the Preservation of the White Race. Founded in Natchez in 1961, the association now has several chapters in southwest Mississippi counties. It holds weekly meetings which are attended by, to quote a newsman, "mighty important people." Last March the group held a fair-sized meeting in Jackson at the Hinds County Courthouse, the courthouse where Byron De La Beckwith had been tried [for the murder of Medgar Evers].

Jackson is home of the Women for Constitutional Government, sort of a women's auxiliary of the Citizens' Council; Patriotic American Youth, a Citizens' Council dominated organization for high school and college students; and the United Front. The front organizes boycotts of any stores who give in to the demands of the "race-mixers"—a Mississippi term for anti-segregationists, or anyone who opposes discrimination. Early in the year the front urged citizens to write to "borderline" senators, stressing opposition to the civil rights bill—among those senators it considered on the "borderline" were both Alabama senators.

The northern part of the state is home for the Patriotic Network and the Association of Tenth Amendment Conservatives. ATAC, an organization of college students, was formed only last April.

The control of these racist organizations even extends to the courts. Mississippi, of course, does not recognize the U.S. Supreme Court. Last March, in Ruleville, when a voter registration worker protested his arrest as being unconstitutional, Mayor [Charles] Dorrough told him, "That law has not reached here yet."

Mississippi, however, does have its own supreme court and its most famous justice is Tom Brady, a Barnett appointee.

Brady was a leading spirit and vigorous organizer for the Citizens' Council and made over 600 speeches for the group during its first years. In his book, *Black Monday*, he wrote, "The Negro proposes to breed up his inferior intellect and whiten his skin and 'blow out the light' in the white man's brain and muddy his skin." Brady further explained, "You can dress a chimpanzee, housebreak him, and teach him to use a knife and a fork, but it will take countless generations of evolutionary development, if ever, before you can convince him that a caterpillar or a cockroach is not a delicacy. Likewise the social, political, economic and religious preferences of the Negro remain close to the caterpillar and the cockroach."

Brady's ideal: "The loveliest and purest of God's creatures, the nearest thing to an angelic being that treads this terrestrial ball, is a well-bred, cultured Southern white woman or her blue-eyed, golden-haired little girl."

Brady's words so impressed people that *Black Monday* became the Citizens' Council's handbook. Brady himself became the Democratic National Committeeman from Mississippi.

But not only Mississippians appoint such judges in Mississippi. President Eisenhower appointed judge Ben Cameron of Meridian to the Fifth Circuit Court. It was Cameron who issued four consecutive stays to block Meredith from entering the University of Mississippi. In one opinion, Cameron wrote that he didn't believe the 14th Amendment's prohibition of racial discrimination should be enforced in the South.

President Kennedy [in 1961] appointed Harold Cox as a Mississippi district judge [Chief Judge of the US Court for the Southern District of Mississippi]. Cox, who was Sen. Eastland's college roommate, early in the year referred to a group of Negro vote applicants as "a bunch of niggers on a voter drive." He explained, "I'm never going to be in sympathy with a bunch of people who act like chimpanzees." Then added, "But I'll oppose with every ounce of my energy any discrimination."

In mid-March, an attorney filed a motion to have Judge Cox disqualified from acting in civil rights cases.

In April, Attorney General Robert F. Kennedy said, "I'm very proud of the judges that have been appointed. We looked into all of them for questions of integrity and whether they would uphold the law of the land."

In Mississippi, justice is one-sided, as politics are one party.

Early in the year, the legislature passed an anti-boycott bill aimed at Negro campaigns against stores that discriminate. But Jackson Mayor Allen Thompson and others had proposed a boycott of "Bonanza" and the show's sponsor because the stars had cancelled a white-only Jackson appearance.

"We might bring some of our friends in court when we are trying to get rid of our enemies," Rep. Frank Shanahan of Vicksburg warned.

However, Thompson McClellan of West Point, the House Judiciary Chairman, pointed out that if any "local" people were accused under the bill they would be "tried in a Mississippi court before a Mississippi jury" and he would have no "apprehension" as to the outcome.

While on the subject of law, it should be mentioned that Mississippi has legal holidays no northern schoolboy would have even dreamed of. They include General Robert E. Lee's Birthday (January 19) and Jefferson Davis' Birthday (June 3). Also, October 26, was declared "Race and Reason Day" by Gov. Barnett back in 1961, in honor of Carleton Putnam. This day could, according to "Ole Ross," "mark the turning point in the South's struggle to preserve the integrity of the white race."

Putnam's white supremacy tract, *Race and Reason: A Yankee View*, had just been published and the author was being honored at a Citizens' Council sponsored banquet, attended by the state's highest dignitaries.

Barnett urged "the people of Mississippi to observe this occasion by reading and discussing *Race and Reason*, calling the book to the attention of friends and relatives in the North, and by participating in appropriate public functions, thereby expressing the appreciation of the people in our state for Mr. Carleton Putnam and for his splendid book *Race and Reason*."

The book was soon to replace Judge Brady's *Black Monday* as the Citizens' Council's handbook.

Mississippi has other heroes from outside the state besides Putnam, a northerner. The first of them is, of course, Gov. Orval Faubus of Arkansas, who became a hero when he defied the federal government at Little Rock.

"If the governors of Southern states had gone to Little Rock," Barnett explained, "and congratulated Gov. Orval Faubus when he called out the National Guard to prevent school integration, federal troops would never have been sent to that city."

Barnett also has praised [Plaquemines Parish boss and segregationist] Leander Perez of Louisiana as, "A truly great American—a man who thinks like you and I do in Mississippi."

Then there is also Alabama Governor George Wallace, "a man of deep convictions and dedication," according to Barnett, "with the courage to back up his convictions." Last April 7, the Mississippi House of Representatives adjourned in his honor.

Mississippians also view themselves as heroes, as Barnett explained last March, "Thinking people throughout America admire Mississippians for standing upon the strong foundation of constitutional government."

But of all Mississippians, former Gov. Barnett is the greatest folk hero, though somewhat expensive, as when he had $10,000 [$78,100 in 2014 dollars] gold-plated bathroom fixtures installed in the Governor's Mansion [as part of a $300,000 ($2.343 million in 2014 dollars) refurbishment]. In June of last year, C. F. Hornsby, president of the Alabama Citizens' Council, presented Barnett a plaque for "courage and patriotism" at the University of Mississippi. In February of this year, Charles M. Hills wrote in the *Jackson Clarion-Ledger*, "Former Gov. Ross Barnett continues to be this state's ambassador for constitutional government and the Southern way of life."

But a new hero within the state is Byron De La Beckwith, accused assassin of Medgar Evers [who was convicted in a third trial in 1994] and a gun-collector who wrote in a letter: "For the next 15 years we here in Mississippi are going to have to do a lot of shooting to protect our wives and our children from bad Negroes and sorry white folks and federal interference." When Beckwith's second trial [in 1964] also ended in a mistrial, he was released on bond and headed north, home to Greenwood.

"When we arrived at Tchula," Beckwith said, "there was a sign saying 'Welcome Home Delay' and when I got to the outskirts of Greenwood, there was another one. It brought tears to my eyes."

Dozens of whites greeted him at the county courthouse and that night he was treated by officials to a steak dinner at one of Greenwood's finest restaurants. Then he moved in with his wife at the Hotel LeFlore.

An up and coming hero is Mayor Allen Thompson of Jackson. Hodding Carter has written: "Jackson is a town obsessed with a determination to maintain existing relationships between the races. Its politics and social order are monolithic. One can count on two hands those Jacksonians who are willing to speak out against any status quo. Almost the sole source of the city's newspaper information comes from a morning and afternoon combination owned by a family whose animation can only be described as an admixture of fundamentalism, furious racism and greed. Rare is the Jackson citizen of any prominence, or even of no consequence, who does not belong to the Citizens' Council."

Even, or naturally, the chairman of a "Keep Jackson Beautiful" campaign is a member of the board of directors of the Jackson Citizens' Council.

Thompson's police force is the object of attention, and, under a new state law, its men and equipment are available to any Mississippi city that requests them. The leading piece of equipment is a $15,000 [$111,450 in 2014 dollars] specially built armored car with a mounted machine gun and two sets of ten port holes—one set for shooting tear gas, the other for tossing grenades. Other equipment includes two troop carriers with search lights, three wire-enclosed flat-bed trailer trucks for hauling off prisoners, and a compound which can hold 10,000 prisoners. The police force consists of 435 men each equipped with a riot helmet, gas mask and shot gun. All this for a town with a population of about 150,000.

"We have a larger than usual police force," Thompson modestly explains.

Thompson even has a color slide presentation on his force which he proudly shows before civic and police groups throughout the South.

"This is the only city in the world where you can guarantee that there won't be any pickets," Thompson says, and his police force sees to that.

The police force in Indianola is also somewhat unique, but unique only for Mississippi, as the department has one Negro on its force.

"We've got that guy down there," an Indianola alderman told the editor of the *Greenwood Commonwealth*. "If he has to shoot a Negro, or he shoots one, you've got an unfortunate shooting, but you don't have a racial incident."

"That is the basis on which Indianola hired its Negro officer," the editor commented. "He has since proved valuable in many more ways."

When the editor suggested that Greenwood police hire a Negro, the sheriff refused, seeing it as the first step to Negroes getting in everywhere.

But thanks to a new law, communities won't have to depend solely on their own police to handle "uppity Negroes" and "outside agitators." The state police have been given additional powers so that the governor, at his own discretion, can send them anyplace he wishes to "handle disturbances." Senator McDonnel charged that the law created "a traveling Gestapo, smacking of Nazi Germany and Russia."

Sen. George Farbrough said, "I think senators do a disservice to the state when they utter things up here about Hitler and other things that should be left unsaid."

Governor Johnson pointed out, "Actually we are seeking to legalize what we have been doing in the past. You sheriffs have always been able to call on the Highway Patrol. This plan will give us swift action."

The law also increased the number of police by 70 percent.

"If we don't pass this bill, it will be fatal to our way of life," admitted Rep. Thompson McClellan.

Rep. Ralph Herrin, however, had a minor criticism. He felt it "should provide 1,000 police dogs to go with the patrolmen."

This then is Mississippi, a unique state, determined to stand apart from the progress of humanity. If the reader takes a trip through the state, he too can discover—to quote from an official state travel ad—"The magic of Mississippi becomes more apparent with every mile you travel through the state."

"Rugged, Ragged 'Snick': What It Is and What It Does"

> *This newspaper article about the Student Nonviolent Coordinating Committee appeared in Chicago in the summer of 1963, about a month after Medgar Evers was murdered and a few weeks before the March on Washington. Its readers knew about the NAACP and Martin Luther King, but few outside the movement understood SNCC at the time.*

STUDENTS FIGHT FOR CIVIL RIGHTS IN TOUGH SPOTS
Chicago Daily News, Sat., July 20, 1963
Ex-Chicago Schoolteacher Leader in Deepest Dixie
By M. W. NEWMAN, Staff Writer

ATLANTA—In a seedy office here, you find the command post of an amazing blue jean army that fights Jim Crow behind enemy lines.

Husky James Forman, 34, sticks out his hand and says hello. This onetime Chicago schoolteacher is executive director of what everyone in the seething "rights" movement calls Snick.

Snick is short for SNCC, which in turn is the initials of the Student Nonviolent Co-ordinating Committee.

That long handle offers protective cover for as rugged, and perhaps ragged, a band of individualists as exists in this country.

The boys and girls of Snick risk their lives deep in the South's Hate Belt in sit-ins, freedom rides, voter registration drives and other unsafe forms of citizenship.

Most of them are college students or former students, aged 20 or so. High school youngsters also take part. They have been shot, beaten, jailed, hounded or denounced by guardians of the Southern "way of life." Their skin color generally is brown, but some are white.

They generally are surprisingly disciplined, but they have their stagey hotheads. SNCC sympathizers were accused of taking part in the booing of Chicago's Mayor Richard J. Daley at a July 4 rally of the NAACP.

In the South, Snick workers often are on the receiving end of boos, boots and even bullets.

One of them, slender Robert Travis, was punctured by a white night rider's rifle bullet. It didn't stop him and he returned to his voter registration campaign in Greenwood, Miss., bastion of white supremacy.

Another SNCC staffer, Lawrence Guyot, removed his overalls and showed newsmen in Jackson, Miss., savage bruises and clots on his brown skin.

Guyot said deputies in Winona, Miss., beat him while he was protesting against the arrest of five other Negroes. Their crime, he said, was entering a "white" waiting room in a bus terminal.

All this happened while the six were on their way to Jackson for the funeral of Medgar Evers, murdered NAACP official.

The undaunted Guyot, according to Snick, went on to take part in a Negro registration drive that has brought fierce resistance from whites in Greenwood.

He wound up in the county work farm after a courthouse "stand-in"— and led a "sit-down" while in custody.

They Practice Nonviolence

These disciplined young people do not strike back when clubbed by rednecks. The most they may do is [words missing in original] Luther King Jr., apostle of nonviolence, and their constitution states firmly: "Through nonviolence, courage displaces fear; love transforms hate; hope ends despair."

Snick's goal, like King's, is to appeal to the white man's conscience—thus setting the stage for equal rights and peaceful co-existence of the races. By any definition, this amounts to virtual revolution, at least in Dixie.

Forman himself has been arrested six times, and this may not even be par for the course. Some Snick workers are in and out of the lockup so often they can't get their laundry done.

To get where they're going, these determined young boys and girls apparently will have to pass through all the jail cells of the racist South.

They will go into towns like McComb, Miss.; Selma, Ala.; Lebanon, Tenn.; and Cairo, Ill., to reach the masses of "degraded, disenfranchised and exploited Negroes" as they put it.

Some friendly farmer may give them a pad to sleep on and dish of chitterlings. Their "uniform" will be overalls or shirt and blue jeans.

They will go up and down the roads—by foot, by jalopy, by bus—talking, explaining, exhorting, trying to get simple rights for brown-skinned citizens living a "slavey" life and buried deep in poverty and despair.

Sometimes, out of this hard and dangerous work, come sit-ins and protests aimed at integrating lunch counters, hospitals and theaters, or at improving jobs and housing for Negroes.

SNCC's campaign to register Negro voters, to end the reign of error and terror that has kept them from Southern polling places, is acutely important. It could help change the South if successful.

That perhaps is why Mississippi officialdom has fought so hard to keep Negroes from voting. Threats, boycotts, economic pressures, jailings and violence all have been used, according to Negroes.

In Greenwood, Miss., a police dog attacked two registration workers. The city's mayor complained that the voter registration drive followed "the Communist line of fomenting racial violence."

Police officers have killed three Negroes in Mississippi counties where the U.S. Justice Dept. has brought voting suits, according to SNCC.

"You're just never sure what the police will do," said a white Chicagoan who had worked with SNCC gadflies in Greenwood. "You never really feel safe.

"And when you sit in the Snick office and see cars filled with white men drive by slowly, you're always wondering what they're going to do."

Tests Keep Them Out of the Booth

Negroes who manage to overcome all these barriers find still another when they seek to register in Greenwood and many other cities—unusually stiff "qualification" tests aimed at keeping them voteless. About three out of four are turned down by the Greenwood registrar.

"And on top of that," Forman says, "Negroes throughout the South have been brain-washed into thinking that voting is none of their business. Our goal is to change their thinking."

SNCC works in this kind of civil rights battleground—and as the rugged Forman puts it matter-of-factly:

"It's dangerous. We know we're risking our lives."

Like most of the young people he directs, he takes violence as it comes.

"There was that time in Selma, Ala., when a mob of 150 white people surrounded some of us in a church," he said.

"We had to get on the phone and call the Justice Department and the FBI in Washington in order to get the local police to take action. After Washington got in touch with them, they dispersed the mob.

"Oh, yes, there also was that time in Monroe, N.C., when a fellow pointed a shotgun at me. Fortunately, it didn't go off."

Forman has been arrested for things like trying to integrate a "white" waiting room. Once, he recalls, all that the police seemed to have against him was that he was riding in a car.

In Greenwood, he said, police grabbed him because he took a picture of a police dog biting a protest marcher. Forman's wife Mildred took over his duties while he lingered in jail. Despite all the arrests, Forman added, he never has been convicted of anything.

Blond Sandra (Casey) Hayden of Austin, Tex., confided that she is the only staffer in SNCC's Atlanta office who never has been arrested. "Texas is such a big place that they just never got around to it," explained this blue-eyed beauty of 25.

Like many SNCC volunteers, she came to the work through religious and ethical beliefs. A number of the staffers are clergymen's sons. Most are Southern born. About 10 per cent are white.

They usually are paid about $35 a week. Most of their peers in the commercial rat race would not even consider that petty cash.

The cool, poised Forman came out of Chicago's densely packed South Side, where Negroes live jammed together.

He was born in Chicago but spent part of his youth in northern Mississippi. He got his first taste of race prejudice when, as a 6-year-old, he went into a Memphis, Tenn., soda fountain to buy a soft drink.

"Even at that age, the porter made me go to the back," said Forman with a shake of his head.

"That really shook me up. I guess I learned early that you have to do something about segregation.

"There has to be some form of mass agitation to get freedom. And you don't have to be ashamed of the word 'agitation.' "

Receives Diploma At Roosevelt

In Chicago, Forman was graduated from Engelwood High School and Roosevelt University. He became a specialist in public administration, served in the Army and worked for a while for the Institute for Juvenile Research on Chicago's West Side. His mother, Mrs. Octavia Rufus, lives at 7437 South Park.

In 1960–61, he said, he was a substitute teacher at Kenwood School, 49th St. and Blackstone. The Negro protest movement in the South already was in swing with student lunch-counter sit-ins, voter drives and mass action influencing Forman.

He heard about sharecroppers in Fayette County, Tenn., near the Mississippi line, who were being evicted in a battle over voting rights.

"I knew that if they could be driven off the land it would be doomsday for Mississippi," he said.

The young teacher took leave and went to Tennessee to organize help for the farmers, some of whom were living in tents and dodging bullets.

His work there drew so much attention that he was drafted to head SNCC, which had been formed in 1960 as an outgrowth of student "sit-ins."

That was the fall of 1961, and SNCC at the time occupied a hole-in-the-wall cubicle on Atlanta's Auburn Ave.

Its present-day offices on Raymond St., while roomier, barely qualify as dilapidated.

SNCC now consists of representatives from some of the student protest groups that have helped to spark today's massive Negro revolt. The budget is about $75,000 a year, with much of it coming from Northern students. They flood in as volunteers during summertime, when as many as 40 per cent of the workers may be white.

SNCC quickly won a name as a major Negro freedom group.

Martin Luther King Jr., president of the Southern Christian Leadership Conference, gave it his blessing and aid. The NAACP Legal Defense Fund took over the job of getting these young people out of jail.

You find SNCC workers on hand wherever the Negro mass movement bursts into action—be it Jackson, Miss., Birmingham, Ala., or Albany, Ga.

What these tough-minded young folk call the "white power structure" (downtown businessmen, bankers, politicians) has become used to the idea of negotiating with them.

"Start your action against things these guys own," is a Snick byword.

In Little Rock, Ark., site of the famous school integration crisis of 1957, sit-ins began in late 1962.

Students from Philander Smith College and Shorter Junior College sat at segregated downtown lunch counters under direction of Bill Hansen, a Snick "veteran." He himself was a student.

A White Citizens Council threatened violence. But the city had suffered a black eye and economic chills since 1957, and some of the prominent people in town indicated readiness to talk.

"At first the city was not willing to yield," according to a SNCC version, "and so renewed sit-ins began in December."

Hansen and a Snick buddy, Worth Long, were arrested. They chose to stay in jail.

After continuing uproar, SNCC reported, the white community agreed to work out a plan to increase jobs for Negroes and integrate lunch counters and other facilities.

In return, the two crusaders had to agree to leave jail.

Agitation Pays Off

They did. Hansen, in fact, moved on to Pine Bluff, Ark. He met there with students at Arkansas A.M. & N. University, a Negro state school.

Sit-ins began in Pine Bluff Feb. 1 at a chain variety store. Eight days later, a SNCC report says, 15 students were expelled from the college.

Eight of these undaunted young rebels, with Hansen and another SNCC worker, then launched a community-wide attack on segregation in Pine Bluff. They zeroed in on restaurants, theaters, hotels. A wave of arrests got under way.

These young people "live cooperatively in two houses in Pine Bluff," a staff report says. They hope to develop a voter registration program and voters' leagues in surrounding counties.

Snick's daring young folk also penetrate into southwest Georgia, heart of the Black Belt and still a very unsafe place for civil rights advocates.

Twelve field secretaries operate out of an Albany, Ga., HQ—a cramped cold-water house with a kerosene stove.

Carver Neblett, 19, is a Negro student from Southern Illinois University in Carbondale. Joyce Barrett, 24, hails from Philadelphia and is white. Jack Chatfield, 20, is a white student from Bradford, Vt.

They and others conduct mass meetings in churches or tents, stirring up hope and belief, battling deep fear.

They canvass from door to door, seeking to build trust. They try to work with teenagers, teachers, ministers, and encourage people to register.

A lot of their time is spent in documenting stories of threats and firings suffered by voter applicants.

It's hard going, and slow, but these young SNCC workers apparently have banished thoughts of self and pelf. They can be likened to missionaries in a dark and dangerous land, risking their lives for a cause bigger than themselves.

They're Angry And Honest

Are they angry? Of course. Zealots? Undoubtedly. Political radicals? Some of them may be. Honest? Obviously.

The contrast with beatniks, panty-raiders and beach rioters is painful— or refreshing, depending on how you look at it.

Certainly these young people are revolutionaries, tackling "the monster in the backwoods" or the downtown white businessmen who hire Negroes only as porters and segregate the races in separate toilets.

Among themselves, SNCC missionaries almost automatically assume that American society is corrupt and commercial. That's the lever they use to pressure white bosses into concessions:

"Hit him in the pocketbook; Babbittry comes before bigotry."

But, notes a thoughtful Atlanta newspaper columnist, who can deny their assumptions?

"For the goals of their revolution," he writes, "are simply the basic rights guaranteed in the Constitution."

Some day, Forman hopes, SNCC will have done so well that it can put itself out of business. That will be the day.

Fannie Lou Hamer Deposition

> *Hamer described the following incident multiple times, most famously during her testimony before the Credentials Committee of the Democratic National Convention in Atlantic City on August 22, 1964. On that day, she, members of the committee, and millions of Americans watching her on TV were all in tears as she asked rhetorically, "Is this America?" This copy is a sworn affidavit, dated May 24, 1964, from the files of COFO's attorneys and was intended to be used in court.*

State of Mississippi,
County of Sunflower

I, Mrs. Fannie Lou Hamer, a Negro, being duly sworn and deposed, to wit:

I am 46 years of age, and reside in Ruleville, Sunflower County. My mailing address is 626 East Lafayette St., and I am married to Mr. Perry Hamer.

On the 9th of June, 1963, I, Mrs. Annelle Ponder, and eight other women were returning from a voter registration workshop which had been in South Carolina. We were on a Continental Trailways bus—which stopped at Winona, Montgomery County [Mississippi], at the bus station. Annelle Ponder, and others of our party, including James West, from Itta Bena, Rosemary Freeman, from near Greenwood, June Johnson, a 15 yr old girl, got off the bus to go to the restaurant. Two, Euvester Simpson and Ruth Day, also of our party, got off the bus to use the rest room. I remained on the bus.

The four that got off the bus to go to the restaurant and had gone to the "white side" of the restaurant, were coming back to the bus. I got off the bus and asked them "what happened." They said that there were some policemen and highway-patrolmen in there. Annelle said policemen with billy-clubs told them to get out of there. I said that this can be reported and Annelle said, "Yes, I am going to get the tag number." The four of them were standing outside to get the tag number and Euvester Simpson was standing with them talking when all five of them were put in the patrol car, which I think was the high-way patrolman car, he also was the one giving orders.

I got off the bus when all at once, an officer from the patrol car said, "get that one too." A county-deputy, Earl Wane Patric and one more got out of the car and opened the door to his car and said, "You are under arrest." I was going into the car when this Patric "kicked me" me into the car. While driving to the jail, they were questioning and calling me "bitch."

We got to the jail, I saw all five of the above in the booking room. As soon as I got to the booking room, a tall policeman walked over to James West and jumped hard on James West feet.

I was led into a room—a cell—with Euvester Simpson. While I was in the cell, I could hear screaming and the passing of licks. Pretty soon, I saw several white men bringing Annelle Ponder past my cell—she was holding unto the jail walls—her clothes all torn—her mouth all swelled up and her eyes were all bloody—one eye looking like itself.

After a while, they came for me. John P. Bassinger, a high-way patrol man (his name on a metal plate on his pocket), the policeman who had jumped on James West feet, and another policeman with a crew-cut haircut. They came into my cell and asked me why I was demonstrating—and said that they were not going to have such carryings on in Mississippi. They asked me if I had seen Martin Luther King Jr. I said I could not be demonstrating—I had just got off the bus—and denied that I have seen Martin Luther King. They said "shut up" and always cut me off. They then asked me where I was from. I said Ruleville. They then left—saying that they were going to check it out.

They then returned. John Bassinger said: "You damn right you are from Ruleville. We going to make you wish that you were dead, bitch." They led me to another cell. Before I had been led out of the cell—I saw a Negro—who I reckoned was a trustee—who stayed around the jail—bring a mop and bucket to take somewhere. When I was brought to another cell I saw two Negro's who were in their 20's or a little younger. John Bassinger—he said—"take this" talking to the youngest Negro. John Bassinger had in his hand a long, 2 feet blackjack—made out of leather—wider at one end, and one end being filled with something heavy. The young Negro said: "You mean for me to beat her with this?" John Bassinger said, "You damn right"—"If you don't, you know what I will do for you."

The young Negro told me to get on the bunk and he began to beat me. I tried to put my hands to my side where I had polio when I was a child—so that I would not be beat so much on that side. The first Negro beat me until he got tired. Then the second Negro was made to beat me. I took the first part of it, but couldn't stand the second beating. I began to move—and the first Negro was made to sit on my feet to keep me from kicking. I remember that I tried to smooth my dress which was working up from all of the beating. One of the white officers pushed my dress up. I was screaming and going on—and the young officer with the crew-cut he began to beat me about the head and told me to stop my screaming. I then began to bury my head in the mattress and hugged it to kill out the sound of my screams. It was impossible to stop the screaming. I must have passed out—I remember trying to raise my head and heard one of the officers, "Bassinger," who said, that's enough. He said get up and walk. I could barely walk. My body was real hard-feeling like metal. My hands were navy blue—and couldn't bend the fingers. I was taken back to the cell.

While I was back in the cell, I could talk to June Johnson, Annelle Ponder, and Rosemary Freeman who were in their cells. I learned that June Johnson had a hole in her head from her beating. I learned that the trustee had used the bucket and mop to mop the blood.

They got us up one night to take our pictures and John Bassinger, who had taken the pictures, forced me to sign a statement which they already made me write, that I had been treated all right. That night was the following Monday night. I tried to write the statement in such a way that anybody would know that I had been forced to write the statement.

The following Tuesday, we had our trial. There was no jury. We had no lawyer. We were charged and were found guilty of Disorderly Conduct and Resisting Arrest.

When we were put in the jail, and when I was put in the jail, I told them that nothing is right around here. The arresting officer had lied and said that I was resisting arrest. I told them that I was not leaving my cell—and that if they wanted me, they had to kill me in the cell and drag me out. I rather be killed inside my cell instead of outside the cell.

On that Tuesday, I heard some white men talk to the chief jailer that they were F.B.I. and had to report what they saw. I was able to see Lawrence Guyot, a field secretary of SNCC who I had known before in voter registration work, and saw him in the booking room and saw that he had been beaten.

On the following Wednesday, James Bevel, Andrew Young, and Dorothy Cotton of SCLC (Southern Christian Leadership Conference) came to see us and to get us (the people who had been on the bus who were arrested) out. But before I left the jail, I was able to see that Lawrence Guyot's head had been beaten out of shape.

In 31st of August, 1962, I had been fired from my plantation job, Dee Marlow's Plantation, Ruleville, because I attempted to register to vote. I had been working for SNCC and SCLC before I had been beaten. At the present time, I am a candidate for Congress in the coming primary, for the second Congressional District.

Doctor Searcy, Cleveland, Mississippi, said that I had been beaten so deeply that my nerve endings are permanently damaged—and I am sore.

Signed, Mrs. Fannie Lou Hamer

Sworn to and signed before me this 24 day of May, 1964

Signed: John D. Due, Jr.

Notary Public

My commission expires: May 22, 1968

SNCC Biography: Bob Moses

This portrait of the person most responsible for Freedom Summer dates from 1964, when SNCC issued a series of short biographies of its leaders to the press.

STUDENT NONVIOLENT COORDINATING COMMITTEE
6 RAYMOND STREET, N.W.
ATLANTA, GEORGIA 30314

MISSISSIPPI DIRECTOR ROBERT P. MOSES

Robert Parris Moses has directed SNCC's Mississippi project since he first went into the state in August 1961 and set up a pilot voter registration project in McComb.

He was teaching in New York City when the student sit-ins broke in 1960, and decided to come South to work for SNCC in 1961.

Moses was born in New York City in 1935 and grew up in a Harlem housing project. He was awarded a scholarship to Hamilton College in Clinton, N.Y., upon graduation from Stuyvesant High School.

Moses received the A.B. degree from Hamilton College in philosophy with honors in 1956, and graduated as vice-president of his class and captain of the varsity basketball team. Resuming active association with the American Friends Service Committee under whose auspices he had participated in work camps in Europe the summer of 1955, he worked in a similar program in Japan in 1956.

In September of that year he began one and a half years' study at Harvard University and at the end of one year received the M.A. degree in philosophy. His mother's death and hospitalization of his father drew him to New York City again where he tutored privately before beginning three years' teaching of mathematics at the Horace Mann School.

Moses came South "to stay" in time to be the first representative of a civil rights group to attempt rural voter registration work in what was then, and still is, the most economically and politically depressed state in the nation.

He has remained in that state since 1961—a major factor in conquering some of the fear that many Mississippians have: civil rights workers will come into a community, "stir up trouble" and then leave. For this reason also, scores of native Mississippians have either been placed on SNCC staff or work actively with "the students" as SNCC workers are widely called by the local people with whom they live and work.

Moses began a vote drive in the hazardous southwest area of Mississippi, stronghold of white terrorist activity, and was beaten by the cousin of the Amite County sheriff when he accompanied two farmers to the courthouse in the town of Liberty in 1961. When SNCC workers moved North to the planter country of the Delta in 1962, Moses and SNCC worker James Travis were shot at. Travis was almost killed.

In 1962 Moses helped draft a plan to combine local groups across the state which had formed in response to vote drives, into the Council of Federated Organizations (COFO). Moses, who directs COFO, also heads the Mississippi Summer Project.

Notes on Biography of Dave Dennis

These notes are unsigned and their context is unclear, but they appear to date from late 1964 or early 1965 and vividly convey the roles Dave Dennis played in the early years of the civil rights movement. They are from the personnel files of CORE's Southern Regional Office.

Notes on biography of Dave Dennis

- 1958 wrote a newsletter for the NAACP in Shreveport but did not participate in the direct action
- spring 1960 participated in mass march of 4,500 students to capitol in Baton Rouge while a student a Southern U.
- in Nov. 1960 while a student at Dillard joined New Orleans CORE chapter, first arrest came that month, remembers his first meal in jail as hog head cheese sandwich on french bread
- he continued in the sit ins and was arrested several more times, picketing too
- May 1961 went with Doris and Oretha Castle on freedom ride from Montgomery to Jackson, arrested in Jackson but after 5 days was extradited back to New Orleans to the Parish prison. They had gotten out of that prison just before leaving to go to Montgomery to join freedom ride, and conditions of release from prison was that they were not supposed to leave the state. Dave had been in the prison for 30 days for picketing without a permit. After extradition was in 2 days before bonded out. Was still a student at Dillard during this and returned there in June to take final exams after all other students had left
- summer 1961 tour in Chicago, New York with Jerome Smith
- picketing in Washington July 1961 with Wash CORE. also during the summer was elected regional rep by national conv or council
- July 1961 back to Shreveport to organize a CORE chapter; first project was desegregation of bus terminal, which they did. in the course of the project Dave was arrested for vagrancy, loitering etc. in one instance he was arrested for "disturbing the peace" while sitting in a parked car; the officer said he was disturbing his peace by being there. It was also during this time that a small freedom ride came through Shreveport led by Rev. B. Elton Cox. it had come from Arkansas and went to New Orleans.

There was a hostile scene at the bus station in Shreveport with about 1000 whites, fortunately there was little violence.

- During the summer at a banquet sponsored by Shreveport CORE at a church two bombs were thrown in the windows while Dave was addressing the banquet. No one was injured but a part of the church burned. After the fire was put out Dave had a plan at that time to use the 50 students as a "non-violent Army" and scatter them in Louisiana and some in Miss. This was the forerunner of the existing CORE Task Force. The national office did not accept the idea at the time and when summer came the students left and the project apparently disintegrated more or less.

- June 1962 went to Mississippi. that summer COFO was organized to work on voter registration and as an instrument of getting grants from VEP [Voter Education Project, a fundraising group backed by the Kennedy administration, major foundations, and civil rights organizations] on a state-wide basis. at that time there were only about half a dozen civil rights staff workers in the state. Dave hired people out of his own salary and then with VEP money when it came. He was working in Jackson, Hattiesburg, Greenville and Ruleville. Others involved at that time were Lawrence Guyot, Bob Moses, Lafayette Surney, Landy McNair and James Jones.

- Dave was arrested between 10 and 15 times during this period, mostly if not all were for various traffic offenses. One time he was arrested and the officer told him, when Dave asked what the arrest was for, "by the time we get to the jail I'll think of something." Prior to COFO there was the Jackson Nonviolent Movement composed of CORE and SNCC, an organization to involve the freedom ride students. It was generally in this period, June–December 1963 that the Miss. food program was organized, one of its first projects was to take food to people in the Delta who had lost jobs trying to register. Also Dave was one of those who first developed the idea of a community center, he along with Moses and James Bevel

- January, Feb., March 1963 Dave continued his general work, Greenwood was added, the quilt cooperative in Ruleville was organized. George Raymond worked for a while before going to Canton. It was during this time, and earlier that Dave met his wife to be Matte Bivins in Hattiesburg, (also her home town) where she worked for SNCC (2 yrs altogether) as Bob Moses' secretary.

- In 1963 Dave went to Canton to start work there and in June George Raymond came down from Ruleville to work Canton. During this period

Dave recruited various people in the state to work or from outside the state to come and work, including: Doris Castle, Annie Moody, Jerome Smith, Jean Thompson, one of the Dearon boys from near Canton, Doris _____ (from Jackson), Barbara McNair, Hezekiah Watkins, and Matt Suarez

- June, July 1963 Dave worked in Jackson organizing the demonstrations at the request of the NAACP. He worked closely with Medgar Evers and Dave remembers that the day he was killed he had been using Medgar's car all day in Canton, and missed most of the mass meeting that night. He returned the car that night and saw Medgar shortly before he (Medgar) went home. Dave remembers that he left a pack of Kent cigarettes in Medgar's car.

- Fall 1963 sometime about here Dave was elected Asst Program director of COFO. in the fall was the first freedom vote, Aaron Henry for Governor, Edwin King for Lt. Gov. After the freedom vote was over Dave turned himself in to the Jackson police, he had been wanted for charges of contributing to the delinquency of a minor since July (probably in connection with the Jackson demonstrations). As it was not convenient for him to go to jail until after the freedom ballot, he had to avoid the police for about four months, the measures to do that included being smuggled out of Jackson in a car trunk. The police searched his apt. looking for him, etc.

- From Jan 1964 to November 1964 Dave served as the Asst Program director of COFO, an increasingly large job as COFO grew in size, preparing for the summer program. In January three workers arrived from New York, Dick Jewett and Rita and Michael Schwerner. Jewett was sent to Canton where he was put in jail for 32 days after he had been there less than 24 hours. Dave had by this time received approval from the national office for his community center program and asked the Schwerners if they would like to work in the community center in Meridian. They agreed and went to Meridian only to find that there wasn't any community center at all, only five empty rooms. They called him and asked him how they were to set it up; since there were no other centers in the state and they were about to establish the first one, there was little Dave could tell them. Perhaps that was best, because left on their own, they established a beautiful center.

- In October 1964 Dave left Mississippi to work in the CORE southern regional office as the southern program director.

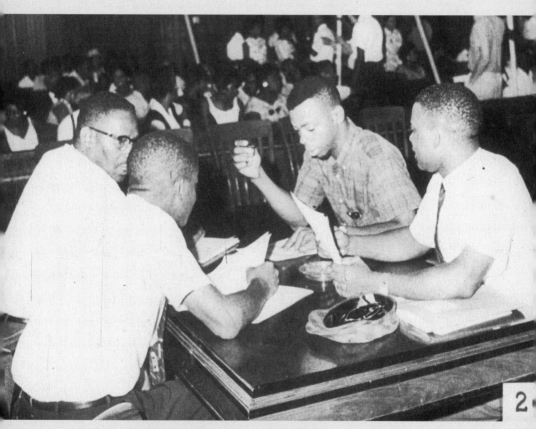

2

Four African American men discuss a document around a table. This image was possibly taken at a meeting of the Mississippi Freedom Democratic Party.

DEBATES, PREPARATIONS, TRAINING

Bob Moses went to Mississippi for SNCC in 1961 and learned through personal experience that sit-ins and boycotts—tactics that had worked elsewhere—brought only murderous reprisals in Mississippi. One of his mentors, veteran Cleveland, Mississippi, activist Amzie Moore, suggested to him that the best way to secure constitutional rights for black Mississippians was the ballot box.

The first document in this chapter is an internal memo that Moses wrote for SNCC's September 1963 executive committee meeting, in which he reviews the group's first two years in Mississippi and suggests SNCC consider a massive voter registration drive "aimed at the overthrow of the existing political structures of the state. They must be torn down completely—to make way for new ones."

To show that African Americans wanted to vote, activists ran a mock election called the "Freedom Vote" in the fall of 1963 parallel to the official election, a tactic they would repeat the next year. Aaron Henry, head of the state's NAACP, ran for governor and the Reverend Edwin King, a white chaplain at Tougaloo College, for lieutenant governor. Several dozen students from Yale and Stanford came to Mississippi for two weeks (trailed by the national press) to help sign up participants. More than 80,000 "freedom votes" were cast, validating Moses's emphasis on voter registration.

That election and the debates that followed it at a November 1963 SNCC staff meeting are summarized in the second document here. The November meeting included arguments for and against a massive voter registration campaign using hundreds of white Northern students. Although not unanimously supported, in December SNCC members began to swing behind the idea and in January the Council of Federated Organizations, an umbrella group of civil rights organizations in Mississippi, authorized

Bob Moses and Dave Dennis to create a "Mississippi Summer Project." The murder of local voting rights activist Louis Allen on January 31 tipped the scales, and the project was launched.

Shortly afterward, Moses called for volunteers and financial support (his appeal to movement contacts is the third document here), which yielded hundreds of applications like Andrew Goodman's (reproduced as the next document). Throughout the spring the project was announced to the media and to Mississippi residents in brochures, articles, and press releases such as the fifth item in this chapter. By the end of May 1964, COFO had recruited more than one thousand volunteers to come to Mississippi, mostly white Northern college students.

During the second half of June, the National Council of Churches sponsored two, week-long orientation sessions for these volunteers at Western College for Women in Oxford, Ohio. Those sessions are represented in the last four documents in this chapter. The first is a letter from New York volunteer Joel Bernard to his mother describing the trainers, the daily schedule, and the political situation. The other three documents show how the inexperienced, idealistic Northerners were introduced to conditions on the ground in Mississippi and taught how to meet them nonviolently. Role-playing instructions forced them to imagine how they would react to tense situations, and the project's Security Handbook showed them how to protect themselves from the hostility they would face.

Finally, several short documents on nonviolence used at the orientation clarify the techniques volunteers would use when confronted and the ideals that motivated their actions. In today's violent world, these may sound naive and utopian—almost as incomprehensible as the savagery of their white-supremacist opponents, who speak for themselves in the next chapter.

Memo to SNCC Executive Committee, September 1963

Memo to S.N.C.C. Executive Committee
Re: S.N.C.C. Mississippi Project
From: Bob Moses

I. Chronology for the past two years:

S.N.C.C. began a voter registration project in McComb in July, 1961, and quickly expanded it to cover a three county area—Pike, Amite and Walthall counties. After an abortive direct action campaign in McComb, we pulled out of the area in November, 1961. During this time we joined S.C.L.C. and C.O.R.E. in a program in Jackson in August, 1961, maintaining a base in Jackson until winter of 1962.

During the winter of '61–'62, we worked with R.L.T. Smith in his campaign for Congress and helped the *Mississippi Free Press* for the first two or three months of its existence. The Smith campaign provided a natural opportunity to expand the voting work already begun in what was then the 4th congressional district. We made contacts in Hinds, Adams, Jefferson, Claiborne, Copiah, and Lincoln counties.

In February, 1962, we helped draft a program for the Council of Federated Organizations and provided them with two S.N.C.C. field workers to begin a project in Hattiesburg. Curtis Hayes and Hollis Watkins were assigned to Hattiesburg and worked there until September, 1962, when the project was turned over to a local person, Mrs. Victoria Gray. Mrs. Gray ran the project until March, 1963, when it was stopped temporarily. This project was resumed in July, '63, by John O'Neal and Carl Johnson.

We began the summer of '62 with voter registration projects in the Mississippi Delta as a part of the Council of Federated Organizations. S.N.C.C. workers were stationed in Vicksburg, Greenville, Cleveland, Ruleville, Greenwood and Holly Springs. These projects are still in operation, with the exception of Vicksburg.

II. The following facts are indisputable:
   A. We have accomplished the following:
   1. The recruitment and involvement of people from Mississippi, some adults, but mostly young people, in S.N.C.C.'s programs in Mississippi and elsewhere.

2. The establishment of "beachheads" or bases for operation in a number of towns and counties in Mississippi.
3. Gained the confidence of many local Negro leaders in the validity of S.N.C.C.'s program.
4. Provided considerable material for suits by the U. S. Department of Justice against Mississippi voting laws and practices designed to keep Negroes from voting.

B. We have learned the following:
1. It is not possible for us to register Negroes in Mississippi. (There is reason to believe that authorities in Mississippi will force a showdown over the right to vote in large numbers similar to the Federal-State show-downs over integration of schools.)
2. All direct action campaigns for integration have had their backs broken by sentencing prisoners to long jail terms and requiring excessive bail. It has not proved possible to get large enough numbers of people committed to staying in jail, or long enough money to overcome these two obstacles.
3. It is expensive to operate in Mississippi.

III. The core of the problem:

The Mississippi monolith has successfully survived the Freedom Rides, James Meredith at Ole Miss, and the assassination of Medgar Evers without substantive change. The election of Paul Johnson reinforces all that is bad in the state: the full resources of the state will continue to be at the disposal of local authorities to fight civil rights gains; the entire white population will continue to be the Klan.

The only attack worth making is an attack aimed at the overthrow of the existing political structures of the state. They must be torn down completely—to make way for new ones. The focus of such an attack must be on the vote and the Delta of Mississippi, including Jackson and Vicksburg.

IV. I propose that the S.N.C.C. adopt the following program for Mississippi:

That S.N.C.C. make its National Headquarters in Greenwood, Mississippi, starting this fall. That Jim Forman, John Lewis and other members of the executive committee spend considerable chunks of time in Mississippi during the coming year.

That S.N.C.C. launch a one-man, one-vote campaign for Mississippi aimed at obtaining the vote in Mississippi by 1964.

This iconic photo shows (left to right): Freedom Summer director Bob Moses; SNCC steering committee member Julian Bond; SNCC field secretaries Curtis Hayes, James Peacock, and Hollis Watkins; and local leaders Amzie Moore and E. W. Steptoe on Steptoe's farm in Amite County in 1963.

That S.N.C.C. organize local political clubs to support a Negro for Congress from the 2nd congressional district and, if possible, a Negro from the 3rd congressional district. That it begin and continue an unceasing operation against the seating of Jamie Whitten as Congressman from the Delta.

That it begin, now, to explore the ways and means of ousting Senator Eastland in the 1966 Senatorial elections.

That it begin now to explore ways and means of electing militant Negroes to local offices in Mississippi in the 1967 elections.

Notes on Mississippi

It's not clear when or by whom this short summary was written. It was preserved among the papers of SNCC's Mendy Samstein, and appears to date between the November 14–18 staff meeting and the December 31 discussion of Freedom Summer by SNCC. It describes the 1963 Freedom Vote campaign and the debate at a SNCC meeting a few days later over whether to recruit white outsiders to help them organize a voter registration drive the following summer.

Perhaps the most significant result of the Freedom Vote campaign [of 1963] was in the area of organizational development. For the first time a genuinely state-wide operation was put into effect. A central office was set up in Jackson with the task of coordinating activities around the state. A Mississippi WATS line [Wide Area Telephone Service[1]] was installed to aid in this purpose. The five congressional district offices, established in September, became organizational bases for penetration into neighboring cities and towns, and in practice expanded their operational scope beyond the city in which they were primarily based. Contacts were made in cities and towns previously untouched by the movement. A beginning was made in the compilation of enormous state-wide contact lists, centered in files in the Jackson office. A collection of phone books from around the state was begun. Lists of all physicians, funeral directors, barbers, beauticians, and ministers in the state were compiled. There were glimmerings of the organizational uses to which the WATS line could be put: 1) as an information relay center 2) for coordination of staff activities 3) for the gathering of information about local problems, either of a community or personal nature 4) for informing people about federal programs 5) for contacting people about the payment of poll taxes 6) for contacting people about

---

1 Before cell phones, a Wide Area Telephone Service (WATS) line enabled the subscriber to make unlimited long-distance calls for a flat monthly fee without going through local telephone operators. Civil rights workers in the field could always reach SNCC, CORE, or COFO offices, whose WATS lines were staffed twenty-four hours a day, to report violence or arrests, summon medical or legal help when workers were beaten or jailed, alert staff in other locations to common threats, and notify the media or US Department of Justice about emergencies. The daily WATS logs from Jackson, Greenwood, and Atlanta document the events of Freedom Summer hour by hour. Logs for nearly every day of the summer are available at www.wisconsinhistory.org/freedomsummer.

registering to vote 7) for setting up meetings in different parts of the state 8) for arranging speakers at meetings 9) for arranging for the movement of staff and people in general from one place to another.

The Freedom Vote campaign, completed on November 4, was followed by a lull in activities throughout the state. On November 10 thirty staff people were brought together for a five day workshop which culminated in a weekend staff meeting.

The November 14–18 Greenville staff meeting was primarily concerned with four problems: 1) the role of whites in the movement 2) the number of Northern students to be brought into Mississippi this summer 3) programs which might lead to greater federal involvement in the state and 4) whether COFO should sponsor an independent political party or work within the framework of the existing parties. None of these problems were essentially resolved at the Greenville meeting. Perhaps the greatest amount of discussion was devoted to the question of the role of whites in the movement. A number of people seemed to question whether whites had any role working within the Negro community. While acknowledging certain educational advantages to the image of black and white working together, they maintained that this image often became one of white leading black and that in order to undermine and ultimately destroy the belief in white supremacy, it was imperative that the movement maintain black leadership. For a while, some argued that whites should only work in white communities.

Some of this conflict over the role of whites arose inevitably as part of the backwash of the Freedom Vote Campaign in which over eighty Yale and Stanford students came into the state to work. But a large part of the conflict, whether understood at the time or not, stemmed from a dissatisfaction with the nature in which decisions were made during the Freedom Vote Campaign. Both the lack of any clearly defined decision-making machinery and the hecticness of the campaign necessitated that decisions, if they were to be made at all, be made in Jackson and on the spot. Inevitably, it seemed to many on the staff as though they were being excluded from the decision-making process. With the concentration of whites in the central office as a result of the expansion in state-wide activities and the concurrent need for specialized people, it seemed to people in the field as though whites were intimately involved in the decision-making process whereas they themselves were excluded. (This impression was not entirely without basis. But to the extent that it was true, it was more the result of necessity—i.e., who was in the office to discuss and implement ideas—than of design.)

No essential changes, however, emerged from this discussion. There was simply no one willing to come out of the field in order to work in the Jackson office. On the other hand there's a strong mandate directed to the entire staff, though in effect primarily to the central office, to attempt to involve more Negro Mississippians (e.g. from Jackson State College) into the movement.

Considerable time was spent at Greenville discussing whether to invite a massive number of Northern whites into Mississippi for the summer of 1964. It was clear from the nature of the publicity derived from the Freedom Vote campaign that the press would respond to the beating of a Yale student as it simply would not do to the beating of a local Negro. The *New York Times* headlined its stories about the campaign with the news that Yale and Stanford students were working "for a Negro gubernatorial candidate in Mississippi." During the Freedom Rally in Jackson which concluded the campaign, TV men from N.B.C. spent most of their time shooting film of the Yalies and seemed hardly aware of the local people and full-time SNCC workers. While it was agreed by all that this was a sorry state of affairs, many contended that such publicity was essential for awakening the national conscience and preparing a climate for greater federal involvement in Mississippi. (It was noted that for the first time the Justice Department had people on hand in the eventuality of trouble.) It was argued that by flooding Mississippi with Northern whites the entire country would be made dramatically aware of the denial of freedom which existed in the state and that the federal government would be inevitably faced with a crisis of sufficient magnitude that it would have to act. Others, however, maintained that the reality of such a program would be chaos, if not actual bloodshed. The staff could never handle a massive number of whites either organizationally (supply them with sufficient things to do) or administratively (house, feed, and bond them all out of jail). The organizational development of the Negroes of Mississippi would be more set back than advanced by such an invasion. Furthermore, psychologically it would be a duplication of the same pattern—one of whites leading blacks—as the one we were trying to destroy. Local Negro leadership would be stifled rather than encouraged.

The argument was never clearly resolved at the Greenville meeting; though many seemed in favor of bringing in a limited number of whites to perform certain specified functions. In general, it was agreed that there needed to be more emphasis placed on recruiting Negroes, and especially native Mississippians.

Also discussed at the Greenville meeting was the need for some dramatic action which would bring about significant federal presence in Mississippi. Howard Zinn introduced the discussion by asserting that organizational protest in Mississippi could not succeed without outside assistance. Techniques that worked in other places (sit-ins, pickets, etc.) would not work in Mississippi because they would not be tolerated by the police power of the state. Therefore, no matter how strong the movement became, it would inevitably require the power of the federal government to restrain the use of police clubs, if it was to make any important gains in the state. The question then posed was how to generate enough pressure to force the government to intervene in Mississippi to ensure Negro voting rights. A number of projects were discussed (see minutes) but nothing specific was adopted at the time.

Bob Moses followed by discussing the need for institutionalizing a number of long-range projects which are now being put into operation (see minutes). Throughout the week-long workshop it was repeatedly recognized that since the achievement of any political gains was still in the distant future, the movement would have to develop its own structure, outside the state, for servicing vital needs. Along these lines the most important project which emerged from the Greenville meeting was the plan for setting up a network of community centers which would perform functions ranging from pre-natal care to political education. In addition, emphasis was placed on making greater use of federal programs, such as FHA [Federal Housing Administration], MDTA [Manpower Development and Training Act], and RAD [Rental Assistance Demonstration program], and on promoting more home industries, such as the one initiated in Ruleville. It was made clear, however, that these added activities were not to detract from (but rather to supplement) our primary concern with politics.

A great deal of time at the Greenville meeting was given over to discussing our relationship with the NAACP. There was strong sentiment that if the NAACP was not going to lend its full weight behind COFO it should not be a member. But in the final analysis it was agreed that the use of the NAACP's name was of benefit to us, and that as long as the NAACP did not openly oppose our program it might be well to tolerate its lack of active cooperation.

Throughout the winter of 1963–64, SNCC continued debating whether to invite more Northern volunteers and run a large-scale voter registration project the next summer. Some members thought the success of the Freedom Vote could be replicated on an even larger scale with more college student volunteers, and with them would come more national press. But others felt SNCC simply wasn't ready to organize and run a campaign employing hundreds of people. Others worried that an influx of educated white outsiders would inhibit the growth of local black leaders.

Then, on January 31, 1964, news came during a SNCC meeting in Hattiesburg that Louis Allen had been murdered. Allen, an activist in the town of Liberty, had witnessed the killing of Herbert Lee by a member of the state legislature and described it to the FBI. After white supremacists heard about this, they gunned Allen down outside his home. "Until then," Bob Moses recalled, "the staff had been deadlocked, at loggerheads with each other; this decided it."[2] The Mississippi Summer Project was launched.

2 Moses, Robert P. *Radical Equations* (Boston: Beacon Press, 2001): 76.

Dear Friend

Dear Friend,

Enclosed is a description of our plans for Mississippi this summer. You might also be interested to learn what we are doing within the state to structure these plans and to prepare for the hundreds of volunteers we are expecting to participate in our program.

Since the beginning of February we have been traveling the state consulting with local leaders, speaking at mass meetings, and in general informing as many people as possible of what is planned for this summer. Local groups everywhere have responded with enthusiasm and are making preparations for the programs and the number of people they would like to see in their community. At the moment we have already lined up housing in various communities for over 200 people and the commitments are continuing to come in. We have also begun to negotiate for facilities in which to locate Freedom Schools and community centers—and at the moment there are many promising prospects.

We have already begun recruitment of high school students for the Freedom Schools. A statewide Mississippi Student Union has been formed and local affiliates are being organized. The Union is expected to serve as a natural source of recruitment. In addition, we are using our local contacts with adults—ministers, teachers, community leaders—and we are planning two statewide student conferences at which recruitment for the Freedom Schools will be the keynote.

We have had several sessions to map out curriculum for both the Freedom Schools and the educational programs of the Community Centers. A weekend conference of various people trained and experienced in education is being planned for March at which further details will be worked out.

Funds are now desperately needed to make all these plans work. We urge you to begin a fund-raising drive on your campus, at your church, among your working colleagues (if you are out of college) or wherever you can. You could open a special "Mississippi Summer Project" bank account and try to raise as much money as you can by June.

Everyone over 18 is invited to apply for the Mississippi Summer Project (though we are asking parental permission for those under 21). If you would like to help recruit others for the project we urge that you give special emphasis to people with the type of skills listed in our application form. Application forms or any further information can always be obtained by writing to Mississippi Summer Project, 1017 Lynch Street, Jackson, Mississippi.

We expect by May 15 to inform everyone of their acceptance or rejection. At that time those accepted will also be informed of where they have been assigned, where they will live, what they will be doing, and under whom they will be working. An orientation period for all summer workers is being planned for sometime in June.

We hope to hear from you soon. If you have any comments, suggestions, or questions please let us know.

Mississippi Summer Project
1017 Lynch Street
Jackson, Mississippi

Application to Work on the Freedom Summer Project

New York Student Nonviolent Coordinating Committee

Summer Project Participant - 1964

G-3

1. Name _Andrew Goodman_ 2. Age _20_ 3. Sex _M_

4. Home Address _161 W 86 St N.Y. N.Y. 10024_

5. Home Phone _EN-2-7265_ 6. Marital Status _Single_

7. Name of Parent or Guardian _Robert W Goodman_

8. Address of Parent or Guardian _161 W 86 St N.Y. N.Y. 10024_

9. High School Attended _Walden School_ 10. Yr. of Grad. _1961_

11. College Attended _Queens College_ 12. Year of Grad. _1966_

13. Major _Anthropology_

14. Honors _____

15. Extra-curricular Activities _Off - Broadway and Queens College Theatre._

16. Graduate School _____ 17. Field _____

18. Occupation (If not a student) _____

19. Previous Civil Rights Activities _Picketing through CORE and High School, Marches on Washington_

20. Summer Assignment:

___ Freedom Schools ___ Community Centers

✓ Voter Registration

___ Communications ___ Research Project

SNCC volunteer application form filled out by twenty-year-old college student Andrew Goodman in early 1964. Goodman was one of three Freedom Summer volunteers murdered by the Ku Klux Klan on June 21, 1964.

Mississippi Summer Project Launched

> *This SNCC press release, dated March 20, 1964, is one of several publications provided to the media, supporters, and local residents during the spring of 1964 to raise funds and build awareness.*

MISSISSIPPI SUMMER PROJECT LAUNCHED

JACKSON, MISSISSIPPI—"At least 2,000" full time civil rights workers will conduct voter registration and political education programs in Mississippi this summer, according to civil rights worker Robert Moses.

The announcement of the "Mississippi Summer Project" came from a day-long conference of the Council of Federated Organizations (COFO) here March 15. COFO is a coalition of national and local civil rights groups working in Mississippi.

COFO leaders said the "Freedom Summer" plans included recruiting 1,000 white and Negro college students to man "Freedom Schools," Community Centers and to work on a voter registration drive. The group will also run two Negroes for Congress in the state's 2nd and 5th Congressional Districts.

COFO Chairman Dr. Aaron Henry of Clarksdale, state NAACP head, said Mrs. Fannie Lou Hamer of Ruleville would oppose Representative Jamie Whitten of Charleston in the 2nd District and Reverend John Cameron of Hattiesburg would oppose Representative William Colmer of Pascagoula in the 5th District. The two Negro candidates will also run in a "Freedom Primary" corresponding with the state's Democratic primary, COFO workers said.

If both lose, they plan to challenge the seating of the winning candidates. "We intend to challenge whether the country will permit people to be elected from districts where Negroes are not allowed to vote," COFO Program Director Moses said.

Moses, who has headed the Student Nonviolent Coordinating Committee (SNCC) vote drive here since 1961, and Dave Dennis of the Congress of Racial Equality (CORE) will head up the summer drive.

Moses and Dennis said the summer campaign would include:

FREEDOM SCHOOLS that will give youth and adults political education as well as courses common to a high school curriculum;

COMMUNITY CENTERS that will provide recreational facilities, instruction in pre-natal care, nutrition, job retraining, arts and craft classes, organized sports and libraries;

FREEDOM REGISTRATION that will register 400,000 Negroes on mock polling list to "prove Negroes in Mississippi will register to vote if they are allowed to."

FREEDOM ELECTION held during the state's Democratic primary on June 2 to indicate Mississippi Negroes are not satisfied with present candidates;

CHALLENGING THE SEATING OF MISSISSIPPI CONGRESSMEN on the floor of the House of Representatives on the basis that many Negroes are denied to right to vote in the state;

VOTER REGISTRATION drives that will attempt to register an added 25,000 Negroes;

EMERGENCY RELIEF AND WELFARE AID for Negroes who face job losses or evictions because of their participation in the vote drive.

Moses said the Freedom Schools, in addition to giving students a chance to learn subjects poorly taught in Mississippi's Negro schools, would teach the "politics of Mississippi" and would begin to build a core of educated leadership in the state. Dennis and Moses said the Freedom Registration drive would try to register "more Negroes than could possibly register" under present discriminatory standards.

Dr. Henry said students were being recruited for the summer at 7 Freedom Centers located at Northern college campuses and in large cities.

COFO plans call for Freedom Summer operation in twenty-nine locations scattered throughout the state's five congressional districts.

Letter from Volunteer Training in Oxford, Ohio

> *Joel Bernard was a New Yorker accepted by COFO to work as a volunteer. In this letter, he describes the training sessions in Oxford, Ohio, and includes a warm portrait of Bob Moses. He spent the summer working on voter registration in Columbus, in northeastern Mississippi.*

June 25, 1964

Dear Mom,

I'm sort of hesitant about writing this way, with carbon papers, and apologize if you are getting a carbon, but you can all imagine how much time I have to write letters while getting oriented.

I arrived in Oxford, Ohio, at 10 in the morning last Sunday, after an all-night ride from NYC in a rented car, with four other people—a man and wife and two students—all quite nice and from the NY area. The ride was very enjoyable—mostly across Pennsylvania, a very beautiful state at night and an especially welcome fresh-country change from NY. West Virginia was very depressing, many ramshackle homes, "country-western" music radio station (WWVA) which happens to be very powerful. Somehow the combination of scenic dissonance and, sort of, music suggesting so much foreign from the city, without arousing any reaction except an unpleasant jarring of the senses, as if it were somehow so representative of depressing, mountain way of life—all added to the desire I felt to get away quickly. My favorite song was (if I remember) "I Overlooked an Orchard in Search of a Rose." It was more than just another city reaction on my part, I believe.

The dorms are very nice—beds with sheets—and the food is excellent. We get up at 7:30, and throughout the day go to general orientation meetings (everybody) and sections (depending upon what post you go to).

The staff—those with whom we will be working throughout the summer, are amazingly competent. Almost all Negroes from Mississippi who have been jailed and beaten many times—but still have a reverence for the movement. All are sort of quiet, with wry senses of humor, and a feeling you get of strength, an ability to get you out of a tough situation.

A word about Bob Moses, the leader of the project. You've really got to meet the man in order to fully appreciate his personality. I'm not exaggerating when I say that he's a Christ-like figure who has won the respect of everyone on the project. An MA in philosophy, he picked up and left a job in a NYC school and a few days later walked into McComb, Miss., (the most dangerous part of Miss.—where five Negroes have been killed in five months). Anyway, he walked into the middle of this and established a civil rights movement. He is of medium short height, a light skinned Negro, with a quiet voice and a perpetually sad, thoughtful face—almost childlike expression of long-felt grief which occasionally lights up in a smile and equally quickly returns to thoughtfulness. I doubt if he's ever raised his voice in his life or shown any other outward signs of excitement, although he's been beaten and harassed often. A really humble person, always wearing farmer's clothes—blue jeans with belt and suspenders. The moment he speaks, silence—and in a few words he has spoken more common sense than everyone else.

Orientation sessions are well-thought-out—we're given general background material of course, but also outside speakers including lawyers (what to do and expect) and the southern lawyer who spoke out in Birmingham and had to leave. A deep attempt to force us to explore our feelings about Negroes, and also "role-plays" (e.g., what to do if you are stopped by a policeman).

I expect to go to Natchez, after first going to Columbia, Miss., for some further training. I just returned from a two day visit to Washington DC, where the group from SW Miss. went to lobby congressmen to put pressure on the Justice Department to send marshals and FBI men to protect us. There was a party when we got in which raised $700 for SNCC. I had an interesting time, feeling quite a center of attention, since I and the others had just returned from Oxford, Ohio, where the orientation had received much press coverage. Mostly typical young suburban types, liberals involved perhaps in government work. Also saw Congressman Ryan and Sen. Keating—who are both active in supporting civil rights. Ryan is really respected—he has badgered the JD [Justice Department] and constantly uses his influence to create or push support for SNCC. I'll probably leave for Mississippi in a few days. Please write or telegraph the press and your congressman expressing "deep concern" over the level of violence in Southwest Miss., which is a stronghold of the Klan, and asking for federal protection. Certain sections of Title 18 US Code very adequately invest the federal government with powers. Of course, all JD officials deny it but don't admit the political reasons for this denial. This summer will, I hope, force their hand.

You might also spread word about the project to friends. We have been getting very decent press coverage, but most people are still unaware of the real situation in Miss. and of SNCC's real purpose. It is important that public indignity be kept high, and we have reason to believe that much of the federal action already has been prompted by personal appeals of ourselves, parents, friends.

I'm in fine shape, perhaps a little grubby, but well fed. I'm looking forward to getting to Miss. and starting work. I hope you all won't worry about me too much and I'll try to send word occasionally. It's been hot here but Washington was an oven. You can write to me, temporarily, c/o Western College for Women, Oxford, Ohio.

Love,
Joel

Possible Role-Playing Situations

> *Movement veterans leading the Freedom Summer orientation were alarmed at the naïveté of the Northern volunteers, most of whom had never encountered segregation and were about to face off with racist sheriffs and angry mobs. They designed a variety of scenarios and forced the Northerners to confront how they would respond.*

[Document 1]

1. The Cell (4 persons, white, same sex)

   —a white civil rights worker is thrown into a cell with three ardent segregationists. As the jailer opens the cell, he identifies the civil rights worker to the inmates—"Got some company for you fellas, one of those northern nigger-loving agitators. Now treat him nice."

2. Police harassment (7 persons, white and Negro, male and female)

   —two state troopers stop a carload of 5 civil rights workers for speeding on a little used highway. (Variation: one of the troopers notices a white girl sitting with a Negro boy on the back seat and proceeds to drag the Negro worker out of the car and beat him to "remind him of how we expect our niggers to act.")

3. The Guest (7 persons, white and Negro, male and female)

   —a white civil rights worker who is staying with a Mississippi Negro family receives an anonymous note or phone call warning him that unless he clears out of town by midnight, the family will be attacked and the house burned to the ground. (Variation: The civil rights worker and the family are having a late supper and a brick is thrown through the window with the message mentioned above. The father of the family immediately jumps up from the table and goes to get his shotgun.)

4. Canvassing (5 persons, white and Negro, male and female)

   —an integrated team of civil rights workers visit a Negro home to try to persuade the adults of the family to register to vote. (Variation: While the team is talking with the family, the plantation owner arrives on the scene with a shotgun.)

5. Other possible situations:

   —an encounter with two white Mississippi students (members of ATAC [Association of Tenth Amendment Conservatives, a white-supremacist student group in Mississippi])

—an ambush of 3 civil rights workers (two whites and one Negro), in which the Negro is singled out and beaten

—a picket line outside a Federal Court House which is attacked by a group of stone-throwing white teenagers (for role playing use dried prunes for rocks)

—suggested non-violent counter-offenses to particular tragic incidents such as the disappearance of the 3 workers near Philadelphia, Mississippi.[3]

[Document 2]

I. Reporter
   1. What would you say if a reporter asked you about staff problems?
   2. What would you say if a reporter asked you about COFO policies?
   3. What would you do if a reporter asked you what do you expect out of the summer project?
   4. Do you think the summer project was a good idea?
   5. Do you like working with Negroes?
   6. Have you found that most Negroes are dirty?
   7. Are Negroes staying with white boys and girls?

II. Police
   1. If a police stopped you and asked you to get into his car, what would you do?
   2. If a cop told you you are under arrest, what would you do or say?
   3. If you are taken to jail, what would you say? What questions would you answer?
   4. If you saw another person arrested, what would you do?
   5. If you were allowed a phone call, who would you call and what would you say?
   6. If you saw a person being beaten, what would you do? by police? by an outsider?

III. Non-violence
   1. How would you react to: teargas, firehoses, dogs, picket line, march to courthouse, verbal intimidations, cattle prod, etc.

IV. Canvassing
   1. How would you approach a person in a community you had never seen before?

---

3   The trainings were in two sessions, June 15–22 and June 23–29, each with different volunteers. The reference to "the 3 workers" suggests that this document was from the second session, which began after James Chaney, Andrew Goodman, and Mickey Schwerner disappeared.

2. How could you make a person understand what voting is by relating things in his everyday life?
3. How would you talk to a real religious person?
4. How would you talk to a community leader?

V. White Local citizens
1. How would you approach a local white citizen?
2. How would you react if approached by a local white citizen?

Security Handbook

> *This manual taught volunteers how to protect themselves. It distilled the bitter experience that CORE and SNCC workers had gained over the previous few years as they worked in the Deep South.*

1. Communications personnel will act as security officers.
2. <u>Travel</u>

    a. When persons leave their project, they <u>must</u> call their project person-to-person for <u>themselves</u> on arrival at destination point. Should they be missing, project personnel will notify the Jackson office. WATS line operators will call each project every day at dinnertime or thereabouts, and should be notified of changes in personnel, transfers, etc. (If trips are planned in advance, this information can go to Jackson by mail. Phone should be used only where there is no time. Care should be taken at all times to avoid, if possible, full names of persons travelling.) Checklists should be used in local projects for personnel to check in and out.

    b. Doors of cars should be locked at all times. At night, windows should be rolled up as much as possible. Gas tanks must have locks and be kept locked. Hoods should also be locked.

    c. No one should go <u>anywhere</u> alone, but certainly not in an automobile, and certainly not at night.

    d. Travel at night should be avoided unless absolutely necessary.

    e. Remove all unnecessary objects from your car which could be construed as weapons. (Hammers, files, iron rules, etc.) Absolutely no liquor bottles, beer cans, etc. should be inside your car. Do not travel with names and addresses of local contacts.

    f. Know all roads in and out of town. Study the county map.

    g. Know locations of sanctuaries and safe homes in the county.

    h. When getting out of a car at night, make sure the car's inside light is out.

    i. Be conscious of cars which circle offices or Freedom Houses. Take license numbers of all suspicious cars. Note make, model and year. Cars without license plates should immediately be reported to the project office.
3. <u>Living at Home or in Freedom Houses</u>

    a. If it can be avoided, try not to sleep near open windows. Try to sleep at the back of the house, i.e., the part farthest from a road or street.

b. Do not stand in doorways at night with the light at your back.

c. At night, people should not sit in their rooms without drawn shades.

d. Do not congregate in front of the house at night.

e. Make sure doors to Freedom Houses have locks, and are locked.

f. Keep records of suspicious events, i.e., the same car circling around the house or office several times during the day or week. Take license numbers, makes, years and models of cars. Keep records of the times these cars appear.

g. If an "incident" occurs, or is about to occur, call the project, and then notify local FBI and police.

h. Depending on project needs and circumstances, it may be advisable for new personnel to make deliberate attempts to introduce themselves immediately to local police and tell them their reason for being in the area.

i. A phone should be installed in each Freedom House, if there isn't one already. If a private phone is used, please put a lock on it. Otherwise, install a pay phone; this will avoid immediate pick-ups on suspicion.

4. Personal Actions

a. Carry identification at all times. Men should carry draft cards.

b. All drivers should have in their possession drivers licenses, registration papers, and bills of sale. The information should also be on record with the project director. If you are carrying supplies, it might be well to have a letter authorizing the supplies from a particular individual to avoid charges of carrying stolen goods.

c. Mississippi is a dry state and though liquor is ostensibly outlawed, it is available everywhere. You must not drink in offices, or Freedom Houses. This is especially important for persons under 21.

d. Try to avoid bizarre or provocative clothing, and beards. Be neat.

e. Make sure that prescribed medicines are clearly marked, with your name, the doctor's name, etc.

5. Relations with the Press

a. Refer questions about SNCC's perspective or policies to the Project Director.

b. Do not argue with the press. Do not exaggerate. Give the facts only.

c. The Project Director and communications person will ask for credentials of press. If you do not know the reporter, check with one of them or ask to see the reporter's credentials.

d. Try to relate your activities to the lives of the local residents. This will not be hard to do, or unnatural, if you remember your role in the state.

6. Information to Police

Under no circumstances should you give the address of the local person with whom you are living, his or her name, or the names of any local persons who are associated with you. When police ask where you live, give your local project or Freedom House address, or if necessary, your out of state address.

7. Relations with Visitors

Find out who strangers are. If persons come into project offices to "look around" try to discover who they are and what exactly they want to know. All offers of assistance should be cleared through the project director.

8. Records

1. Any written record of importance should have at least four copies. Keep original, send copies to Jackson, Greenwood and Atlanta. Bear in mind that the office might be raided at any time.

2. Keep a record of interference with phone lines and of notifications of FBI. This information will go to Jackson via the communications person.

9. Policy

1. People who do not adhere to disciplinary requirements will be asked to leave the project.

2. Security precautions are a matter of group responsibility. Each individual should take an interest in every other person's safety, well-being, and discipline.

3. At all times you should be aware of the danger to local residents. White volunteers must be especially careful.

Nonviolence: Two Training Documents

> *To some workers, nonviolence was just a public relations device, a tactic designed to evoke sympathy and support in observers. To others, it was a moral imperative and a way of life. These short pieces were used to introduce volunteers to the breadth and power of nonviolence.*

[Document 1]

1. NONVIOLENCE

Non-violence is a deliberate way of securing social change and of reaching others. It is active, not passive. It sometimes looks passive, when those who receive violence refuse to retaliate. Their refusal is a positive act of communication. They are saying to the other person that regardless of what he does, they believe that he is the temporary victim of an evil or negative force, but that if he wants to, he can overcome that force. Their own refusal to retaliate encourages him to try and shows him that it is possible.

Practicing non-violence requires discipline in order to keep control in the face of provocation. If we retaliate with violence, we convert our struggle into a test of physical strength. But our whole purpose is to make society behave in a more responsible—which means a more moral—way. Thus we exert moral force in order to bring about a moral response in others, and thus a more moral society. If we act irresponsibly, we confirm the prejudices of those who want to deny our rights because they claim we are incapable of exercising them morally and responsibly. If we act responsibly, we do more than to repudiate that argument, and to persuade others that we do have the capacity to act justly and correctly. We also strengthen ourselves—we confirm by our actions, our belief in ourselves and our values, and our readiness to put our legitimate rights and privileges to proper use.

Non-violence is a way of speaking to others and to ourselves. We must continue to speak while we act, and never close the door to a dialogue with the rest of the community. Non-violence testifies to our readiness always to speak in a spirit of constructive conciliation and cooperation. There are six maxims of non-violent behavior:

1. Our attitude toward officials and others who may oppose us will be one of sympathetic understanding of the burdens and responsibilities they carry.

2. No matter what the circumstances or provocation, we will not respond with physical violence to acts directed against us.

3. We will not call names or make hostile remarks.

4. We will adhere as closely as we are able to the letter and spirit of truth in our spoken and written statements.

5. We will always try to speak to the best in all men, rather than seeking to exploit their weaknesses to what we may believe is our advantage.

6. We will always attempt to interpret as clearly as possible to anyone with whom we are in contact—and especially to those who may oppose us—the purpose and meaning of our actions.

[Document 2]

2. Case Study: Statements of discipline of non-violent movements

The purpose of this material is to stimulate discussion of the values and practices of the movement. Is the movement the germ of a new society? Would we want a whole society in which people related to each other as they do in the movement?

I. Student Nonviolent Coordinating Committee statement of purpose:

"We affirm the philosophical or religious ideal of nonviolence as the foundation of our purpose, the presupposition of our faith, and the manner of our action. Nonviolence as it grows from the Judaeo-Christian tradition seeks a social order of justice permeated by love. Integration of human endeavor represents the crucial first step towards such a society.

Through nonviolence, courage displaces fear; love transforms hate. Acceptance dissipates prejudice; hope ends despair. Peace dominates war; faith reconciles doubt. Mutual regard cancels enmity. Justice for all overcomes injustice. The redemptive community supercedes systems of gross social immorality.

Love is the central motif of nonviolence. Love is the force by which God binds man to himself and man to man. Such love goes to the extreme; it remains loving and forgiving even in the midst of hostility. It matches the capacity of evil to inflict suffering with an even more enduring capacity to absorb evil, all the while persisting in love.

By appealing to conscience and standing on the moral nature of human existence, nonviolence nurtures the atmosphere in which reconciliation and justice become actual possibilities."

II. CORE Rules for Action (excerpts):

1. Investigate the facts carefully before determining whether or not racial injustice exists in a given situation.

2. Seek at all times to understand both the attitude of the person responsible for a policy of racial discrimination, and the social situation which engendered the attitude. Be flexible and creative, showing a willingness to participate in experiments which seem constructive, but being careful not to compromise CORE principles.

3. Make a sincere effort to avoid malice and hatred toward any group or individual.

4. Never use malicious slogans or labels to discredit any opponent.

5. Be willing to admit mistakes.

6. Meet the anger of any individual or group in the spirit of good will and creative reconciliation; submit to assault and not retaliate in kind either by act or word.

7. Never engage in action in the name of the group except when authorized by the group or one of its action units.

8. When in action obey the orders issued by the authorized leader or spokesman of the project. Criticism [may be referred later] back to the group.

III. Staff decorum suggested for SNCC SW Georgia Project:

(1) There will be no consumption of alcoholic beverages.

(2) Men will not be housed with women.

(3) Romantic attachments on the level of "girl-boy friend relations" will not be encouraged within the group.

(4) The staff will go to church regularly.

(5) The group shall have the power of censure.

IV. Pledge of Freedom Riders imprisoned in Parchman Penitentiary (also discussed in Unit VII):

Having, after due consideration, chosen to follow without reservation, the principles of nonviolence, we resolve while in prison:

- to practice nonviolence of speech and thought as well as action;
- to treat even those who may be our captors as brothers;
- to engage in a continual process of cleansing of the mind and body in rededication to our cause;
- to intensify our search for orderly living even when in the midst of seeming chaos.

V. From the Discipline of the San Francisco-to-Moscow Walk:

General statement. The purpose of the Walk is to appeal to the mind and conscience of the American people. It is also a part of a nonviolent philosophy to have respect for all human beings and to seek to communicate with them, not to put up barriers between them and ourselves. It is recognized that dress, manners, ways of speaking, etc., of the Team members have a bearing on the impact, emotional, intellectual and spiritual, which they make on those with whom they come in contact on the walk. We do not think any committee is in a position to lay down detailed rules on such subjects and in any case sensitivity in our relations to persons and commitment to the project and the way of nonviolence constitute the only true source of right action in these matters.

Specifics. Our attitude toward officials will be one of sympathetic understanding of the burdens and responsibilities they carry.

No matter what the circumstances or provocation, we will not call names, make hostile remarks, nor respond with physical violence to acts directed against us.

We will adhere as closely as we are able to the letter and spirit of truth in our spoken and written statements.

We will always try to speak to the best in all men, rather than seeking to exploit their weaknesses to what we may believe is our advantage.

Epilogue (ask students if this sums up the foregoing): "The revolution is a need of being no longer alone, one man against another; it is an attempt to stand together and be afraid no longer. . . ." (Ignazio Silone).

Hattiesburg, Mississippi, police march toward voting rights demonstrators in the rain in January 1964.

3

OPPOSITION AND VIOLENCE

Opponents swung into action as soon as Freedom Summer was announced. In April 1964, Mississippi's legislature introduced laws making the most common forms of protest illegal (the first document in this chapter). The state patrol and local police beefed up their arsenals; Jackson even bought a tank. "We're going to be ready for them," the city's mayor said about Freedom Summer volunteers. "They won't have a chance."[1]

The press, pulpit, broadcasters, and nearly all other media denounced Freedom Summer. In his autobiography, SNCC's Stokely Carmichael recalled this as "a deliberate, systematic, unchallenged campaign of disinformation put out by the local media, much of which originated with the governor (through his Sovereignty Commission) and ran through the legislature, down to local mayors and petty politicians. . . . [It was] a calculated exploitation of people's anxiety and confusion to whip up anger and bloodlust."[2]

Because it's hard for most people today to appreciate the degree of racism that motivated Freedom Summer's adversaries, significant space is given here to letting them speak for themselves. What should be clear after reading this chapter is that black Mississippians and Freedom Summer workers were immersed in a situation of potential violence that could erupt at any moment into kidnapping, firebombing, and murder.

The second document here, an issue of the *Klan Ledger*, lays out the Ku Klux Klan's program to defend racial purity. Thousands of Mississippians were members of the Klan in 1964 and were probably swayed by its appeals to religion, history, and fear. The next item is an address by the head of the Citizens' Councils—a sort of white-supremacist Chamber of Commerce. It uses calmer language than the Klan's to justify institutionalized racism. The

---

1   "Allen's Army." *Newsweek* (February 24, 1964): 30.

2   Ture, Kwame (Stokely Carmichael). *Ready for Revolution* (New York: Charles Scribner's Sons, 2003): 360–361.

testimony by black residents summarized in the fourth document explains how federal officials, local police, courts, white businesses, and racist groups seeking to instill terror conspired to deny African Americans their basic constitutional rights.

On the project's first day, June 21, Freedom Summer workers James Chaney, Andrew Goodman, and Mickey Schwerner were abducted, tortured, and murdered by local police and Klan members in Neshoba County. Their last hours are described in Louis Lomax's article excerpted here. Bob Moses's plea to parents a few days later, an attempt to leverage their influence and force the federal government to protect volunteers (the next document), was a failure: the Justice Department and FBI continued to insist it was not their place to enforce laws at the local level.

In fact, Mississippi FBI agents and police usually shared the white-supremacist views of their neighbors. Extreme examples of those views are revealed in the next section: hate mail sent to civil rights workers and their families (including the parents of the murdered Andrew Goodman).

The last document in this section is a short journal and a letter written by Walter Kaufmann, a California volunteer who worked in the town from which the three murdered workers had departed. It describes an atmosphere of violence that greeted volunteers in many parts of the state.

Readers whose knowledge of the civil rights era comes only from school-books should be able to see from these accounts that the civil rights struggle wasn't just waged in marches on Washington or arguments before the Supreme Court. It was fought on the streets of small Southern towns, a war zone where, as the title of one memoir puts it, "we had sneakers, they had guns."[3] Justice was won because thousands of common people challenged their inherited beliefs, overcame their fears, and put their bodies on the line to liberate themselves.

---

3 Sugarman, Tracy. *We Had Sneakers, They Had Guns: The Kids Who Fought for Civil Rights in Mississippi* (Syracuse, NY: Syracuse University Press, 2009).

Mississippi Readies Laws for Freedom Summer

The following excerpt is from a longer COFO report listing bills introduced in the Mississippi legislature to oppose Freedom Summer. Its comments were written by COFO staff. The fact that many of these provisions violated the US Constitution didn't seem to matter to Mississippi officials.

Please note that only those bills starred with an asterisk have actually been signed into law, as of June 2, 1964. Several other bills which have been passed in either or in both houses will probably become law before adjournment of the current session, expected in late June or early July.

1. ANTI-ECONOMIC BOYCOTT BILL - Senate Bill No. 1607 (Still in Committee) - This bill attempts to outlaw economic boycotts by Negroes against white businesses which discriminate.

*2. ANTI-LEAFLETING LAW - Senate Bill No. 1545 (Passed and Signed) - This bill prohibits the distributing of leaflets calling for economic boycotts.

*3. ANTI-PICKETING LAW - House Bill No. 546 (Passed and Signed) - A bill prohibiting picketing of public buildings.

4. SECOND ANTI-PICKETING LAW - (Passed in House, sent to Senate) - An almost identical law to be used if the above law is declared unconstitutional.

5. BILL AUTHORIZING SPECIAL DEPUTY SHERIFFS IN ALL COUNTIES - House Bill No. 246 (Still in County Affairs Committee) - A bill to allow unlimited deputy sheriffs "to cope with emergencies."

*6. BILL TO "RESTRAIN MOVEMENTS OF INDIVIDUALS UNDER CERTAIN CIRCUMSTANCES"—THE CURFEW LAW - House Bill No. 64 (Passed in both Houses and signed) - This bill would allow police to restrict freedom of movement of individuals and groups and to establish curfews without formally declaring martial law.

7. BILL "TO PROVIDE FOR APPOINTMENT OF SECURITY AND PATROL PERSONNEL FOR STATE INSTITUTIONS" - House Bill No. 617 (Passed in House and sent to Senate) - This bill provides for "security patrol officers" to be appointed at all State institutions by the Public Safety Commissioner.

8. BILL TO AUTHORIZE A COMPLETE RADIO STATION FOR POLICE IN ANY COUNTY - House Bill No. 101 (Passed in both Houses)

*9. THE "MUNICIPAL AGREEMENT" ACT - Senate Bill No. 1526 (Passed by both Houses and signed) - A bill to allow municipalities to share police forces and firefighting equipment during "riots and civil disturbances."

10. THE "REFUSAL TO COMPLY WITH CERTAIN REQUESTS" BILL - House Bill No. 777 (Passed in both Houses) - A bill to outlaw passive resistance in civil rights demonstrations.

*11. THE HIGHWAY PATROL ACT - House Bill 564 (Passed in both Houses and signed) - An omnibus bill enlarging the Highway patrol and expanding its powers, and allowing the Governor to order the patrol into local situations without the request of local authorities.

12. ANTI-FREEDOM SCHOOL BILL NO. 1 - Senate Bill No. 2136 (Still in Judiciary Committee) - This bill makes illegal the Freedom Schools and Community Centers planned by COFO for the coming summer.

13. ANTI-FREEDOM SCHOOL BILL NO. 2 - Senate Bill No. 1969 (Still in Education Committee) - This is an earlier attempt to ban the Freedom Schools.

14. A BILL TO RAISE QUALIFICATIONS FOR MEMBERS OF COUNTY BOARDS OF EDUCATION - Senate Bill No. 1702 (Released from Education Committee) - Among other things, this bill would require Board members to be high school graduates. The bill has had trouble in the Senate.

15. A BILL TO PERMIT SEGREGATION OF PUBLIC SCHOOLS BY SEXES - (Approved by the House Education Committee) - The bill is to be used in the event Mississippi schools are forced to integrate racially.

16. BILLS TO ALLOW STATE SUPPORT OF PRIVATE SCHOOLS - (Introduced into the Senate) - This is a series of bills to allow state funds to be used in support of private schools if public schools are closed to avoid integration.

17. BILL TO REVOKE THE CHARTER OF TOUGALOO COLLEGE - Senate Bill No. 1672 (Still in Judiciary Committee) - This bill was introduced in retaliation for civil rights activities of students and faculty at integrated Tougaloo College.

18. BILL TO END ACCREDITATION OF TOUGALOO COLLEGE - Senate Bill No. 204 (Passed in both Houses) - This bill would change the accreditation system in the state so that Tougaloo could be dropped from accreditation.

19. INVESTIGATION OF UNIVERSITY OF MISSISSIPPI PROFESSOR CRITICAL OF THE STATE - (Concurrent resolution introduced in the House) - An attack by legislators against a critical university professor.

20. ANTI-SUMMER PROJECT BILL - TO PROHIBIT ENTRY INTO THE STATE - House Bill No. 870 (Still in Judiciary "A" Committee) - This bill attempts to prohibit entry into the state of volunteers for the Mississippi Summer Project on the grounds that their purpose is "willful violation of the laws of the state."

21. THE "CRIMINAL SYNDICALISM" BILL - Senate Bill No. 2027 (Passed in Senate, reported out favorably by House Committee) - This bill makes illegal any association which advocates or practices crime or violence. It is aimed both at white extremist groups and at civil rights organizations.

22. BILL TO PROHIBIT THE CAUSING OF CRIMES FROM OUTSIDE THE STATE - Senate Bill No. 2026 (Passed in Senate, reported out favorably by House committee) - This bill, like the Criminal Syndicalism bill, could be applied to both white extremists and civil rights workers.

23. AN ACT TO PROHIBIT "ENTICEMENT" OF A CHILD TO VIOLATE THE LAWS AND ORDINANCES OF THE STATE - House Bill No. 786 (Still in Judiciary "A" Committee) - This bill attempts to keep minors from participating in civil rights activities by punishing teachers, parents, and civil rights workers.

24. BILL PROVIDING FOR COURTS TO TREAT JUVENILES ARRESTED IN CIVIL RIGHTS CASES AS ADULTS - House Bill No. 960 (Passed by House, now in Senate) - This bill removes from Youth Court jurisdiction minors under 21 years of age charged under those laws most often used for arrest of civil rights workers.

*25. APPROPRIATION FOR THE STATE SOVEREIGNTY COMMISSION - $50,000 - Senate Bill No. 1896 (Passed in both Houses and signed) - An emergency $50,000 appropriation to the State Sovereignty Commission, the official watchdog of segregation in Mississippi, to fight the Civil Rights Bill now pending before Congress.

26. SUPPORT FOR GOVERNOR WALLACE - Concurrent Resolution in the House (Passed by the House) - A Resolution commending Wallace for his Wisconsin "victory."

27. BILL TO PAY COSTS OF COUNTY REGISTRARS AND CIRCUIT CLERKS CONVICTED UNDER THE 1957 and 1960 CIVIL RIGHTS ACTS - Senate Bill No. 1880 (Passed in Senate, now in House) - This bill would allow the State to actively support county officials who refuse to comply with Federal Court orders to register Negroes on an equal basis with whites.

28. THE "LIBERTY AMENDMENT" TO OUTLAW FEDERAL AGENCIES AND THE INCOME TAX - House Concurrent Resolution No. 16 (Passed

in both Houses, now in joint committee) - This proposed amendment to the U.S. Constitution would require the U.S. Government to dissolve or sell all agencies which might compete with private enterprise. The personal income tax would also be ended.

29. BILL TO END URBAN RENEWAL - House Bill _____ (Passed in House, sent to Senate) - A bill ending urban renewal in Mississippi to avoid "federal encroachment."

*30. BILL TO INVALIDATE THE 24TH AMENDMENT WHICH BANS THE POLL TAX - Senate Bill No. 1783 (passed in both Houses and signed) - This bill appears to comply with the 24th Amendment which bans the poll tax in Federal elections. But the bill in fact provides for a similar form of registration which would have the same exclusive effects as the poll tax itself.

31. BILL TO REDUCE THE NUMBER OF NEGROES ON MISSISSIPPI JURY LISTS - House Bill No. 937 (Passed in House, sent to Senate) - This bill attempts to reduce the number of Negroes on Mississippi jury lists by changing the qualifications for jury members.

*32. BILL TO PROVIDE PRISON TERMS OR STERILIZATION FOR PARENTS OF ILLEGITIMATE CHILDREN - House Bill No. 180 (Passed by House, revised version passed by Senate, Senate version finally approved by both Houses and signed) - This bill in its original House form gave parents of a second illegitimate child the choice between three to five years in the State Penitentiary and sexual sterilization. A Senate version, striking the sterilization clause and reducing the penalty to a misdemeanor, was finally approved and signed.

33. BILL TO PROVIDE STERILIZATION FOR THOSE CONVICTED OF A THIRD FELONY - House Bill No. 788 (Still in Judiciary En Banc Committee) - A bill to provide mandatory sterilization of those convicted of a third felony.

34. BILL TO REDUCE THE PENALTY FOR RAPE - House Bill No. 145 (Defeated in the House) - A defeated bill which would have reduced the penalty for rape. The present penalty is either death or life imprisonment.

*35. BILLS TO ALLOW ARRESTED CIVIL RIGHTS WORKERS TO BE TRANSFERRED TO PARCHMAN PENITENTIARY - House Bills No. 321 and 322 (Passed in both Houses and signed) - These bills provide that city and county officials may transfer prisoners to the State Penitentiary in the event of "crowded or inadequate" facilities.

36. BILL TO ALLOW DISCLOSURE OF JUVENILE COURT RECORDS TO STATE AGENCIES - Senate Bill No. 2016 (Passed in Senate, amended version passed in House) - This bill would allow disclosures from records of juvenile offenders to any office or agency of the State, at the discretion of the Youth Court Judge. The purpose of the bill is to allow the Board of Trustees of the University of Mississippi to consider the civil rights arrest records of Negro applicants.

*37. BILL TO REFORM PARCHMAN PENITENTIARY - House Bill No. 227 (Passed in House, revised bill passed in Senate, House version finally passed in both Houses and signed) - A "reform" bill for Parchman Penitentiary which, however, allows continued use of the lash on prisoners. The bill centralizes control of the Penitentiary under the Governor.

The Klan Ledger

> After its long opening prayer, this four-page newsletter from
> September 1964 explains what the Ku Klux Klan believed and why.
> With thousands of Klan members in Mississippi that year, beliefs
> such as these were widespread. White supremacists frequently
> appealed to religion to validate their claims and often accused
> Freedom Summer volunteers of being Communist inspired, if not
> directly controlled by the Soviet Union.

The Klan Ledger
An Official Publication of the WHITE KNIGHTS of THE KU KLUX KLAN
of Mississippi
DEDICATED TO THE PRESERVATION OF CHRISTIAN CIVILIZATION
EARLY AUTUMN EDITION

The "long, hot summer" has passed. Can we measure the results now,
or will it take a number of years to weigh the outcome and success? The
COFO has no laurels to their credit, and the general public of Mississippi
has had a fill of their very existence. In fact the COFO can be summed up
as a complete failure. For this we owe thanks to the general public and the
failure of the good people of Mississippi to accept the scum from our land
as teachers and leaders in our community which was built to its magnificent
splendor by the sweat and blood of our great White Fathers. For the success
of our struggle against this scum, we offer our thanks to Almighty God, our
Creator and Saviour.

THIS THEN IS OUR PRAYER
ALMIGHTY AND ETERNAL FATHER, AGAIN WE ENTER INTO
THY PRESENCE TO WORSHIP YOU IN SPIRIT AND IN TRUTH.
KNOWING THAT AS THY CHILDREN AND THY HOUSEHOLD
THAT WE CAN BE GUIDED BY THY WORD, THAT WE CAN BE
INSTRUCTED BY THY SPIRIT THAT YOU ARE IN CONTINUAL
COMMUNION WITH THY PEOPLE, THAT THY SPIRIT IS WITH US
ALWAYS, EVEN UNTO THE END OF THIS AGE. BECAUSE OF THY
PRESENCE AND BECAUSE OF THE RELATIONSHIP OF THY SPIRIT
WITH OUR SPIRIT WE ARE NOT ONLY GUIDED AND PROTECTED.
BUT THY SPIRIT HAS CAUSED A MEDITATION IN US TO PRAY FOR

THOSE THINGS WE HAVE NEED OF, EVEN WHEN WE ARE NOT AWARE, FOR THIS GUIDING PROTECTION, FOR THIS SHIELD OF THY PRESENCE WE ARE THANKFUL. WE PRAY OUR FATHER, THAT YOU SHALL AWAKEN US IN THIS GREAT HOUR OF OUR NATIONAL NEED TO THE PROBLEMS THAT FACE US AND THE CAUSE OF THESE PROBLEMS. GRANT OUR FATHER, THAT WE SHALL HAVE LEADERSHIP THAT SHALL RESPOND TO THE AWAKENING OF THY PEOPLE TO DELIVER OUR LAND TO THE POWERS OF DARKNESS AND THE FORCES OF EVIL, TO LIFT HIGH AGAIN THE STANDARDS OF THY KINGDOM THAT WE MIGHT LEAD THE WORLD IN RIGHTEOUSNESS. WE THANK THEE OUR FATHER, FOR THE ASSURANCE OF VICTORY OVER THE POWER OF DARKNESS, FOR THE ASSURANCE THAT NO WEAPON THAT OUR ENEMY BRINGS AGAINST US SHALL PROSPER, FOR THE REALIZATION OF THE FINAL VICTORY OF THY KINGDOM AND THE DEFEAT OF EVIL, AND FOR THE REALIZATION THAT THY THRONE IN THE EARTH IS FOREVER AND THAT THY ADMINISTRATION IN THE HOUSEHOLD IN WHICH YOU HAVE ESTABLISHED IN THE EARTH AND ITS INHERITANCE SHALL REMAIN BEFORE THEE SO AS WE COMMIT OURSELVES IN THY HAND WE PRAY FOR THY GUIDANCE, FOR THY WISDOM AND FOR THY KNOWLEDGE AND FOR THE MIGHTY IMPOWERING OF THY SONS AND DAUGHTERS PROMISED FOR THIS VITAL HOUR, SO WE SAY THY WILL BE DONE IN EARTH AS IT IS IN HEAVEN. IN THY NAME WE ASK IT. AMEN.

Since Adam and Eve partook of the fruit of knowledge against God's will, there has been much trouble upon the face of this planet, Earth. Since that time it has been the nature of mankind to rebel against the things that do not please and make comfortable the human body and mind.

We human beings are very apt to overlook things taking place today that could destroy us tomorrow, and accept a compromise in order to avoid a struggle. Actually, there is no such thing as compromise in regards to principle, a thing has to be right or wrong! No solution short of the right solution will long survive; yet, every day of our lives we are asked by the Disciples of Dictatorship to compromise our principles for the sake of their own personal and political gain. When we compromise our principles and beliefs for the sake of "getting along," we lose our most precious possession, freedom.

In the light of history, this great nation of ours is the most superb creation of man's knowledge, spirit, and labor—thanks to our wonderful Constitution (the original Constitution). Not one word of that constitution should be, or should have been changed in compromise for any reason whatsoever. Especially not to please or comfort our Godless, deadly enemy, the Communist Party of the world. I believe it is plain to everyone, now, that the Communist are, and have been from the outset, behind the racial violence and unrest in our nation; the purpose of which is to divide and conquer. I might add, they have done a terribly devasting job so far.

The big word that has gone around during most of my lifetime has been "reform." Just what are we to reform? Christianity? God, perhaps? America and Americanism, our inheritance from our ancestors? The rules and regulations of government they left us in our Constitution? Maybe these laws are not perfect, but they have served longer and better than any others in history. No book of rules (or laws) have ever been, or could ever be devised to please everyone. Yet, our Constitution, until a few years ago, served best for everyone. Before things were hopelessly fouled up and changed, the only gripes came from "do-nothings" and Communist agitators. Now, I doubt that any of us will live what would have been considered a normal life until things have been changed back, to the way they were before our leaders began legislating "common sense."

All of us should undertake the task of returning our government to its original form, for if we fail, we may well have lost ALL. This might well be the "Last Frontier" and not the bright, shiny one we have been promised by self-serving politicians.

As Mississippians and Americans we must work together as an intelligent people (which we are) for the betterment of all the people of our state and our country. We must all move together, one step at a time and build a bridge across the deep canyon . . . the long leap to try to jump across may plunge us all into defeat and destruction.

I wonder if Adam and Eve in their haste to disobey God in partaking of the fruit of the tree of "Knowledge" didn't overlook a tree marked "Better Knowledge." I wonder if we are not overlooking a simple, Christian way of settling the differences that are dividing our nation. We need a Christian statesman who can unite—not a divider. Lord, help us find one.

Use the greatest power you have left in the coming election for a President of these United States, vote for the man who stands for AMERICANISM and the AMERICAN CHRISTIAN WAY.

We are going to serve notice that we are not going to recognize the Authority of any Bi-Racial group, <u>Nor the Authority of Any Public Official Who Enters Into Any Agreement With Any Such Communist Organization</u>. We Knights are working day and night to preserve law and order here in Mississippi, in the only way that it can be preserved: by strict segregation of the races, and the control of the social structure in the hands of the Christian, Anglo-Saxon White Men, the only race on Earth that can build and maintain just and stable governments. We are deadly serious about this business. We have taken no action as yet against the enemies of our State, our Nation and our Civilization, but we are not going to sit back and permit our rights and the rights of our posterity to be negotiated away by a group of "Jewish" priests, bluegum black savages and mongrelized money-worshippers. Take heed, Atheists and Mongrels, we will not travel your path to a Leninist hell, but we will buy <u>You</u> a ticket to the Eternal if you insist. Take your choice, <u>Segregation</u>, <u>Tranquility</u>, and <u>Justice</u>, or, <u>Bi-Racism</u>, <u>Chaos</u> and <u>Death</u>.

And I know the <u>Blasphemy</u> of them which say they are <u>Jews</u>, and are not, but are the <u>Synagogue of Satan</u>! Fear none of those things which <u>Thou</u> (Christians) <u>Shalt Suffer</u>. Behold, the <u>devil shall cast some of you into Prison</u> that ye may be tried: (Rev. 2:9, 10).

Behold, I will make them of the <u>Synagogue of Satan</u>, which say they are Jews, and are not, but do <u>Lie</u>; behold, <u>I will make them</u> to come and worship before Thy feet, and to know that I have loved Thee. (Rev. 3:9)

Today's so-called Jews persecute Christians, seeking to deceive, claiming Judea as their homeland and that they are "God's Chosen." They "do <u>Lie</u>," for they are <u>not</u> Judeans, but <u>Are</u> the <u>Synagogue of Satan</u>!

Does this sound like they are God's <u>issue</u> ruling with him? No, my Friends, you are God's issue ruling with him. You are his Israel and don't let anyone ever tell you different.

Today, few Americans understand the beautiful truths of "The Sovereignty of the Individual" as intended by our Bible-Indoctrinated Founding Fathers when they wrote our Constitution. In the light of "Individual Sovereignty" we must face the Anti-Semitic bogy head-on.

Our Constitution protects a Jew as well as any other individual. If a Jew is not capable of functioning as an individual, and must take part in <u>Conspiracies</u> to exist on this earth, that is his problem. Our Constitution

<u>protects</u> the individual but not conspiracies! It is only a matter of time, when, through natural processes under our Constitution, <u>all conspiracies</u> will dissolve into nothingness. And, any President, cabinet member, court justice, senator, congressman, or any other person caught in them will have to pay the consequences for their lack of wisdom and foresight. As an informed Christian puts it—any Jew who says our Constitution is anti-semitic is off his rocker, and should see his psychiatrist. No relief there, for persisting as a Jew consulting Antichrists, he will discover in fact our Constitution <u>is Christian</u>; <u>is Anti-Jew</u>, and Anti-Synagogue of Satan.

You have lost your Freedom, Americans. "Freedom, once lost by a great Nation, is seldom regained." (Daniel Webster)

Tyranny, Treachery, Trickery, Treason is the order of the day in Washington, D.C. Honor, Integrity, Race, Country, America's Christian Religion, are becoming out moded.

Your most precious blood bought individual Freedom—of choice, of association, of individual Independence, of free speech and free press, of control over your children's welfare, of the sacredness of your home and private property, right to run your own business—of the <u>"right to be let alone by Government,"</u> ALL ARE being insidiously but surely eroded and usurped by your overpaid public SERVANTS in an all-powerful central government. Your national Sovereignty and Security have been bartered away by these same U.N. (Not U.S.) public servants. More and more you become a regimental <u>number</u> in a Socialist-Communist Dictatorship. Satan and Antichrist stalk the land. American citizens once were CONSTITUTIONALLY masters, of their Government, including the courts—but not now.

WHAT ARE YOU DOING ABOUT ALL THIS?

We are dedicated to stop this.

How many times have you heard that intergration is inevitable? This is the big lie, created by the Communist conspirators and parroted by Liberals, Socialists, Pinks, Punks, Do-Gooders and Bleeding-heart Clergymen in the hope that you will repeat It. Many people will repeat an often heard phrase without even evaluating it for truth. Repeat a lie often enough, it will be believed! (An old satanic policy.)

Once people believe that intergration is inevitable, the main struggle to install it has passed. We should not accept this concept any sooner than we would accept intergration, for the idea is father to the act. The first thing you can do in the fight against intergration is to refute this insiduous piece of propaganda. The only thing inevitable is mongrelization IF WE INTERGRATE!

Volumes could be, and have been written concerning the evils of intergrating a society, but the most conclusive and damning testimonials as to the utter folly of such a practice are as handy as your family Bible and the World History Book.

God found intergration of the races so abominable that he had the entire populace of several cities destroyed—every man, woman and child! What other lesson do we really need?

Christian values do not change over the years, it is just as wrong to lie, cheat, steal, commit adultery, murder, or intergrate today as it was centuries ago. It always will be!

Those of us who sit back and do nothing to stem these socialistic acts of God-less-ness are just as guilty as the evil perpetrators. To say we don't want to get involved is a weak and invalid excuse—we are involved. Christians have always been involved in the conflict between the forces of Good and the forces of Evil. We must take action to the limit of our ability to defeat these Satanic forces that confront us, to do less is to lend tacit approval to the plans of those who would destroy us through mongrelization.

If you are not a Bible student, reflect on the lessons given us through the recorded history of our world. Egypt was at one time the greatest empire on earth, but the white citizens began to intermarry with the Negro slaves and trouble began. Even in that ancient time the Pharaohs realized the danger inherent in such a practice and prohibited it by proclamation. Alas, all too late. Corrupted, mongrelized Egypt fell and will never rule as a world power again.

The Roman Empire withstood great military armies and onslaughts from without, until the noxious host of mongrelizers within its own camp caused its social structure to crumble with moral decay.

What sets the United States apart from these and other great world governments? So far it has been racial integrity built on an abiding Christian faith. Now we would inject into the body of our own government the evil virus of race mixing, that would produce therein a cancer for which there is no cure.

There is no such thing as token intergration. No such thing as a little intergration. ANY intergration is, in truth, the beginning of total intergration and its irrevocably destructive culmination—mongrelization.

The wolf in sheep's clothing is at the door. Mongrelization under the cover of school intergration is the monstrous wolf that seeks entrance into the fold, where it would not stop until it had devoured the entire flock. Don't you be the one to open the door to this ravening wolf, or even to help. This evil creature, mongrelization, disguised in the vermin-infested sheep's clothing must be destroyed. It will take the combined efforts of each and every Christian patriot to do this job. The responsibility of preserving our White Christian civilization for ourselves and generations of children yet unborn rests squarely upon our shoulders, yours and mine. We must not fail, for upon our hands will be the blood of the innocent! School intergration is the opening wedge to mongrelize us. You ask what one person can do. One person was responsible for having the Holy Bible removed from our schools. What you do is important. Do what you can, if it is no more than steadfastly voicing your disapproval of intergration. Do your part to kill the idea that intergration is inevitable. No matter how dark things look at times, remember you are on the right side—the winning side. God will bless you for your effort in the continuing battle to maintain Christian racial integrity.

We would like to inform the general public that this organization has had no part in the bombing of Churches, schools and homes for which we have been blamed. The recent bombing of a church and home in McComb, Mississippi is a good example of outside agitation.

THIS IS WHY WE HAVE THE WHITE KNIGHTS OF THE KU KLUX KLAN OF MISSISSIPPI.

IN A DEBATE WITH JUDGE DOUGLAS AT CHARLESTON, ILLINOIS, SEPTEMBER 18, 1858, MR. ABRAHAM LINCOLN EXPRESSED HIS VIEWS AND HIS STAND ON THE RACIAL QUESTION, IN PART AS FOLLOWS:

"I am not nor ever have been in favour of bringing about in any way the social and political equality of the white and black races! I am not nor ever have been in favour of making voters or jurors of negroes, nor of qualifying them to hold office, nor to intermarry with white people. I will say in addition to this that there is a physical difference between the white and black races which I believe will forever forbid the two races living together on terms of social and political equality; and inasmuch as they cannot so live, while they do remain together there must be the position of the inferior and superior, and I am, as much as any other man, in favour of having the superior position assigned to the white race."

DEDICATED TO MAINTAIN AND EXTEND THE DIGNITY, HERITAGE AND RIGHTS OF THE WHITE RACE OF AMERICA.

Thomas Jefferson, Benjamin Franklin, John Adams, James Monroe, even Booker T. Washington favored segregation.

DON'T DESTROY [this publication]—Pass it along—Enclose in your letters—Give to your pastor, your politician, your school teacher. Maintain the dignity, heritage and rights of the White Race.

The Citizens' Council: A History

> *White Citizens' Councils were established all across the South after the Supreme Court's 1954 ruling on school desegregation. In principle, they defended segregation as an expression of states' rights: Washington officials should not be permitted to dictate how local communities run their schools and other civic activities. In practice, they gave bankers, employers, and merchants a way to work together to punish black residents by firing them, foreclosing mortgages, canceling credit, et cetera. In this 1963 speech, Robert B. Patterson, head of the White Citizens' Councils movement, reviews its history and mission.*

The Citizens' Council: A History. An Address by Robert B. Patterson, Secretary, The Citizens' Councils of America, Executive Secretary, Association of Citizens' Councils of Mississippi, To the Annual Leadership Conference of the Citizens' Councils of America. Jackson, Mississippi, October 26, 1963

Ladies and gentlemen, fellow members of the Citizens' Council:

Last month the Citizen's Council had one of the finest compliments paid it that it has been my pleasure to hear. Ralph McGill, left-wing publisher of the *Atlanta Constitution*, charged in a speech in Wellesley, Massachusetts, that "Citizens' Council leaders have begun a cleverly planned campaign to exploit irrational northern fears of Negro demonstrations." And "Mississippi is ruled by a network of White Citizens' Councils. Their political control and their coercive power in economic affairs is so vast as to be difficult to comprehend."

Coming from Ralph McGill this must be considered a tribute to the effectiveness of the organization of which you are a part.

Many of you here have been part of this organization from the beginning, nine years ago. Our basic strategy, to inform and organize white people in this country, has changed but little during this time. It might be worthwhile now to briefly review the organization's history.

On July 11, 1954, the first Citizens' Council was formed in Indianola, Mississippi, by fourteen men who met and counselled together on the terrible crisis precipitated by the United States Supreme Court in its Black Monday decision of May 17, 1954 [*Brown vs. Board of Education*, which mandated desegregation of public schools]. For the first time in American history, racial segregation, the way of life regulating the daily activities of tens of millions of American citizens, black and white, in a well known pattern of familiar and satisfactory conduct, had been decreed illegal.

Despite the long range dangers to our constitutional safeguards apparent to many men, North, South, East and West, in legislation by judicial fiat, the immediate and pressing danger to men and women in Mississippi and the rest of the South was the potential flood of negro invasion into our schools, parks, swimming pools, restaurants, hotels, trains, buses, into our very neighborhoods and homes, and into public office.

To thoughtful men, concerned for the safety and welfare of their families and their property, the prospect opened up by this politically inspired decree appeared utterly unacceptable.

"The best of prophets of the future is the past." History proves that the supreme power in the government of men has always been public opinion. Public sentiment is the law! It was felt that only through local grass roots organization could public sentiment be mobilized and expressed.

These fourteen men, having no idea that such a small beginning would, in a few months time, expand miraculously into a virile and potent organization, worked out the basic ideas underlying the Citizens' Councils method of operation.

The idea for the four committees was born: Membership and Finance, Legal Advisory, Political and Legislative, Information and Education. Within the scope of these four fields of activity lies the real heart and muscle of the Citizens' Councils.

The concept of assembling non-political community leadership into a unified body to provide the best thinking on the local level, dealing with local problems, became deeply rooted.

It was acknowledged that the impending threat was of such magnitude that our elected officials would be unable to deal with it without the unyielding and organized support of thousands of responsible white citizens to counter the steadily mounting pressure and unceasing attacks from left-wing groups, which were and are liberally financed, skilled in revolutionary techniques that are literally a closed book to most of our political leaders, and irrevocably dedicated to our destruction.

The word spread. Neighboring towns and counties heard of the plan and began to organize. When some twenty counties had organized themselves, the idea of a State Association was conceived.

On October 12, 1954, the Association of Citizens' Councils of Mississippi was organized at Winona, Miss. That was the date on which the officers of Citizens' Councils from the various counties in the State of Mississippi got together and formed the first State Association.

The original purpose of the State Association was to provide an agency to act as an information center and as a co-ordinating agency for the various local Councils.

These men realized that logic and common sense was on the side of the South, in addition to the written Constitution of the United States.

It was felt that it was the duty of the Citizens' Councils to rally support from patriotic citizens in the South and then with this support to present the case for the South to our Nation.

Through the State Association, speakers were made available to carry the message to interested groups and to civic clubs all over Mississippi and nearby sister states. A steady stream of printed information on the nature of the racial integration crisis was disseminated from the State Headquarters.

The first major accomplishment and the first project undertaken by our Councils on a State level was the passage of the Constitutional amendment to raise voter qualifications in Mississippi. Although this same amendment failed to pass in 1952, it passed by a tremendous majority when the people of Mississippi, through the Citizens' Councils, were informed of the necessity and reason for its passage. It is impossible to estimate the value of this amendment to future peace and domestic tranquility in this State.

During the first two years of existence, the Citizens' Councils showed an impressive statistical growth. In less than two years sixty-five of our eighty-two counties in Mississippi were organized, with a membership of over 80,000. Councils were organized in each Congressional District in the State.

The Citizens' Councils movement had by then spread into a number of other states. On April 7, 1956, the Citizens' Council of America was organized in New Orleans. The Citizens' Council movement, backed by a large membership, received national publicity, and the State and National Offices corresponded regularly with interested citizens in 50 states, Iceland, South Africa, Mexico, England, Rhodesia, Germany and Australia.

The Citizens' Council has published many writings, pamphlets, documents and other literature which give factual, convincing reasons for the absolute necessity of maintaining segregation. We have mailed tons of literature into all 50 states and to every civic and patriotic organization in every county in Mississippi, as well as to interested individuals and public officials in every county in Mississippi and in every state in the Union. A nationwide television and radio program "The Citizens' Council Forum" was and is produced for nationwide distribution. A nationwide monthly publication "The Citizen" was established. We have helped to mobilize public opinion so that it has expressed itself from every possible direction against every attempt at integration. We are striving to present the case for racial separation to the entire Nation.

Members and officials of the Citizens' Council have traveled throughout the Nation telling them what we have accomplished and helping them to organize. We are exchanging ideas and methods to be used in the struggle that lies ahead. Citizens' Councils have been formed in Louisiana, Texas, Alabama, Arkansas, Florida, Georgia, South Carolina, North Carolina, Tennessee and Virginia. Other States have similar organizations. From everywhere comes encouragement and moral support for our cause.

While certain Council members may feel that they have contributed little as individuals, the fact that they have organized and have developed a voting membership has given our movement the numbers necessary to prove that we mean business, and their contributions have financed our program.

Many of our local Councils have anticipated and prevented racial tensions from developing in their communities. We have proved to all concerned citizens that the NAACP and these other integrationist groups are left-wing, power-mad organs of destruction that bring only ill will and hardship to the negro people.

Representatives of the Citizens' Council have made hundreds of talks and speeches before Councils and groups of all sizes, kinds and descriptions, from the small crossroads schoolhouse meeting attended by 25 God-fearing and determined farmers to massive rallies numbering in the thousands.

Press relations have been established with newspapers, wire services, radio and TV stations throughout this Nation. Editorial support as well as adequate and fair news treatment has been noted. A number of national magazines are now presenting the case for segregation.

Inroads of the NAACP, CORE, SNCC and other similar groups upon local negro sentiment have been checked. School officials have been bolstered considerably by Council efforts in this direction, and by the creation of a strong moral tone of unified public resistance to the arrogant behavior of the NAACP.

An outstanding accomplishment of the Citizens' Council movement that has become increasingly acknowledged is the channeling of popular resistance to integration into lawful, coherent and proper modes, and the prevention of violence or racial tension.

The contrast between the right kind of organization and no organization has been particularly noted in states and communities which have been slow to anticipate the future of race relations within their boundaries.

We must strengthen and build our organization for a long, hard fight.

It is the duty and responsibility of every Citizens' Council member to encourage his friends, correspondents and relatives in other cities and states to organize so that they can do their part in this righteous cause.

"Organized aggression must be met with organized resistance." The NAACP and other left-wing groups are well organized and highly financed. The budget for the year 1963 for seven of these groups exceeded 8 million dollars.

There are 40 million white Southerners and additional millions of white Northerners, Easterners and Westerners whose attitude towards racial integration is exactly like ours. These millions, or a fraction thereof, if properly united can be a power in this Nation, but they must be thoroughly organized from the town and county level up. It must be an organization supported and controlled by the people and not by any politician or political party. The Citizens' Councils think and plan as a group and then they are able to act as individuals within their various churches, schools or any other organization to which they may belong. This has already proved effective in many, many instances.

Counties and towns that have not organized should take pride in organizing so that others will not have to bear their burden for them. A citizen should be as proud to serve in this cause as he or she would be in military service for this country. We are fighting for our children and grandchildren, our nation, our churches and our schools. No white person can stand aloof from the struggle. There are no white spectators, for if racial amalgamation comes about there will be no white survivors.

The fate of this Nation rests in the hands of those white people today who oppose racial amalgamation. If the white people of these United States submit to the unconstitutional, destructive forces of integration, the malignant powers of mongrelization, communism and atheism will surely destroy this Nation.

Integration represents darkness, regimentation, totalitarianism, communism and destruction. Segregation represents the freedom to choose one's associates, Americanism, State sovereignty and the survival of the white race. These two ideologies are now engaged in mortal conflict and only one can survive. They cannot be fused any more than day can exist in night. The twilight of this great white Nation would certainly follow. There is no middle ground.

We still have the "summer soldier and sunshine patriot" with us. We have those who say "I'm behind you but my pension, my boss, my church, my customers, danger, etc."

This country was founded and sustained by courageous men and women. In these perilous times our nation needs the type of American as described by a great patriot of a century ago. In closing I quote Daniel Webster in July of 1850:

AN AMERICAN

"I was born an American; I will live an American; I shall die an American; and I intend to perform the duties incumbent upon me in that character to the end of my career. I mean to do this with absolute disregard of personal consequences. What are the personal consequences? What is the individual man, with all the good or evil that may betide him, in comparison with the good or evil which may befall a great country, and in the midst of great transactions which concern that country's fate? Let the consequences be what they will, I am careless. No man can suffer too much, and no man can fall too soon, if he suffer, or if he fall, in the defense of the liberties and constitution of his country."

YOU CAN HELP!
Contribute to ASSOCIATION of CITIZENS' COUNCILS, P. O. Box 886, GREENWOOD, MISS.

Summary of Major Points in Testimony by Citizens of Mississippi to Panel of June 8, 1964

> *In order to raise the consciousness of policy makers and alert officials to the threat of violence, Freedom Summer leaders organized a symposium in Washington at which local residents testified about repression in Mississippi. A panel of distinguished public figures listened and asked questions and the press covered the event, but it failed to prompt federal officials to protect activists or defend the civil rights of African Americans. This excerpt distributed by COFO is a useful summary of the intimidation, harassment, and brutality that black Mississippians faced every day.*

MASSIVE RESISTANCE BY WHITE OFFICIALS AND CITIZENS TO VOTER REGISTRATION BY NEGROES

Among tactics used to prevent Negroes from registering to vote are technical violations of court orders, threats through publication of registrants, economic reprisal, and violence.

In Forrest County, Mississippi twenty-two questions are asked of the registrant, and a registrar may require an applicant to answer questions on over 200 sections of the Mississippi code. In that same county, the first suit to compel registration was started in 1961. The case was heard in 1962, and a ruling given in 1963. The county requires that the names of applicants be published in the local paper for fourteen days before they are given consideration. In the meantime, applicants become the target for police action, and are subjected to economic reprisal and personal danger. Of 1,000 Negroes who have had the courage to face these conditions, only 150 have been registered.

One witness testified that after she applied to register to vote, the owner of the plantation where she had worked for eighteen years and where her husband had worked for 30 years, ordered the family to leave unless she withdrew her application. She fled that night.

A white student from Tougaloo College, active in voter registration, testified that while driving in a car with a Pakistani student she had been followed and then blocked by two cars. They had been forced out of the car and their lives threatened. After saying that the non-white student was an Indian, they had been permitted to proceed. The student believes killings by whites will occur this summer, and that only intervention by the Federal Government will prevent them.

A field secretary for Student Nonviolent Coordinating Committee was shot in the back of the head and shoulder while driving home from a voter registration meeting. The three men who had shot at him from a passing car and who had been arrested were released on bond. The incident occurred early in 1963. The trial was set for November, was postponed, and has not yet been held. This witness urged that only United States marshals could prevent further tragedies.

One elderly man testified that after registering to vote his home had been bombed, shots had been fired through the window, and his house put on fire. After asking the FBI to investigate, he was charged with arson by the sheriff and arrested. He continues to be harassed and threatened.

POLICE BRUTALITY

Witness after witness testified to the brutality of the police against any man, woman or child who participated in the struggle for civil rights. They were marked for attack at times when they were not participating in any group action or demonstration.

Thus, a man active in voter registration was stopped on the highway at night by a hostile group of men with chains and guns who threatened beatings and death to him and his friends. The witness testified that beatings by police and State Highway Patrolmen were common.

A young man travelling from Cleveland through Ruleville on his way to Jackson was arrested and charged with violation of the local curfew. When he insisted he was only traveling through, he was hit in the ribs with a pistol and punched on the street by the police officer. He was told, "Nigger, you're lying" and was threatened with death. After a night in jail he was fined for violating curfew and driving past a non-existent stop light.

A middle-aged woman testified that on her way back from a student registration workshop, she had been arrested while sitting inside the bus for having asked where she could buy food at a bus stop. She was kicked by police on the way to the county jail. She was moved by the police from one cell and taken into another where the police gave two male Negroes black-jacks and ordered them to beat her. Her skirts were pulled up by the police to expose and degrade her.

Two boys, aged thirteen and fourteen, testified to intimidation and bullying by police. One was arrested, imprisoned and had his arm twisted by the police when he participated in a school demonstration in June, 1963. The second, while participating in a NAACP silent march to the courthouse, had been beaten and kicked by the police and then put in jail.

A young worker for CORE testified that he was ordered out of Yazoo City by the police and gratuitously kicked by a police officer. His driver's license had been taken, and the police had written across it the word "agitator" before returning it.

A CORE worker testified he was hit on the head and across the face by a gun for having asked the police why his car was being held. He was then taken to jail and charged with resisting arrest and intimidating an officer. This young man was told by a City detective, who warned him that he would be killed if he did not leave town that night, that he was misleading "happy people." The next night, on his way to Jackson, he was stopped by police and kicked.

A young Negro woman was taken out of her home and whipped by the sheriff, after he had forced her to undress, on the charge of her employer that she had stolen some money. The white doctor to whom she went refused to treat her, and she had to go to a Negro doctor to get help.

A young boy, active in civil rights, had been injured in a demonstration during the summer of 1963. He was left on a stretcher in the hospital after the police had demanded he be discharged without medical care. When the nurse left the boy he was beaten and threatened with dogs by the police.

A woman active in a sit-in demonstration in CORE was beaten while police watched. She was then arrested and taken to the police station before she was sent to the hospital.

FALSE ARREST AND FALSE CHARGES AS HARASSMENT

Persons active in civil rights are constantly subjected to false arrest, high bail bonds, unjust fines, and persecution for complaining against violence done to them. One witness testified that the Chief of Police had entered her home while she was having coffee with her neighbor and arrested her on the charge of conspiracy not to buy in the downtown stores. She was handcuffed and held in $2,000 bond. The case was later dismissed.

When a witness was denied use of the rest-room at a gas station where she had stopped to get gas, and was also refused change for the $10 bill with which she had paid, she then threatened to report it to the police. She was told by the attendant that he did not cater to the Nigger trade. She was struck on the temple and in the face. Fifty minutes after having reported this to the Chief of Police he arrived at her home and arrested the complainant on the charge of disturbing the peace. She was denied the medical care she needed as the result of her injuries, was convicted and fined.

A CORE worker, driving home legally and correctly, was stopped by a Highway Patrolman, arrested for reckless driving, handcuffed, and kicked. A complaint to the Department of Justice, sent in November 1963, has never been answered.

THE ABSENCE OF EQUAL PROTECTION AND JUSTICE IN THE COURTS

Despite action by the Department of Justice against white men who had beaten five Negroes who applied to register, and despite the testimony of 3 witnesses to sustain the complaint, the case was dismissed by Federal Judge Clayton on the ground the evidence was insufficient.

When a witness who had been beaten by a gas attendant complained to the Chief of Police, she was arrested and fined. Although she took out a warrant against her assailant in June, 1963, he has never been brought to trial.

The trial of three white men charged with shooting a SNCC field worker early in 1963 has been postponed repeatedly, and still has not been held. A man whose home was bombed and set on fire was charged with arson and held in jail under high bond. The charges were ultimately dropped.

THE F.B.I. AND DEPARTMENT OF JUSTICE HAVE FAILED TO PROVIDE PROTECTION OR SUPPORT THE NEGRO OR WHITE AMERICAN IN THE STRUGGLE FOR CIVIL RIGHTS

A white man was beaten up for working in the civil rights movement. His face was swollen and bleeding. When he went to the FBI, accompanied by a well-dressed University Professor and by a lawyer, the FBI agent asked which of the three was the one who had been beaten up.

Witnesses testified that local FBI agents said they could not take action, but could only forward complaints. On complaints to the Department of Justice, not even answers were received. In March 1964, a complaint was filed with the Department of Justice after students had been subjected to police brutality and after four students had been shot at on the Jackson State College campus for protesting the absence of a stop-light. To the date of the citizens' panel on June 8th, 1964, no answer has been received.

TESTIMONY ON THE F.B.I.

One witness active in the NAACP testified that although she had notified the Department of Justice of an assault in the summer of 1963, she had never received an answer.

One CORE witness testified that statements on police brutality were taken by the local FBI men, who claimed that the statements had been sent on to Washington. Since then, nothing has happened. Complaints made directly to the FBI or through the Council of Federated Organizations or to the Department of Justice have received no response.

A brutal attack by two white men on two Negroes, resulting in permanent injuries, was reported to the FBI. The FBI agent stated he could do nothing more than send a report to the Memphis office. The witness, one of the injured men, was told by the FBI to report the attack to the Sheriff, whose answer was "Your family's supposed to be dead." There has been no response to the complaint to the FBI made on February 5th, 1964.

One incident testified to at the hearing concerned a Negro who had been killed, when unarmed, by a member of the Mississippi legislature. A Negro witness to the slaying refused, when arrested, to perjure himself by testifying that the victim had been armed at the time; because he refused, his jaw was broken by jailors. After further threats, he was coerced into revising his testimony and gave a false statement at the trial to the effect that the victim had been armed. Later, he went to the FBI and told the true facts, and asked for protection. He was subsequently shot. His widow, testifying at the hearings, stated that the Sheriff had told her that her husband would not now be dead if he had not gone to the FBI.

A student from Tougaloo College testified to the constant burning of crosses at the College and to frequent shootings from passing cars—shots aimed at faculty houses, dormitories, etc. When the police and State Patrol were asked for help but gave none, efforts to get help from the FBI proved fruitless for three weeks. The FBI arrived, and expressed interest, only after a picture of the burning crosses had been published in the *New York Times*.

"Road to Mississippi"

Black reporter Louis Lomax (1922–1970) researched and wrote a long article on the murders of James Chaney, Andrew Goodman, and Michael Schwerner in 1964. The following is an excerpt detailing their final hours on June 21, 1964. After leaving the Oxford, Ohio, orientation session a day earlier than everyone else, the three young men went to Longdale, Mississippi, to investigate the firebombing of a church that had agreed to host a Freedom School. This excerpt opens as they start their return trip to the town of Meridian.

No one moves unnoticed in Mississippi and the arrival of strangers causes a general alarm in the community. This is particularly true when the police have been broadcasting the strangers' every move over a short wave band used by members of the Klan and the White Citizens' Council. But the local Negroes were also watching. Some of them were hiding in the bushes, others were pretending to be idly driving by. A few sympathetic white people were also watching. And from their sworn statements the following time-table can be constructed:

12:00—Schwerner, Goodman, and Chaney arrive at the site of the burned-out church shortly before noon. They spend about an hour examining the ruins and talking with people who have gathered.

1:30—Schwerner, Goodman, and Chaney turn up at church services at a nearby Negro church. There they pass out leaflets urging the people to attend voter registration schools. (The name of the church and the persons who allowed the three civil rights workers to speak are known but cannot be released because of concern for the safety of the persons involved, as well as for the church building.)

2:30—Schwerner, Goodman, and Chaney are given dinner in a friendly home and then leave for Meridian.

3:00—A person who knows all three civil rights workers sees them as they come along Route 16 from the Longdale area and make a right turn onto Route 491 which will take them back to Route 19 and Meridian.

As soon as they swing onto Route 491, the three civil rights workers are intercepted by Deputy Sheriff Cecil Price, Schwerner's ancient and implacable foe. Schwerner is at the wheel and, as he had done on both May 19 and May 31 when he was in the area for civil rights meetings, he elects to out-run the deputy sheriff. But this time Price can act with total license. His boss, Sheriff L. A. Rainey, is at the bedside of Mrs. Rainey who is hospitalized. Four Negroes witness the chase and have later sworn that Price shot the right rear tire of the speeding station wagon.

3:45—The disabled station wagon is parked in front of the Veterans of Foreign Wars building on Route 16, about a mile east of Philadelphia. Witnesses see two of the civil rights workers, now known to be Schwerner and Chaney, standing at the front of the station wagon, with the hood raised. The third civil rights worker, Goodman, is in the process of jacking up the right rear tire to change it.

Deputy Sheriff Cecil Price (he has by now radioed the alarm) is standing nearby with his gun drawn. Informed of the incident, one Snow, a minor Deputy Sheriff, comes running out of the VFW club where he works as a bouncer. Price and Snow are then joined by State Patrolman E. R. Poe and Harry Wiggs, both of Philadelphia. (The entire episode was broadcast over the shortwave citizens' band which is relayed all over the state. There is evidence that police in Meridian, Jackson, and Philadelphia, as well as Colonel T. B. Birdsong, head of the State Highway Patrol, were in constant contact about the incident. It is also clear that white racists who had purchased short-wave sets in order to receive the citizens' band broadcasts were also informed and began converging on the scene.)

Deputy Sheriff Cecil Price (by his own admission) makes the arrest. (But there is confusion as to precisely where the arrest took place. Three landmarks, all within a square mile radius, are involved. Some witnesses say they saw the civil rights workers drive away from the VFW club to a Gulf station about a mile away. Others say they saw the arrest take place diagonally across the street from a Methodist Church in Philadelphia. At first blush these accounts seem contradictory. But to one who has tramped the roads and swamps of Mississippi in search of evidence—and I have done this more times than I care to recall—the accounts make sense.) What happened was approximately this:

Price, Snow and the State Police decide that too much attention has been drawn to the incident in front of the VFW hall. They allow the civil rights workers to drive into the Gulf station location. The station wagon pulls into the gas station while the police cars park across the street. The Methodist Church in question is a hundred yards farther down the road on the other side of the street and an illiterate observer would identify the church as the landmark and say the arrest occurred across the street from the church.

4:30—Price arrests the civil rights workers. One of the State patrolmen drives the station wagon into Philadelphia. (This means that the tire had been changed and it accounts for the report that the wagon was at the Gulf station.) The three workers are herded into Price's car and the second State patrolman follows the Price car into town in case the workers attempt a break.

They arrive at the Philadelphia jail. Chaney is charged with speeding, and Schwerner and Goodman are held on suspicion of arson. Price tells them he wants to question them about the burning of the Mount Zion Methodist Church, an incident that occurred while they—all three of the civil rights workers—were on the campus of Western College in Oxford, Ohio.

The three civil rights workers are to report back to Meridian by four o'clock. When they do not appear their fellow workers begin phoning jails, including the one in Philadelphia, and are told that the men are not there. Meanwhile the rights workers—charged with nothing more than a traffic violation—are held incommunicado. What happens while these men are sweating it out in jail for some five hours can now be told. And it is in this ghostly atmosphere of empty shacks, abandoned mansions and a way of life hinged up on fond remembrances of things that never were, that the poor white trash gets likkered up on bad whiskey and become total victims of the southern mystique.

The facts have been pieced together by investigators and from the boasts of the killers themselves. After all, part of the fun of killing Negroes and white civil rights people in Mississippi is to be able to gather with your friends and tell how it all happened in the full knowledge that even if you are arrested your neighbors, as jurymen, will find you "not guilty."

The death site and the burial ground for Andrew Goodman, Michael Schwerner, and James Chaney have been chosen long before they die, months before in fact. Mississippi authorities and the white bigots have known for months that the invasion is coming. Mississippi officials have made a show of going on TV to let the nation know that they are ready and waiting with armored tanks, vicious dogs, tear gas and deputies at the ready. But there is another aspect of Mississippi's preparation for the civil rights "invaders" that they elect not to discuss: Mississippi, as Professor James W. Silver has written, is a closed society. Neshoba County is one of the more tightly closed and gagged regions of the state. Some ten thousand people have fled the county since World War II. The five thousand or so who remain are close kin, cousins, uncles, aunts, distant relatives all. For example, it is reported that Deputy Sheriff Price alone has some two hundred kin in the county. This is a land of open—though illegal—gambling. Indeed, the entire nation watches as a CBS reporter on TV walks into a motel and buys a fifth of whiskey, all of which, of course, is illegal. This is a land of empty houses, deserted barns, of troubled minds encased in troubled bodies.

Once they receive word that the civil rights workers are coming, members of certain local racist groups begin holding sessions with doctors and undertakers. The topic of the evening: How to Kill Men Without Leaving Evidence, and: How To Dispose of Bodies So That They Will Never Be Found.

Negro civil rights workers who can easily pass for white have long since moved into Mississippi and infiltrated both the Klan and the White Citizens' Council.

Their reports show that doctors and undertakers use the killings of Emmett Till and Mack Parker as exhibits A and B on how not to carry out a lynching. Not only did the killers of Parker and Till leave bits of rope, and other items that could be identified, lying around, they threw the bodies in the Pearl (Parker) and Tallahatchie (Till) rivers. After a few days both bodies surfaced, much to everyone's chagrin.

The two big points made at the meetings are (1) kill them (the civil rights workers) with weapons, preferably chains, that cannot be identified; (2) bury them somewhere and in such a way that their bodies will never float to the surface or be unearthed.

Somewhere between ten and eleven o'clock on the night of Sunday, June 21 (if one is to believe Deputy Sheriff Price and the jailers), James Chaney is allowed to post bond and then all three civil rights workers are released from jail. According to Price the three men are last seen heading down Route 19, toward Meridian.

Why was Chaney alone forced to post bail? What about Schwerner and Goodman? If they were under arrest, why were they not required also to post bail? If there were no charges against them, why were they arrested in the first place? More, if Chaney was guilty of nothing more than speeding, why had his two companions also been placed under arrest? But these are stupid questions, inquiries that only civilized men make. They conform neither to the legal nor to the moral jargon of Mississippi—of Neshoba County particularly. (The report that Chaney was allowed to make bail and that then all three civil rights workers were released is open to serious question.)

They left the jail in the evening. That is clear, but, and here is the basis for questioning the story: It is one of the cardinal rules of civil rights workers in Mississippi never to venture out *at night*. The most dangerous thing you can do, a saying among civil rights workers goes, is to get yourself released from jail at night. These three were trained civil rights workers and it is difficult, if not impossible, to imagine that they walked out into the night of their own volition.

Nevertheless, we have the fact that they left the jail and just about three miles from Philadelphia they fell into the hands of a mob.

It is not known precisely how many men were in the mob. Six, at least, have been identified by eyewitnesses. But because they have not been charged with the crime, their names cannot now be revealed.

The frogs and the varmints are moaning in the bayous. By now the moon is midnight high. Chaney, the Negro of the three, is tied to a tree and beaten with chains. His bones snap and his screams pierce the still midnight air. But the screams are soon ended. There is no noise now except for the thud of chains crushing flesh—and the crack of ribs and bones.

Andrew Goodman and Michael Schwerner look on in horror. Then they break into tears over their black brother.

"You goddam nigger lovers!" shouts one of the mob. "What do you think now?"

Only God knows what Andrew Goodman and Michael Schwerner think. Martin Luther King and James Farmer and nonviolence are integral parts of their being. But all of the things they have been taught suddenly became foreign, of no effect.

Schwerner cracks; he breaks from the men who are holding them and rushes toward the tree to aid Chaney. Michael Schwerner takes no more than 10 steps before he is subdued and falls to the ground.

Then Goodman breaks and lunges toward the fallen Schwerner. He too is wrestled into submission.

The three civil rights workers are loaded into a car and the five-car caravan makes its way toward the predetermined burial ground. Even the men who committed the crimes are not certain whether Chaney is dead when they take him down from the tree. But to make sure they stop about a mile from the burial place and fire three shots into him, and one shot each into the chests of Goodman and Schwerner.

> The search for their bodies would dominate the national media until August 4, when their remains were found buried in an earthen dam in a remote corner of Neshoba County.

Memo to Parents of Mississippi Summer Volunteers, Late June 1964

> *Shortly after the three men disappeared, project director Bob Moses reached out to parents of volunteers and asked them to contact representatives in Washington and demand federal intervention. It seemed quite possible that many more young people would be murdered. To demonstrate the severity of the situation, he included a list of violent acts perpetrated in the first few days of Freedom Summer.*

TO: PARENTS OF ALL MISSISSIPPI SUMMER VOLUNTEERS
FROM: COFO, 1017 LYNCH STREET, JACKSON, MISSISSIPPI

Immediate action is needed by all those concerned with the safety of the Mississippi Summer Volunteers. Unless the President and the Attorney General can be convinced of the need for Federal protection of civil rights workers in Mississippi, the events of Philadelphia are almost certain to be repeated over and over again in the next two months.

We are asking all parents to use their influence in the coming week to pressure President Johnson and Attorney General Kennedy into a commitment to protect workers <u>before</u> violence occurs, instead of waiting until the worst has happened before they offer their help. To help you understand what can be done, it is necessary to stress the following points:

<u>The mood of Mississippi today is one of mounting tension</u>. Acts of violence or near violence are increasing. We have enclosed a two-page report on incidents from <u>one twenty-four hour period</u>. The 16 incidents in the report show that violence is not limited to any section of the state and that intimidation takes an unlimited variety of forms.

<u>The Federal Government did not act quickly enough in the Philadelphia case</u>. We are enclosing a chronology of the attempts of COFO to obtain an FBI investigation or other Federal aid in the Philadelphia incident [not included here]. This report shows that it took 24 hours—undoubtedly the critical 24 hours—to get the Federal Government to act. FBI agents in Mississippi are always white, generally Southern, and usually from Mississippi itself. Like local law enforcement officers, these agents often serve to obstruct, rather than aid, the administration of justice in civil rights cases. The enclosed chronology deals only with Federal contacts; local police changed their story continually and were useless in the attempt to locate the missing persons.

The Federal Government does have the ability to act quickly and effectively in support of civil rights. The third enclosure lists some provisions
for Federal action in civil rights cases [not included here]. It shows that the
FBI does in fact have the necessary authority to provide protection for civil
rights workers. Moreover, the President could act on executive authority
to provide further protection, for instance through the appointment of
Federal Marshalls.

On the reverse side of this sheet, an incident in Itta Bena is described. In
this case, the FBI did help protect Summer Volunteers, and actually arrested
three white men who had threatened Summer Project workers. The Itta
Bena incident shows that the proper Federal agencies can act effectively
when they choose to do so. The difference in the role played by the Federal
Government in the Philadelphia and Itta Bena incidents was due not to
differences in Federal authority, but resulted from the pressure of private
citizens on the Government in the last few days.

It is difficult to stress sufficiently the urgency of our request. Without
immediate action, the lives of civil rights workers will be further and
senselessly endangered; and we will have failed in one of our primary
goals: to offer some semblance of protection to the Negroes of Mississippi,
who have suffered for decades from the kind of incident which occurred
in Philadelphia.

For instance, there have been five "unsolved" murders of Negroes in the
southwest part of the state since the beginning of the year. These murders
received no national publicity until the beginning of the Mississippi
Summer Project. Only our presence in Mississippi ensures the continued
concern of the nation for the Negroes of that state, and the chance that the
Federal Government will move effectively to provide protection for their
lives and civil rights.

For this reason, in spite of the danger involved, we are fully committed to
continuing the Mississippi Summer Project. This does not mean that we will
attempt to provoke the state. Our program remains what it has been from
its first inception: an attempt to bring educational and political opportunity
to Mississippi's Negroes, where they have never had these things before.

Our workers will participate in voter registration projects and will teach
in Freedom Schools and Community Centers. We are specifically avoiding
any demonstrations for integrated facilities, as we do not feel the state is
ready to permit such activity at this time. All workers, staff and Summer
Volunteers alike, are pledged to non-violence in all situations.

As a further precaution, we are limiting work to a small area around each project center. All Summer Volunteers have gone through an intensive training session on conditions in Mississippi and the responses and actions they should take to allow them to work most safely in the state. A large legal staff is being maintained in the state to help those who get in trouble.

We are asking that movement at night be kept to a minimum. We are continuing a check-in system which allowed us to know almost immediately that the Philadelphia party was missing. However, though all precautions will be taken, we are determined to continue our work; and we need your help. We request that you do the following things:

1. Contact local papers and radio and TV stations and make certain that the full story about Mississippi is being carried in your community. Use the enclosed documents and the experiences of your own children in Mississippi to indicate the goals of the Summer Project and the continued resistance it is certain to meet. Stress in particular the need for Federal protection.

2. Contact the President, and Attorney General, and your own state and national representatives and demand immediate Federal protection for all people in Mississippi. Organize friends and relatives to make the same demand.

We are asking the following three things from the Federal Government:

1. That Federal Marshalls be stationed throughout the state. These Marshalls should be present in all cases where violence is likely. They should be clearly empowered to make all necessary arrests, including the arrest of law enforcement officers. They should be on call at any hour of the day when civil rights workers feel they are endangered.

2. That the FBI and Justice Department officials be instructed to provide full and immediate help in all incidents where danger is involved. FBI agents should use their power of arrest. Even more important, they should investigate immediately when so requested.

3. That President Johnson confer immediately with COFO leaders. This meeting has been requested several times in the last two months. The president declined to meet with COFO representatives, though they predicted that violence would occur early in the summer if Federal aid were not forthcoming.

The choice before Americans this summer seems very clear. They can either accept at face value the statements of the Attorney General that the Federal Government does not have sufficient power to protect the citizens of the country within its own borders—in which case the consequences will fall on those of us who live and work in Mississippi. Or they can use the influence and power they have over their own government to ensure that the events of Philadelphia are not repeated within the coming hours and days in Mississippi.

Robert Moses, Director, Mississippi Summer Project

INCIDENTS REPORTED TO THE JACKSON OFFICE DURING A 24 HOUR PERIOD:

Ruleville

June 24, 2 AM: A car driven by whites circled noisily around the Negro community for about two hours, hurling bottles at cars and into homes. Seven incidents were reported to the police, but they never arrived on the scene.

June 25, 2 AM: Williams Chapel, near the home of Mrs. Fannie Lou Hamer, Negro candidate for Congress, was firebombed. Volunteer fireman quickly had the fire under control. The church was a center of voter registration activity.

Drew

June 24: 30 voter registration workers from Greenville made the first efforts to register Negro citizens in Drew and met with open hostility from local whites. Verbal abuse and threats were hurled at them from circling cars and trucks, some of which were equipped with "vigilante" gun racks. One white man stopped his car and said "I've got something here for you" brandishing a gun.

Greenwood

June 23–24: 2 separate cars of magazine reporters were chased at speeds up to 90 mph by a car driven by whites on their way from Ruleville to Greenwood. The reporters were returning from a public meeting in Ruleville held that evening. Local whites are reported to be trying to intimidate voter registration workers by circling again and again around the SNCC office at night.

Greenville

June 24: Summer volunteer Morton Thomas, who left Greenville to carry on voter registration work in nearby Hollandale, had to return to Greenville because the Mayor and police force in Hollandale said he could not sleep or work in the Negro community. The Mayor claimed that there was a city ordinance to that effect.

Canton

June 24: A car frequently used by CORE workers was struck by a bullet about 9:15 PM approximately 2 miles outside of Jackson on the road to Canton. The car was driven by a Canton Negro, Eddie Lepaul. The shot came from the grass at the side of the road.

Moss Point

June 24: Last night a Canton policeman threatened to strike CORE worker Scott Smith with a shotgun. The policeman accused him of trying to take over the town, and of having told a white man to get out of town. Smith denied the charges.

June 24: The keeper of the Knights of Pythias Hall reported seeing a white man set fire to the building soon after midnight. Damage was minimal, as the keeper soon had the fire under control. The building was to be used for a coming mass meeting. SNCC volunteers had just passed out leaflets announcing the meeting.

Two Negro teenagers were arrested for allegedly having insulted a white woman. They were released the next day after bond was posted.

Two white summer volunteers, Howard Kirschenbaum and Ron Ridenour, were arrested shortly before midnight on the 23rd and subjected to a night of mental harassment and intimidation in the Jackson County Jail, Pascagoula. They were released the next day, with no formal charges.

Collins

June 24: 40 M-l Rifles and 1,000 rounds of ammunition were stolen from the National Guard Armory in the early hours of the morning.

McComb

June 24: At least five bomb threats have been reported in the two days since the Monday night bombings in McComb.

Vicksburg

June 24: SNCC staff workers coming back from a mass meeting at nearby Yorkena spotted a suspicious-looking 1959 Buick with no license plates. The same car parked for some time in front of the Freedom House that night.

Jackson

June 23: A Negro man was hit twice in the head by gunfire, while following a car driven by two white men who had just fired into a Negro cafe on Valley St. The wounded man, Marion Tarvin, 26, was released from University Hospital with a bullet still in his scalp.

June 24: About noon a group of white men tried to enter the house of Mrs. Grace Helms at 714 Weaver St., and other homes in the area. They threatened to return again and again until they found some Negro boys with whom they had fought the night before. The previous night the police had picked up the Negro boys involved in the fight, but had not even taken the names of the whites.

Selected Hate Mail

The first letter here was sent to SNCC chairman John Lewis following a newspaper story about the training of volunteers in Oxford, Ohio. The others were written to the parents of volunteers Shelton Stromquist and Andrew Goodman. The letters to Andrew Goodman's parents were mailed just a few days after his body was discovered on August 4, 1964.

June 16, 1964

Mr. Lewis:

It is to the credit of the majority of your race in the Dayton [Ohio] area that they had enough good sense to stay away from your Communistic race-mixing attempt on Sunday, June 14th. They are beginning to wake up to the fact that it is immoral, unjust, stupid, against the Laws of Nature (each to his <u>OWN KIND</u>), and absolutely Communist-dictated!

For your information, we had observers at your Communistic "song-fest" and were kept regularly informed as to the actions and general stupidity, not only of members of your race, but also of the morally rotten outcasts of the White Race that went with you. These "White Negroes" are the rottenest of the race-mixing criminals. All race-mixers will some day be brought to justice for their crime against humanity and all future generations, and, since race-mixing is morally more CRIMINAL than MURDER, it would give me great satisfaction if I were selected to sit on such a jury.

You are right about one thing—this is going to be a long, hot, summer—but the "heat" will be applied to the race-mixing TRASH by the <u>DECENT</u> people who do not believe in racial mongrelization through racial prostitution, which is in violation of all concepts of justice, decency, and Common Sense. When your Communist-oriented GOONS get to Mississippi, I hope they get their just dues as infiltrators of an enemy power, which they will be in FACT.

Charles J. Benner/signed

Charles J. Benner

Chairman, Unit 42

National States Rights Party

Dayton 2, Ohio

6/26/64

May God help us, The Churches are selling us out.

Why is your son out to bring ruin upon the last remnant of culture which was capable of creating legislation such as made our land great and a place to which even your people seemed to see fit to come to. What have your people done here? The evil powers of this world are out to destroy the only outpost left where any degree of freedom is left. Only the people who created the constitution evidently are capable of maintaining it.

Freedom is not free, free men are not equal, and equal men are not free. The white race is to be distroyed by the mongrelizers of this world.

U.N. soldiers from Red China, the Congo, Cuba and elsewhere are maneuvering in the south poised ready for you and your son and others like you to give the word.

I am north and south.

Signed, the name is Miller

6/29/64

Dear Mrs. Stromquist,

What kind of parents are you anyway? You should be ashamed to show your head out the door.

You have raised another trouble maker who deserves to get the same fate that the 3 other trouble makers got [Chaney, Goodman, and Schwerner]— the sooner all trouble makers are eliminated this way, the better off this country will be.

You should go see a psychiatrist to straighten out your thinking. People who condone their children's evil pranks of going out of their way to inflict such an evil on the human races as trying to force niggers on them, as your children are doing, deserve the worst, and I hope every one of you gets it.

I would vomit in a nigger's face if I were forced to touch one. How can you ever eat out of those hands again?

If your evil son doesn't get murdered as he deserves, I hope he brings you a nigger wife and a house full of the baboon kids.

It was the almighty God who first segregated the negro in the first place. Are you so sick in the head that you cannot see that integration with one of these is the biggest evil of all? And not being satisfied to sin yourself, must you try to force others to sin too, by raising brats to go out and force niggers on the human race?

Sure I believe in evolution, but the human race evolved from porpoises. The niggers from apes. And I also believe in living and let living. May you and yours burn in hell forever for the evil crimes you are perpetrating on the human race.

If you like these niggers so much, why don't you invite them to your town and take them off our hands. We will be glad to trade you all of them for your worst hoodlums, jailbirds, prostitutes, or what have you.

[unsigned]

> *Unsigned postcard sent to the parents of Andrew Goodman*

You tried to be smart. You want to mix the whites with the colored. Your kid got it, alright. Ha ha ha. Good for him, you S.O.B. You bastards, you should all be wiped out. You will. Ha ha ha ha.

> *Postcard sent to the father of Andrew Goodman three days after his son's body was discovered*

Mr. Goodman -

You got what you wanted! You encouraged Andy to go South, as a trouble-maker. Why don't you take up the slack? Put your actions where your big mouth is! They would give you a big welcome in Mississippi. Yours would be cut-off, too. You have a lot of years to regret your stupidity!

Norman Looly

Notes and Letter from Neshoba County, August 15–22, 1964

> *CORE volunteer Walter Kaufmann came to Mississippi from California to distribute food and clothing to local residents. When COFO staff in Meridian (where the murderers of Chaney, Goodman, and Schwerner ran the police force) asked for additional help, he volunteered. This is Kaufmann's account of his first week on the front lines in Neshoba County, including his descriptions of the memorial service held after the bodies of the three men were found on August 4.*

[Document 1]

Date: Sat. Aug. 15th.

Arrived Jackson, Miss. COFO office approx. 10:30 pm Sat., 5 min. later a volunteer worker was assaulted with a baseball bat directly across the street from the COFO office. Twelve stitches were taken in his head. The office is in the heart of the Negro ghetto. The assailants were white.

Ten minutes later, Silas Magee [McGhee], field secretary for SNCC, was shot in the head in Greenwood, Miss. Five min. later, a Negro was shot in the leg on Lynch Street, only one block from the office. Simultaneously a cross was burned at Terry and Lynch Streets, only four blocks from the COFO office.

Sun. Aug. 16th.

Left COFO office 10am for Mileston, Miss., to interview Hardiman Turnbolt [Hartmann Turnbull], an elected delegate to the National Democratic Convention for the Freedom Democrat Party. He is a lifetime resident of Miss., semi-illiterate but a natural leader and a dynamic personality. He says that he is fed up with the treatment of the Negroes and just can't take any more. Earlier this year, he led a group of 14 Negroes to the courthouse in Holmes County to register. The sheriff lined them up, pulled his gun, and asked, "Who wants to be first?" Hardiman Turnbolt immediately stepped forward and said, "Me." The sheriff was so surprised that he did not shoot but holstered his pistol and told them all to go home.

2 weeks later, his home was fire-bombed, and as he, his wife, and twelve year old daughter were fleeing the burning bldg., he was fired upon by whites. He repelled them by firing back, which he has done on two occasions since then.

3:30pm. Attended memorial services for Chaney, Schwerner and Goodman at the site of the church that they had inspected before they disappeared. The rostrum was set amid the ruins of the burned church.

Chaney's mother delivered a very heart-tugging speech. At the end she asked that the people of Miss. and the world should not let her son have died in vain, but that if she had to do it alone she would see that the job that her son had started would be finished.

Mon. Aug. 17th.

Spent most of the day driving all over the northern and central Miss., trying to find space for the food and clothing. Finally settled on a house in Canton Miss. next door to the Freedom House, which is being converted into a community house. Drove back to Jackson, where Dave Dennis rented a car for us. (We had been using his bullet-riddled one.)

Tues. Aug. 18th.

Truck arrived approx. 10am and we had barely finished unloading (the whole community and two ministers from Cleveland pitched in) when the pickup trucks from the outlying communities began arriving. Loaded trucks most of the day and then attended the COFO conference at Tougaloo College that nite. (Very interesting.)

Wed. Aug. 19th.

Drove up to Madison County to inspect and photograph the ruins of Mt Pleasant Baptist Church, one of the 17 churches to be burned since June 1st (see photos) [not shown].

The Freedom School classes are now being held under the trees beside the ruins on the only four benches which were saved from the fire. This school has an enrollment of 32 pupils, ranging in age from 13 to 47. (Attention Tony Perot.)

Back to the conference at Tougaloo in the pm (have interesting notes).

Thurs. Aug. 20th.

Intended to rest today and head for Cleveland tomorrow. While Randy and I were sitting in the cafe next door to the COFO office in Jackson, Rudy Lumbard rushed in with news of a crisis in Philadelphia, Miss., in Neshoba County. (This is the hell-hole and Klan stronghold where Chaney, Schwerner and Goodman were murdered. This is near the location of Hardiman Turnbolt's harassment. This is the area of almost daily disappearance of Negroes who have supposedly "gone north," and never heard from again. In the words of Hardiman Turnbolt, "When Gabriel blows his horn, more Negroes will rise up from the Pearl River than all the graveyards put together." This [is] the realm of Sheriff Rainey, who was last to see the three civil rights workers alive.

This God-forsaken county was given up as impossible and too dangerous to work by COFO in 1961. Four days ago COFO decided to try again. The Evers Hotel was leased for an office and Freedom School and COFO workers moved in.

The Evers Hotel was vacant and consisted of nine <u>small</u> rooms located on the second floor above a grocery store. Ever since the workers moved in they have been harassed and threatened by whites with shotguns and rifles who drove by in autos and trucks, while Sheriff Rainey and the FBI looked on from their parked autos down the street. This morning at 11am, Sheriff Rainey ordered the workers to vacate the building by 1pm on the grounds that they were trespassing on private property, or be arrested. The workers refused to leave.

Consequently when Rudy asked for a volunteer to go with him to Philadelphia, I volunteered. Dave Dennis was really worried and told us that we did not have to go if we didn't want to. We both insisted on going.

Arrived Phila. approx. 3:30pm and could feel the tension in the air. The sheriff had not arrived and although they were laughing and joking, you could see the strain on the faces of the workers.

The sheriff did not appear today and at 8pm the project director, Jim Collier, called a staff meeting to set up some form of security watch for the building. It was decided that two guards would be stationed on the roof of the building with flashlights and a walkie talkie to contact a man standing by the phone to call the FBI, the police and alert COFO hdqts in Jackson. Two shifts were set up, one from 12:00 to 2:30 and another from 2:30 to 5:00am. Eddie Doss of Atlanta and myself volunteered for the second shift.

We prepared for what looks to be a rough nite. The door was locked, barricaded and barbed wire strung in the stairwell leading to the second floor. (God only knows, since this is the only way out of the building.) Now I know the true meaning of the song "We Shall Not Be Moved."

[Document 2]
Aug. 22, 1964
Philadelphia, Miss.
Neshoba County

Despite numerous bomb threats, a constant stream of white visitors in cars, many with guns, and pseudo-legal attempts to evict us, the Philadelphia project is now firmly established and functioning with a great deal of assistance from the community—some of which arrives several times a day in the form of quantities of fried chicken, corn bread, peas, okra and other such essentials.

A week ago today, our first night here in the Evers Hotel, we were visited by three car loads full of armed whites. They gawked for half an hour, brandished their weapons and made obscene gestures and left. Such calls increased each night until two days ago when the traffic outside the hotel decreased appreciably. During the middle of the week, the parade of cars outside the hotel seemed like a bad movie. A comedy of terrors. Wednesday was worst. A regular parade with local whites driving by followed by FBI cars checking license plates (local negroes had just brought us some watermelons) and keeping watch. Sometimes the FBI cars were followed by Sheriff Rainey and Deputy Price, both of whom are under constant scrutiny for possible (I think probable) involvement in the killing of the three boys. At one point Price, frustrated by the fact that we, along with about thirty local negroes, were all sitting outside watching the show and laughing, suddenly shot by with his siren screaming, raising billows of dust, hoping, I suppose, to scare us.

At night we keep guard posted to give ourselves time to make necessary phone calls and perhaps even prevent the bombings that we feel are inevitable. So far, the FBI has been co-operative keeping surveillance on the area at night and getting statements from us about the activities of the local police and other whites who are viewed as a threat to our presence in the county.

Meanwhile, we have gotten a slow but sure start on the Freedom School through our Bookmobile, a small panel truck which we load with books and drive through the community. At several points we stop, let children check out books, teach freedom songs, give short talks, organize games, and end each meeting with the singing of "We Shall Overcome."

It is difficult to get full participation. The people want to cooperate and do all they can to help us, but they are often afraid. Many peer nervously out the window as we speak to them, a few are too frightened to even respond. We are somewhat apprehensive too, especially about going out into the rural community. We now use walkie-talkies and other electronic equipment. Recently three negroes, including one negro woman, were savagely beaten in this area. Then, of course there is the tragedy of the three workers. Only this week a very white looking negro was mistaken for one of us and brutally assaulted in broad day light on the main street of Philadelphia. Three churches have been burned to the ground in this county during the Summer.

Voter registration has just begun and already some local residents have agreed to be block captains and organize precincts for the FDP.

Since regular school begins next week, the Freedom School will not actually begin until we can see when the students will be able to meet. This presents a problem, as many pick cotton after their classes. Classes will probably be held in the evening. Meanwhile we have set up a library in one of the rooms of our "hotel." Many have checked books out already. There is a real thirst for information on the negro and his history.

There has been tremendous support from the community. Our so called hotel has at present no toilet, kitchen, running water, nor anything else save walls, roof and floor. Since our second day here, when we stopped using the little restaurant because of a bomb threat the owner received, we have depended entirely on the community for our basic necessities. Soon we will install our own facilities. Homes have been readily open to us for showering and shaving, hot water is made available across the street, iron and boards, as well as volunteers to launder have been made available. Each day at lunch and supper some one always appears with fully cooked meals for us. Today at lunch there was some confusion and two different persons each appeared with two separate full cooked luncheons. Besides this, there is a great feeling here, a kind of solidarity is emerging among the negroes, a sense of community. They know that our presence insures the presence of the FBI and thus the perpetual terror is for the time being mitigated.

I will write more later. A personal letter will follow.

COREdially,

Walt

A police officer with a bullhorn addresses protesters during
Greenwood Freedom Day, July 16, 1964. More than one hundred
local residents and Freedom Summer staff and volunteers were
taken to jail that day on the bus shown in the background.

VOTER REGISTRATION

At the end of June, Freedom Summer staff and volunteers fanned out into thirty-three cities and towns, nearly all which ran voter registration projects. In the majority of Mississippi's counties, less than one percent of eligible black citizens were registered to vote. The county-by-county breakdown in the first document here demonstrates the extent of the problem.

COFO's leaders knew that this could not be remedied in a single summer. But they hoped to educate local people about the electoral process, take thousands to county courthouses to try to register, and document illegal actions that they could use in future lawsuits. Another short-term goal was to begin breaking down the fear and apathy that kept black Mississippians away from the polls. The next two documents in this chapter are instructions given to volunteers on how to canvass neighborhoods, run voter education meetings, conduct themselves in public, and build a grassroots movement. These may have been used during orientation sessions in June.

The application form that prospective voters filled out is given next. Questions 18 and 19, which had to be answered to the satisfaction of the local registrar, were specifically designed to reject black applicants. Registrars often decided that illiterate white people answered them correctly, while college-educated African Americans failed. The fifth document is part of a report by two Northern ministers that describes voter registration activities in Hattiesburg, including picketing, canvassing, courthouse visits, literacy tests, and mass meetings.

Two letters written by Northern college students to their parents recounting day-to-day voter registration work in black neighborhoods at opposite ends of the state follow. They describe not just the routine of canvassing but also the people volunteers met and how they themselves matured by working with them. Finally, notes from a 1965 speech by Charles McLaurin,

SNCC project director in Ruleville, recall the first time he took applicants to a courthouse.

As expected, comparatively few black Mississippians were added to the voting rolls during Freedom Summer. But consciousness was raised about the importance of voting, entire communities were mobilized to attempt to register together during "Freedom Days," abundant evidence of legal violations was gathered, and newspapers back in volunteers' hometowns informed readers around the nation about conditions in Mississippi.

Negro Voters by District and County, 1963

> *This table was distributed to Freedom Summer staff and volunteers to show the extent of disenfranchisement and the size of the challenge they faced.*

Negro Voters by District and County
(The following statistics are from the *Congressional Quarterly*, week ending July 5, 1963, p. 1091–3.)

First [Congressional] District (Northeast)

County	Negro Pop. Over 21	Negro Voters Regis.	Percent
Alcorn	1,750	61	3.5%
Attila	4,262	61	1.4%
Calhoun	1,767	0	0%
Chickasaw	3,054	0	0%
Choctaw	1,105	10	.9%
Clay	4,444	10	.2%
Itawamba	463	47	10.2%
Lee	5,130	231	4.5%
Lowndes	8,362	70	.8%
Monroe	5,610	9	.2%
Noxubee	5,172	0	0%
Oktibbeha	4,592	107	2.2%
Pontotoc	1,519	6	.4%
Prentiss	1,070	18	1.7%
Tishominga	359	6	1.7%
Webster	1,174	2	.2%
Winston	3,611	57	1.6%

Second District (Northwest)

County	Negro Pop. Over 21	Negro Voters Regis.	Percent
Benton	1,419	150	10.5%
Bolivar	15,939	612	3.8%
Carroll	2,704	3	.1%
Coahoma	14,404	1,800	12.3%
DeSoto	6,246	4	.06%

Grenada	4,323	61	1.4%
Holmes	8,757	41	.5%
Humphreys	5,561	2	.04%
Issaquena	1,081	0	0%
Lafayette	3,239	134	4.1%
Leflore	13,567	268	1.9%
Marshall	7,163	90	1.2%
Montgomery	2,627	11	.4%
Panola	7,250	2	.03%
Quitman	5,673	435	7.6%
Sharkey	3,125	3	.1%
Sunflower	13,524	164	1.2%
Tallahatchie	6,483	5	.07%
Tate	4,326	0	0%
Tippah	1,281	176	13.7%
Tunica	5,822	22	.4%
Union	1,626	6	.4%
Washington	20,619	2,563	12.4%
Yalobusha	2,441	4	.2%

Third District (Southwest)

Adams	9,340	1,050	11.2%
Amite	3,560	1	.03%
Claiborne	3,969	50	1.2%
Copiah	6,407	20	.31%
Franklin	1,842	146	7.9%
Hinds	36,133	5,000	13.8%
Jefferson	3,540	0	0%
Lincoln	3,913	516	13.2%
Pike	6,936	207	3.0%
Walthall	2,490	3	.1%
Warren	10,726	1,100	10.3%
Wilkinson	4,120	110	2.7%
Yazoo	8,719	178	2.1%

Fourth District (Central)

Clarke	2,988	34	1.1%
Jasper	3,675	6	.2%

Kemper	3,221	10	.3%
Lauderdale	11,924	1,200	10.1%
Leake	3,397	150	4.4%
Madison	10,366	500	4.8%
Neshoba	2,565	8	.3%
Newton	3,018	32	1.1%
Rankin	6,944	43	.6%
Scott	3,752	28	.7%
Simpson	3,186	61	1.9%
Smith	1,293	24	1.9%

Fifth District (Southeast)

Forrest	7,495	24	.2%
George	580	13	2.2%
Jones	7,427	872	11.7%
Lamar	1,071	0	0%
Marion	3,630	400	11.0%
Pearl River	2,473	0	0.0%
Perry	1,140	127	11.1%
Stone	868	41	4.5%
Greene	859	40	4.6%
Wayne	2,556	0	0.0%

Voter Registration Summer Prospects

> *This COFO document and the next were addressed to new volunteers and may have been written for the June training sessions in Ohio.*

Voter registration, this summer as always, will form the backbone of COFO's efforts. Mississippi will not change until the distribution of power on the voting rolls is changed, and all the stopgap measures we can plan will not alter this fact. As the situation stands, we will probably not be able to actually register large numbers of Negroes this summer; what we can do is encourage large numbers of attempts. Every Negro who attempts to register represents a victory; every rejected application means another ounce of pressure on the State, another mandate for action for the Justice Department. The job of the voter registration worker is to get the people to try.

No one can give you specific instructions on what to do in your area this summer; do as much as you can. What is possible depends on the mood of the area, on the level of fear, on the intensity of white resistance. There is no set one way—fake it.

The stock work of ordinary voter registration is the simple day-to-day business of canvassing, informal teaching, and taking groups to the courthouses. The problem at this level is not the sheriff or the Ku Klux Klan, but the fear and apathy of the Negro community. Until a local leadership is developed, you, as the "outside agitator," are the leadership. You must become acquainted with the Negro community—develop a general feeling of trust and confidence in you. This is the first step toward developing the community's confidence in you. This is the first step toward developing the community's confidence in itself—toward the creation of a self-sustaining local movement. The worker must give the impression of being courageous but not foolhardy, competent but not all-knowing. Be yourself, do your job, preach Freedom, and the community will come. Keep in mind that you have just begun to tear down a set of attitudes that has taken three and a half centuries to build. Talk and keep talking; there are enough people anxious to shut you up without your own timidity interfering. Also keep listening, and remember that fear will often cause words to mask real responses and that you must learn to hear what is beneath the words.

Your job is communication. Find for yourself the best ways to spread the word. It may be best to work through a group of strong potential leaders; you may have to screen the whole community to find them. It may be that no local people are willing to step out and risk the special attentions of the white community; move those willing to move <u>as a group</u> until there is enough Negro solidarity to make "stepping out" feasible.

You will find in time that the simple process of delivering small groups of Negroes to the courthouse is not enough. The people become frustrated, discouraged, weekly mass meetings pale when the community can see no absolute progress in registration—what's the use? The entire community must somehow be involved, a feeling of real movement must be restored. Calling a "Freedom Day" may revitalize the town as well as providing a probable basis for a Federal suit. The essence of a Freedom Day is that it gives the entire Negro community a sense of solid achievement—at the end of the day everyone participating feels that he has really <u>done</u> something— that the whole town has worked together to win a victory.

The Southern Christian Leadership Conference holds bi-weekly citizenship training sessions at Dorchester, Georgia. See if you can find local people with leadership potential who might benefit from such training. Most of the outstanding local leaders developed so far have been products of Dorchester. The trainee's travel expenses are paid by SCLC, and he returns from the session capable of conducting semi-formal citizenship classes. If and when you find a likely candidate, contact Annelle Ponder in Jackson.

Finally, keep in mind that weekly reports to the Jackson office are essential. One research-communications person on your project will have the assignment of sending in these reports. Your responsibility will be to keep track of the information he requests and to channel it to him. Some of the information that is crucial is contacts made, meetings held, white reactions. If this material is not filed in Jackson, we will lose the benefits of the work you have done when you leave the state.

Whatever you do, make every effort to carry it through to a finish of some sort; if any program must be dropped or abandoned, make sure to explain to the community <u>why</u> it must be. Maintain a feeling of motion, of purpose; when the community sings "We Shall Overcome" it should mean it, it should believe it.

Techniques for Field Work:
Voter Registration

> *These instructions to volunteers who canvassed door to door could have been applied all across the segregated South. They concisely describe how a mass movement to end segregation was built.*

Safety

1. Know all roads in and out of town.
2. Know location of sanctuaries and safe homes in the county.
3. Make arrangements for regular checks with the Jackson office and/or the county office.
4. Decide whether night or day work is preferable.

Canvassing

1. Take pencil and paper to record <u>any</u> information that seems pertinent.
2. Remember that you are asking people to take their time to listen to you. You should try to present yourself in a way that will make them want to talk with you.
3. If a person closes the door in your face or will not talk with you, try to find out elsewhere why he did it. Everybody can be approached, but it may take much time and patience to reach some people.
4. If a person talks but shows obvious reluctance, don't force a long explanation on them. Come back another day to explain more. Soften them up through repeated exposure. This builds confidence and builds a relationship.
5. If a person invites you in but then doesn't listen to you, try asking questions to get their attention. Try talking about other things and eventually working back to your program.
6. If a person listens and seems interested, try to give them something to do to keep their interest up. Use them to help you contact other people. Use them to talk with the rest of their family.
7. If a person already knows what you are telling him, find out how he knows it. Perhaps there is already a group in existence that nothing is known about. Perhaps there are channels of communication that could be valuable in the future.

Under the watchful eyes of white observers, two African American men fill out voting applications at the Forrest County courthouse in Hattiesburg, Mississippi. The sign advises them that their names will be published in the newspaper for two weeks, information that often facilitated reprisals by segregationists.

NOTICE

Applications for Registration must be completely filled out without any assistance or suggestions of any person or memorandum.

After 10 days applicants names and addresses are published for two consecutive weeks in the newspaper. They cannot be ruled on until 14 days after the second publication. Therefore it can take as long as 3 days before we can give you an answer as to your application being accepted or rejected.

Your indulgence is appreciated.
The REGISTRAR

8. When canvassing try to have a single idea in mind, e.g. getting people out to a mass meeting that evening or setting up a workshop. Don't overwhelm a person with too much at any one time.

Workshops

1. Arrange any materials (pencils, paper, application blanks, etc) beforehand so that the workshop isn't hung up for lack of these fundamentals.

2. Emphasize that any question is a good question. Encourage people to speak up, to ask questions, to bring out their own ideas.

3. Whenever possible, use the local residents to lead the workshops, to answer the questions, to take charge. Ultimately the people will be left alone, they can never start standing by themselves [i.e., COFO staff and volunteers will leave local communities, so residents need to be trained as leaders while they're still present].

4. Go slowly enough to include everyone. Ask questions, get the people to call a halt—use any technique to judge whether your speed is correct.

5. Many times people like to open and close workshops with a song and a prayer.

6. Praise people freely. Compliment them for any small thing. This business is new for most people and they are easily intimidated.

Taking People to Courthouse

1. Arrange transportation when necessary.

2. Be prompt if a time is agreed on.

3. Encourage people to go at least by twos, there is strength in numbers.

4. Accompany people to the door of the registrar's office where possible. At least go as far as the local authorities will permit.

Sworn Written Application for Registration

> *This is the text of the official application used in Mississippi court-houses. Questions 18 and 19 enabled registrars to unilaterally reject applicants; there was no provision for appeal.*

Anyone who is over 21 years of age or will be 21 years by the date of the General Election, November 5, 1964, can register to vote. If you are over 60 years of age, you do not have to pay a poll tax to vote.

1. Write the date of this application:
2. What is your full name?
3. State your age and date of birth:
4. What is your occupation?
5. Where is your business carried on?
6. By whom are you employed?
7. Are you a citizen of the United States and an inhabitant of Mississippi?
8. For how long have you resided in Mississippi?
9. Where is your place of residence in the District?
10. Specify the date when such residence began:
11. State your prior place of residence, if any:
12. Check which oath you desire to take:

  (1) General

  (2) Minister's

  (3) Minister's wife

  (4) If under 21 years at present but 21 years by the date of the election

13. If there is more than one person of your same name in the precinct, by what name do you wish to be called?

14. Have you ever been convicted of any of the following crimes: bribery, theft, arson, obtaining money or goods under false pretenses, perjury, forgery, embezzlement, or bigamy?

15. If your answer to Question 14 is "Yes," name the crime of which you have been convicted and the date and place of such conviction or convictions:

16. Are you a minister of the Gospel in charge of an organized church or the wife of such a minister?

17. If your answer to Question 16 is "yes," state the length of your residence in the election district:

18. Write and copy in the space below Section _____ of the Constitution of Mississippi: (Instruction to Registrar: You will designate the Section of the Constitution of Mississippi and point out same to applicant.)

19. Write in the space below a reasonable interpretation (the meaning) of the section of the Constitution of Mississippi which you have just copied:

20. Write in the space below a statement setting forth your understanding of the duties and obligations of citizenship under Constitutional form of government: (FOR EXAMPLE: A good citizen pays all taxes, obeys all laws, and votes in every election.)

21. Sign and attach here the oath or affirmation named in Question 12:

22. I, _____, have resided in the Election District of _____County.

The Applicant will sign his name here _____

STATE OF MISSISSIPPI

COUNTY OF _____

Sworn to and subscribed before me by the witness named _____

on this _____day of_____, 19_____.

County Registrar

What Were We There To Do?

> *David Steffenson and Paul Murphy were not COFO volunteers but Northern Methodist ministers working with an ecumenical project that supported voter registration in Hattiesburg, Mississippi. This is an excerpt from a long, mimeographed report that they sent back to colleagues in the North. It provides a clear snapshot of voter registration work in one of the state's larger cities.*

What Were We There To Do?

In the Minister's Project we worked independently of, but alongside the Council of Federated Organizations (COFO), which is a united effort on the part of the leading civil rights groups in the South. The COFO staff and volunteer workers in Hattiesburg is made up largely of people in the Student Nonviolent Coordinating Committee (SNCC or "Snick").

We were there to do three things with them. We walked in the integrated picket line in front of the courthouse part of each day. This line was set up to remind the County Clerk, Theron Lynd, that he was being watched and to give moral support to the Negro community. It was also a witness to the fact that white Americans did care about human rights. Until April 10, except for an avoidable incident in February, this was the first peaceful civil rights picket line in the history of Mississippi.

In the afternoon we helped the COFO workers canvass the Negro neighborhoods to find people who would agree to apply to register. He would explain the procedure to those who agreed and discuss the issue with those who were reluctant. We were also looking for those who had already tried to register to have them sign affidavits as evidence to use against Theron Lynd in the federal courts. (He is presently being tried in federal court for contempt of an order to cease his discriminatory practices.)

In Mississippi one must fill out a form with 18 questions on it to get on the voting rolls. The 18th question is the kicker. It asks the applicant to read any section of the state constitution the registrar chooses and then to interpret it in simple language to the satisfaction of the registrar. Of course no Negro can satisfy him. We were told that he would sometimes add questions such as, "How many bubbles in a bar of soap?" And he would disqualify anyone for the least error such as putting "M" instead of "Male" on the form. Also, any applicant has his name published in the paper which allows his employer to fire him or informs the local toughs where to lob their bombs.

The canvassing interested us because we met people face to face. We ran across open welcome on the part of some to deep fear on the part of others. We could understand the man who said he had been everywhere but heaven, but he was in hell now. And we were heartened by the elderly and crippled Negro minister who put the gospel of love into simple and eloquent terms as he agreed to go down and register somehow. We wish we'd had more time to call.

In the evenings we took part in the COFO mass meetings in various Negro churches to whip up enthusiasm for the program in the Negro community. The singing of the freedom songs during these meetings were an inspiration, and we learned much about the feelings of the concerned Negro. One evening some of the SNCC workers demonstrated some of the non-violent techniques (though our program was not this type of demonstration). It was chilling to see high school youth acting out methods of curling up on the ground so as to protect their vital parts from police kicks and clubs, how to protect themselves from the police dogs lunging at their throats without resisting or fighting back (by Mississippi law the dogs have the same status as the police), and how to protect themselves from the knives of local white toughs in a non-violent way.

The white ministers also tried to communicate with white leaders in the community. Our activities here were cut short by our arrest, but we did have some insightful experiences. We spent one delightful evening in the home of the local rabbi who is a northerner trying to do something constructive in a difficult position. Paul also had a short interview with the Mayor in which he told Paul how, "If anyone understands the Negras, it's me," and then proceeded to demonstrate his ignorance. Some of our Presbyterian friends that week talked with a local minister, originally from the North, who has had quite a change of heart in recent weeks. He tried to visit us in jail the first evening and was in the audience at arraignment in court—both acts of great courage in his position.

Dear Dad

> *Robert Feinglass was a college student from Illinois assigned to voter registration work in Holly Springs, in northern Mississippi. This July 1964 letter is one of several he wrote home describing his day-to-day life during Freedom Summer.*

Rust College
Holly Springs, Miss.
Dear Dad,

Please excuse the carbon; I have not much time.

I want to tell you about Mississippi and about the Freedom Movement here. It is not easy; my impressions are many and very strong. I have met the best and worst people here, the greatest courage and the greatest terror—sometimes in the same person. This Mississippi is a beautiful land of red earth and a thousand greens, made ugly by the squalor and hate which dominate the races who live here.

I work in voter registration. Three of us work together; one is a Negro. In as many cases as possible the Negro is made the project director, and such is the case here. The policy is a wise and effective one. On a normal day we roll out of bed early in the morning. We may have slept in the Freedom House, or in the home of some generous and brave farmer (two essential requirements for anyone to offer us hospitality). We study the map of the county, decide where we will work for the day. We scramble for breakfast and hit the road.

The work is long and hot. We drive from farmhouse to farmhouse. I have averaged almost 200 miles a day on the car. The roads are in despicable condition. We know where the colored people are by those roads: where the pavement stops the Negro sections are likely to begin. And if there is not even gravel on the roads, we can be reasonably sure that we are in a safe neighborhood. Such is not always the case, though, and more than once we have been cursed and threatened by someone for knocking on a white man's door.

When we walk up to a house there are always children out front. They look up and see white men in the car, and fear and caution cover their expressions. Those terrified eyes are never quite out of my mind; they drive me as little else could. Children who have hardly learned to talk are well-taught in the arts of avoiding whites. They learn "yassah" as almost their first words. If they did not, they could not survive. The children run to their parents, hide behind them. We walk up, smile, say howdy, and hold out our hands. As we shake hands I tell them my name. They tell me their names and I say Mr. _____, how do you do. It is likely the first time in the life of this farmer or housewife a white man has ever shaken hands with them, or even called them "with a handle to their names." This does not necessarily bode well to them; they are suspicious. Chances are they have heard about the "freedom riders" passing through. The news is usually greeted with mingled fear, excitement, enthusiasm and gratitude. But the confrontation is more serious and more threatening. They think, if Mr. Charlie knew . . . , and they are afraid. They have good reason to be. Murders of Negroes in Mississippi are not news. No one cares, and no one is surprised. Much as teenagers in our northern cities cruise the streets and whistle at girls, white teenagers down here abuse Negroes. They go night-riding five in a car, and woe to him caught alone on the road. They throw bottles at homes and people; they even shoot into cars. There is not a lawman in the state who would arrest them for such an activity. Young girls never go out alone at night. All this appears before them as we speak, and it is this they fear. Many, too, are share-croppers, who must turn over a third to a half of the year's harvest to a man who does no work at all, but who owns the land they till. These may be evicted, and have often been for far less serious offenses. Nearly everyone black in Mississippi is at least a year in debt. The threat of suspended credit and foreclosure is a tremendous burden; our presence adds much to the load. A wage for a laborer is usually $2.50 to $3 a day for work from six to six. There is no job security, no sick benefit (often if you get sick you get fired), no old age pensions. Very often Negroes know nothing about welfare or social security. They have no insurance against misfortune.

Yet they listen when we speak. We tell them we are from the North. We tell them that the nation has finally become interested in them, and concerned over their plight. We talk about taxes, and cotton allotments, and usury, and schools and hospitals and federal agencies. We talk about dignity. People listen, and they wonder. They are not sure. What does it mean when a white man tells them the truth, when he asks them to help him, to help themselves. Why is he here. What does he really want. What will come of it. We tell them about the Freedom Democratic Party, about the Convention Challenge in Atlantic City. We talk about a Negro sheriff and blacktop roads and respect. They listen and they wonder. They think of their children, of the danger, of the odds. And more often than not, they sign up for the Freedom Democratic Party.

This new party in this state is going to be the salvation of the black man and of the white. There is not the bitterness here that there is in Chicago, in Harlem. People in the North have tried and failed. Here they are trying for the first time.

Twice in the last five days we have held precinct and county meetings, in DeSoto and Tippah counties. DeSoto is very poor, and 62% Negro. Tippah is surprisingly wealthy and about 20% Negro. The meetings attracted about 110 people in DeSoto and about 40 people in Tippah (after only three days work).

Our job is a seven-day, fifteen-hour job, except when there are mass meetings (at least twice a week), when it is longer. We have extensive reports to write up (in quadruplicate; we need a ditto reproducing machine badly), staff meetings, strategy planning. It is the most stimulating, satisfying work I have ever done. Nothing is ever enough; there is no such thing as a job finished: there is only progress. We are involved here in a process of uniting, joining, becoming a mutually interested community. The song says it well: we shall overcome.

Yours,

Bob

Dear Mom and Dad

> *Ellen Lake was a volunteer from a suburb of New York City. She was assigned to Gulfport, on Mississippi's southern coast. In this letter to her parents, she discusses how voter registration work changed her and gives vivid portraits of some of her black neighbors.*

2905 Harrison St.

Gulfport, Miss.

July 4, 1964

Dear Mom and Dad,

I've been waiting and thinking about this letter for a long time. I'd like to try to communicate to you—and crystallize for myself—some feelings and attitudes which have become apparent to me during these last weeks.

First about myself: You both know how critical I always have been of other people—always expecting a high level of performance and rather arrogant when the level is not reached. Thus, I was a little worried, coming down here, where—because of a completely different cultural environment—people couldn't possibly meet those standards, or even aim toward them. That is, I was worried that I would tend to be extremely critical of the people around me, even though intellectually I knew how ridiculous it was.

But, this has not occurred. My standards and expectations have been acclimated to my surroundings. When I talk to someone while I am canvassing, I am able to accept them completely as they are, without mentally correcting their grammar or becoming impatient when they cannot answer what seems a very simple question on a questionnaire. In a sense, I hold any judgment in store; if Mrs. X can read, fine; if not, I can enjoy talking to her about her life and experiences. Perhaps, I've been finding that people everywhere have more in common than I once thought. Humanity is so much more basic than education or intellectual achievement.

Related to this: I have met some of the most amazing, great people among my canvassees. Out of nowhere, seemingly, come little old women with so much warmth and wisdom that I almost cry. There's little Mrs. Rachel Fairley, who is about 65 and wonderful and crisp and brisk, yet full of God and sympathy. She's always praying for me—and for the three lost near Philadelphia—and I can't help feeling that her prayers must be doing some good, they're so sincere and deeply felt.

Yesterday, around 7 p.m. I marched up on the steps of a dark little falling apart house. Mrs. Brotherns—the lady of the house, I later learned—invited me in. (Everyone, without exception in the Negro community, overflows with hospitality and friendliness. I keep being invited in for "some barbecue" or a cold drink or a rest on the front porch.) She was already registered, but her husband was not. He was a beautiful man of about 59, great trusses of graying hair and a completely beardless face. He was crippled with arthritis and thus could not write and could not read either.

I told him about going down to the courthouse and asking to register, while admitting that he couldn't read or write. (Supposedly the registrar is required to record such a person's name and address—which may be used later in a federal suit against the State's registrars.) But it's a difficult thing to ask anyone to do, because it's embarrassing to admit to illiteracy. But Mr. Brotherns did not hesitate. Later, after he'd written his "X" on the Freedom Registration Form (to become a member of the Freedom Democratic Party), he said, proudly, "That's what I've always wanted to do—vote."

"Can I vote soon?" asked his adopted third grade son.

"Not for a long while," Mr. Brotherns said. "Can I do it when I'm fourteen?" the little boy said eagerly.

"Then I can sign my 'X' like Daddy."

"No," said Mr. Brotherns firmly and proudly. "You're learning to write."

It was really quite beautiful. Just then it began to pour and the pageant continued inside—in a small dark room, lighted only by a brief flame in the fireplace, where Mrs. Brotherns was cooking dinner. The three adopted children sat on the floor and read from their school books or counted on bottle tops, while the two old people looked on with love. The whole scene was from another century—especially because the little boy had a self-made bow and arrow, bent from a stick and tied with some cord. He proudly shot an arrow into the bushes across the street as I watched.

Another lady—Mrs. Ella Mae Hart—is also illiterate, but staunchly marched into the circuit clerk's office not once but twice on Friday. She is extremely fat, and had a hard time getting up the steps into the office and then had to rest before she could puff out her message—that she'd come to register, though she couldn't read or write. She wasn't daunted when the registrar told her she couldn't register and he refused to take her name and address. When she got home, she told me firmly that she intended to come nightly to our adult literacy classes. And so she will.

African American residents line up outside the Leflore County courthouse to try to register to vote on July 16, 1964, Greenwood Freedom Day. Only three were allowed inside at a time, and most never reached the door because county officials deliberately slowed down the application process.

I have the most strange feeling, when Negroes talk about white folks' injustices toward them. I can't figure out how I look to them—am I transparent or am I a "white Negro?" No matter—either way, it's fascinating and deeply moving to be on the other end—to hear maids talking about how mean their employers are or how poorly they are paid. I've always before heard the white end of this conversation, but now the Negro end is so much more real and more meaningful. Perhaps for the first time, the people who have always appeared to me as servants are becoming people. They have dropped out of their roles and are individuals. One lady said to me today, "I guess there's nothing for poor folks but work; we can't rest till we die." I'd never before come upon such an attitude, expressed to me; and I think it's extremely important that I now have. It makes me so much more aware of people and their sufferings than I have ever before had to be.

I brought two women down to register on Tuesday, and sat and watched them while they slowly worked through the twenty-two question form. It took them over an hour on a form which they had already been drilled on quite carefully. After about three-quarters of an hour I began to get a little annoyed and restless, and began to wonder how a questionnaire could take so long. Then I realized how different an experience it was for these two to be taking a written test—with pencil in hand and having to express themselves, if only in phrases. I have been through so many hours of this kind of testing that I take it for granted that others are used to the type of thinking it requires. But these two women have just not travelled in a world of paper-work and tests, and the experience was completely new for them. How different worlds can be.

I guess that's why I'm here—to bridge these two distant worlds—with understanding and knowledge and love.

Love,
Ellen

To Overcome Fear

> *Charles McLaurin began his voting rights work in the Delta in 1962
> as one of SNCC's first field secretaries in the area. Here, he describes
> his anxiety taking local residents to a courthouse for the first time.
> He soon became a trusted veteran, ran the Ruleville COFO office
> during Freedom Summer, and was eventually arrested more than
> thirty times for his political work.*

The first people that I accompanied to the Sunflower County Courthouse in Indianola, Miss., gave me the spirit and courage to continue.

I will always remember August 22, 1962, as the day that I became a man. It was on this day that I was to test myself for courage and the ability to move in the face of fear and danger, danger such as I had never faced before.

About 7:30 a.m. that morning, I had been around to the homes of people who had given me their names as persons willing to go to the courthouse and attempt to register to vote. I was very disappointed, I had only been able to find three of the ten. The others, because of fear, had left home rather than say so to me.

Since I was going down to the Courthouse for my first time I too was afraid; not of dying and not of the man (Mr. Charlie) per se, but of the powers the sheriff's department, the police department, the courts; these are the powers and the forces which keep Negroes in their so-called places. The night riders [the Ku Klux Klan] would not be so fearful if it wasn't for the sheriff who would be on their sides, or the policemen who would arrest the Negroes who had been shot by the mob, for breach of the peace. The Negro just happened to be in the wrong place at the right time. So for this reason and many others, this poor Negro must face a hostile police court, he must stand before a prejudiced judge and be sent to the County Farm or the State prison, for a crime committed by others whose skin happened to be lighter and brighter, this is the system and the effects of that system and of the people subjected to the system.

So much for the in-between. About 8 a.m., I had only three people to go to the courthouse, this was the day I learned that the numbers were not important. I learned that a faithful few was better than an uncertain ten.

These three old ladies whose ages ranged from 65 to 85, knew the white man and his ways, they knew him because they had lived, worked, and raised families on these plantations, and on this day, they would come face to face with his sons and daughters to say, "We Must be Free." Now!

Tommie Johnson, son of one of the ladies active in the movement in Ruleville, was to carry us down in his car. About 8:30 Tommie came to where I was staying and we went to pick up the three old ladies. After we had them in the car, off we went, down the highway south on 49 highway.

We drove past an American service station operated by three white brothers known as the Woolenhams. These were bad brothers. They were known to beat up Negroes getting off the Greyhound bus when it put them off there. They also pulled guns on Negroes who asked for air in their car tires. As we passed this station, I could not help but watch to see if they noticed the car, for this car had taken six brave ladies down weeks earlier, and all the white people knew it. On and on, passing the people in the cotton fields; trucks and busses along the sides of the highway; men, women and children moving to rhythm of the beat of the hoe; working, hoping, and forever saying, "Lord, my time ain't long," this work will soon be over, I'll be free.

Now Doddsville, five miles south of Ruleville. Doddsville is the home of U.S. Senator Eastland, James O. Eastland, that is.

The light turned red just as our car reached the intersection and we stopped. A strange little place this was, five or six buildings, old and run down from the years when cotton was King and the Negroes were even more plentiful than they are today. Doddsville, where many years ago the burning of Negroes was a Sunday spectacle, where whites young and old delighted at this evil, which killed the spirit of the old Negroes and set the stage for the place-fixing of young ones not yet born.

On and on my eyes taking in as much at a glance as possible. The old ladies talking telling the stories of the years gone by; me with knees shaking, mouth closed tightly so as to not let them hear the fear in my voice. I am feeling the movement of the car and the rumbling of the motor as we move on and on towards our destination, Indianola, county seat of Sunflower County. As we move past the little town of Sunflower one of the old ladies said, "Won't be long now." At that moment my heart seemed to stop; fear so much fear, realizing what danger could lie ahead for us, especially me. A smart Nigger trying to change a way of life liked by everyone; at least it seemed that way.

Indianola, the city limits of Indianola, state of Mississippi; county of Sunflower. I am the police. These are the words of Indianola's trusted police officer, Officer Shark. As we move into the town past the numbers of gas stations along 82 highway, I could almost speak now. I was going to face the man (Mr. Charles) in the Courthouse. I was filled with fear, but this I must do; do this or continue to <u>die</u>. Not that I was dead and walking, as such; but one who is alive in real life but dead in mind, dead in ability to say, to do or to act in a way that would give attention to one's presence in society.

We turned off the highway and again we drove south, this time through a neighborhood, a white neighborhood. Then around a corner and there was the courthouse, the police station and the sheriff's department. All of the big powers together. We pulled up in front of the Courthouse. The building was an old faded brick type with a four door that opened on a different street.

As I opened the door to get out, I got a feeling in my stomach that made me feel weak, sweat started to form on my forehead, and my [hands?] became moist. At this point I was no longer in command, the three old ladies were leading me, I was following them. They got out of the car and went up the walk to the courthouse as if this was the long walk that lead to the Golden Gate of Heaven, their heads held high. I watched from a short distance behind them; the pride with which they walked. The strong convictions that they held. I watched as they walked up the steps and into the building. I stopped outside the door and waited, thinking how it was that these ladies who have been victimized by white faces all of their lives would suddenly walk up to the man and say, <u>I want to vote</u>. This did something to me. It told me something. It was like a voice speaking to me, as I stood there alone, in a strange place and an unknown land. This voice told me that although these old ladies knew the risk involved in their being here, they were still willing to try. It said you are the light, let it shine and people will know you, and they will follow you. If you show the way, they will go, with or without you.

So they did. I ask one night; I told them what to do and when that day came I followed them. The people are the true leaders. We need only to move them; to show them. Then watch and learn.

The ladies came out of the courthouse and found me day dreaming. They told me that the man in the office had told them that the office was closed; at that I went to see. I tried to open the door but it was locked. I knocked but no one opened the door. I went back to where the ladies were and we went back to the car.

As we drove away I looked back at this place, called Indianola, for one day real soon I would make a speech on these grounds. Surrounded by hundreds. That dream came true 3½ years later, when we held one of the greatest Freedom days in the state around the courthouse.

Children play outside an unidentified Freedom School.
The schools usually taught a broad curriculum that
included not only black history and core subjects
but also arts, crafts, and physical education.

5 FREEDOM SCHOOLS

Some planners of Freedom Summer initially thought that alternative schools for black students were a peripheral activity, one that at best might channel some new young people into canvassing for voters or picketing. But the people who designed the curriculum had a much grander vision—that Freedom Schools would undermine the oppressive conditioning African Americans had internalized and release a tidal wave of questioning, insights, creativity, and commitment. They were right, and in some ways Freedom Schools were the most conspicuous success of the summer project.

The first piece in this chapter was written by SNCC's Charlie Cobb, who is often credited with the idea of Freedom Schools. It shows how racist "common sense" was nurtured in order to benefit the white elite who profited from it and to limit the hopes and dreams of black residents. Cobb then calls for a new kind of education in which students examine their own lives and challenge the unspoken assumptions that bind them. He also drew up a detailed "Prospectus for a Summer Freedom School Program" that became the basis for the summer's activities.

The next document, from the spring of 1964, is the draft text for a fundraising appeal to support the Freedom Schools program. Conditions in four towns are described, showing the location, costs, and likely enrollments of projected schools. Then follow three documents used to train teachers at the volunteer orientation sessions in Ohio. The first is the table of contents of the complete curriculum package given to teachers, which provides an overview of the topics taught in Freedom Schools. Next are two full lesson plans from the package showing how Cobb's vision was worked out in practice.

Although organizers had initially assumed that only high school students would attend, Freedom Schools attracted people of all ages. Young children came for arts and crafts or reading programs, and adults came for basic literacy classes or voter registration training. Nearly 3,000 students took classes from 175 teachers in 40 schools.

In August, to cap the summer program, students organized a Freedom School Convention in Meridian. A long letter from Hattiesburg teacher Cornelia Mack describes that convention, her own students, and the community centers in her area. The final document in this chapter, written at the end of the summer by Liz Fusco, who coordinated the Freedom Schools program, is an internal SNCC assessment of their effects on kids, teachers, and communities. She refers back to Cobb's prospectus, describes how the curriculum was developed, and then explains why she thinks the Freedom Schools may be the most significant achievement of the Mississippi Summer Project.

Some Notes on Education

Why are some things common knowledge and others unthinkable? How do we get the ideas that tell us some things are good, others bad; that some dreams are attainable, others impossible? In this short reflection, SNCC's Charlie Cobb explores how African Americans living in the segregated South were indoctrinated for generations, and how the pernicious effects of that oppression could be undone. The length and tone of this piece are typical of position papers that SNCC members circulated among themselves before meetings. This one likely dates from late 1963 or early 1964.

What we have discovered over the last few years of our activities in the South, is that oppression and restriction is not limited to the bullets of local racists' shotgun blasts, or assaults at county courthouses, or the expulsion of sharecroppers from plantations, but that it (oppression and restriction) is imbedded in a complex national structure, many of the specifics of which are oft times difficult to discern, but which govern every facet of our lives. What is relevant to our lives is constantly defined for us; we are taught it in every waking hour; it is pounded in us via radio, T.V., newspapers, etc., most of which are the tools of our oppressors. Definitions are articulated to us through the use of terms such as, "qualified," "responsible," "security," "patriotism," "our way of life," "the American way of life," "Nigger," "leader," "politics," and a thousand others, infinitely more subtle and complex. Our lives are pointed out for us in a million irrelevant directions, and what we are finding we have to deal with, if we're talking about change (whether in Mississippi or New York) is, <u>Who points out and determines the direction of our lives; how do they do it and get away with it?</u>

The most immediate implication of an exploration into this question seems to be an examination into the day to day realities of our existence as only we can know it. One of the things that is vividly clear to us in the south today is that we are denied through the use of political machinery. The part of this machine that we have come into direct contact and conflict with has been state political machinery. This state machine has done at least three things that we've experienced at many levels. It has kept us (1) <u>separated</u> (through the use of segregation laws, by playing white against black, by perpetuating the myth that we can never get together without knowing what they know—e.g. in other words without being "qualified" and they define that word); (2) ignorant (communications media orient us to the irrelevant, the "qualified" gear us to become "responsible" to them, the lie of "white folks business" is perpetuated, we wander confused, aspiring to "the american way of life" rather than our own, our schools are committed to a policy of non-think, and students to an attitude of no-questions); (3) afraid (through the use of gestapo-like law enforcers, by binding us in THEIR laws and customs, which operate above us because we're not "qualified," tacitly endorsing terror—e.g. the White Citizens Council getting money from the Mississippi State Sovereignty Commission, the perversion of justice in the courts). We have found that we cannot even talk about an end to oppression and restriction in the south without these structures feeling responsible to the people of the south (or the nation). Government structures (which include all the institutions that relate to it, e.g. schools, churches, banks, communications media, big business—these control the thinking and create the values) cannot feel this responsibility, for they have isolated themselves from people in the interest of maintaining their positions. Consequently, we are governed from a kind of isolated authority which has wrapped us in structures that evade our efforts to function in them at any level. In this lies the crux of our disenfranchisement. As we begin to trace what this governing monster called "american way of life" we are discovering that avenues of knowledge, as to what it is and how it works specifically, are not available to us. We have begun to suspect that the key to dealing with it does not lie in plowing through all the intricacies of how it operates top to bottom, which we mostly cannot see anyway, but rather, with its effects locally, and our daily oppression.

You're in Mississippi, or Alabama, or Georgia, or Arkansas, defined by somebody as "nigger." This reality is understood only in terms of what it is, for there is no place to understand why it is. Attempts to understand why, means the asking of questions, the exposure of inconsistency, and the asking of more questions. To encourage questions, is to encourage challenge, which is to encourage overthrow. To talk about why a policeman hits a Negro across the head is to talk about why that policeman does not feel responsible to Negroes, and who he is responsible to, and why they don't feel responsible to Negroes, and what can be done to make them feel responsible, or who can be placed in those positions that will feel responsible, and how they can be placed in those positions, and whether or not those positions are necessary. This kind of question and exposure undermines those persons in isolated authority, because people might organize themselves around the fact that they can make these authorities irrelevant; which is to leave them with no authority at all. This is the latent threat of the Negro Movement in the south, for "keeping the niggers in their place" is just an extreme of keeping people in their place, all of which is keeping everybody from dealing with what is relevant in their lives, or even finding out what relevancies they have to deal with. This kind of questioning threatens, so this kind of questioning is not allowed. Discontent has been forced underground, where it rumbles, and is felt more than seen.

Yet, sometimes, this undercurrent of discontent is expressed; maybe by a handful of kids wearing SNCC buttons to school, or by someone standing up in civics class wanting to talk about voting, or the "freedom riders." It gets scribbled on a piece of paper sometimes: "If the white man is free, why can't the black man be?"

And sometimes, these expressions soar:

I wish that I was free
free as I can be
I'd fly, oh I'd fly
away over the sea
I'd fly over the mountains
I'd fly over the sea
And I'd be as proud
proud as I can be
But I'm not a free bird
not as free as I can be
that is why,
oh that is why
these chains are binding me

If given a chance these expressions can be beautiful. Yet too often, it is muttered bitterly, and in a vacuum, as Earnest George of Mississippi mutters: "Can't teach me a damn thing in school that a nigger in Mississippi don't know already." The Brewer brothers of Tallahatchie County got the education they needed. They heard while being pounded to the floor of a plantation store by a group of white men, shortly after a trip north, "You're back in Mississippi now nigger."

What other knowledge is needed, and can be expected of Earnest George, the Brewer brothers, and millions like them as long as they must exist in a society built to cage them? Their function has been reduced to acting on what is defined for them—defined by the cop with the stick.

OUR RESPONSIBILITY TO RELEVANT EDUCATION

People in the south, essentially black people, are beginning to build their own life. They are setting their own standards of "qualifications." They have found that they have not been able to participate in the life that they have always known. Up to this point of new building, the contradiction of all the kinds of education that they have experienced (from an attack by a cop, to public schooling) has been that it bore no relevance to functioning in a society that was not theirs. As people have started motion and agitation in their communities, they have discovered that they need an education that is geared to the relevancies they discover while building this new life <u>if they are to function and participate in it</u>. For, education is not the development of intellectual skills, but a preparation for participation in living.

Profiles of Typical Freedom Schools:
Hattiesburg, Meridian, Holly Springs, and Ruleville, Spring 1964

I. Hattiesburg

Hattiesburg, Mississippi, is a town of around 30,000—which makes it one of the five or six largest cities in Mississippi. It is near the gulf coast cities which are the "moderate" part of the state, but Hattiesburg itself is a deep-dyed conservative town. It is Governor Paul B. (Stand Tall with Paul) Johnson's home town. It is the site of Mississippi Southern University, whose law school faculty has engineered the so-far successful defiance of Ross Barnett in the James Meredith case (also acts as consultants for the State of Miss. in other civil rights cases). Mississippi Southern also is the school where Clyde Kennard, a Negro, applied in the late 1950's. He was subsequently sent to Parchman Penitentiary on a flimsy burglary conspiracy charge, contracted cancer in prison and died. Mississippi Southern has since rejected the application of another Negro, John Frazier, five times. Hattiesburg is the seat of Forrest County. Despite its large (by Mississippi standards) university and a fairly firm economic base in commerce and manufacturing, Hattiesburg "feels" like a small, agrarian-oriented community.

Hattiesburg has had a long, tough history of civil rights activity, primarily centered around the denial of the right to vote. The Circuit Clerk of the County (registrar of voters), one Theron Lynd, has made himself the test case for all recalcitrant Mississippi registrars. As early as 1961, the Department of Justice instituted proceedings against him, charging discrimination against Negroes. After much litigation, the federal government won its case and Lynd was ordered to register persons whose applications a U.S. District Judge had processed and found acceptable. Lynd consistently refused to obey these court orders, was convicted of civil contempt and STILL would not register the persons in question. The Department of Justice then instituted criminal contempt proceedings against him which are still pending. At this point, however, the civil rights groups moved independently. On January 22 [1964], designated Freedom Day in Hattiesburg, COFO people from all over the state, national civil rights leaders, but mostly the people of Hattiesburg, started a picket line around the Forrest County courthouse which, with some interruptions, is still going on. This picket line represented a breakthrough for civil rights demonstrations in

Mississippi, because it was the first to last more than 10 minutes—the police did not arrest everybody. Later, after the State legislature passed a special statute outlawing picketing of public buildings, the picketers were arrested, but that passed, too, and the picketing has resumed.

The COFO project in Hattiesburg is one of the largest and most active in the state, with a high proportion of adult participation and leadership. The town is organized, with 100 block captains, 15 citizenship teachers, and uncountable canvassers, picketers and ministers from outside the state. Two [African American] candidates for national office (one for Congress and one for Senate) have come out of the movement in Hattiesburg. The atmosphere is enthusiastic and the people work very hard. Because the project is so active, there is a lot of demand for the Freedom Schools, and the Hattiesburg people have, therefore, planned a series of Freedom Schools. The facilities are presently planned for Sunday School rooms in churches around town and in surrounding counties. Project leaders in Hattiesburg are especially interested in supplementary classes for local adults and staff members in basic literacy and current issues. The project has found housing for 110 summer workers (all of which will not work in the city of Hattiesburg, however). The project has also laid hands on a movie projector and a tape recorder for the summer project. Since the community is able to support the program better than in other areas of the state, the needs are not proportionately as great, even though it is a large Freedom School project. The main needs are for equipment and transportation to outlying schools and schools in other counties. The total budget is for $2,000 to pay for food, transportation, equipment and inescapable expenses such as phone bills.

II. Meridian

Meridian is a city of 50,000, the second largest in the state. It is the seat of Lauderdale county. It is in the eastern part of the state, near the Alabama border, and has a history of moderation on the racial issue. At the present time, the only Republican in the State Legislature is from Meridian. Registration is as easy as anywhere in the state, and there is an informal (and inactive) "biracial committee," which, if it qualifies, is the only one in the state.

Voter registration work in Meridian began in the summer of 1963 (for COFO staff people, that is), and by autumn, when Aaron Henry ran in the Freedom Vote for Governor campaign, there was a permanent staff of two people in the city. In January, 1964, Mike and Rita Schwerner, a married couple from New York City, started a community center. In Meridian's mild political climate, the community center there has functioned more smoothly than either of the two community centers which COFO has organized in tougher areas. The center has recreation programs for children and teenagers, a sewing class and citizenship classes. It also has a library of slightly over 10,000 volumes, and ambitious plans for expansion if more staff were available. The COFO staff in Meridian uses Meridian as a base for working six other adjoining counties.

The Freedom School planned for Meridian will have a fairly large facility, in contrast to most places in the state. The Baptist Seminary is a large, 3-story building with classroom capacity for 100 students and sleeping accommodations for staff up to about 20. Besides this, there is a ballpark available for recreation. The school has running water, blackboards and a telephone. The center has a movie projector and screen which it probably would lend. The library lends books to anyone for two-week periods. The question of rent has not been decided for the school. Even if there is no rent, however, we can count on a budget of around $1,300, for food for students, utilities, telephone and supplies.

III. Holly Springs

Holly Springs is a small town, the seat of Marshall County. The Methodist Negro College, Rust College, is located in the town. It's a very attractive campus, and the students and faculty have been very active recently (since it's a church-operated school, one can expect somewhat more cooperation of Rust than the state schools). Holly Springs is currently acting as the clearinghouse for all our library books and Freedom School materials. There has been no permanently based COFO project with a full-time staff worker in Holly Springs; all the action has been the work of the local people. The roots in this community are somewhat recent, reflecting the fact that in the Northern, hilly part of the state, intensive civil rights work is just beginning.

In Holly Springs there are two houses available for a total of 75 students (and housing for 15 teachers). The rent will be $400, a major expense. The houses will go if we can't raise the rent money. Besides rent, the normal expenses and food will make the project cost about $1,000.

IV. Ruleville

Ruleville is a small Delta cotton town in Senator Eastland's home county (Sunflower County). The sheriff in Ruleville is the brother of the man believed to have killed little Emmett Till in 1955—a man with a great reputation in his own right for brutality toward Negroes. By any standard, Ruleville is a tough Delta town. Its main attraction for us is that it is the home of Mrs. Fannie Lou Hamer, the Mississippi Freedom Democratic Party's candidate for Congress in the Second Congressional District. Mrs. Hamer's own history is typical of much of the harassment of Negroes in the Miss. Delta: When Mrs. Hamer tried to register to vote in 1962, she was fired from her job. She and her family were run off the plantation where they had worked for years. She persisted, and became one of the great leaders of the Mississippi movement, but in the meantime she was arrested, beaten, her home shot into, her husband fired.

Voter registration activity began in Ruleville in 1962. The project is well-established in the community, even though the town is so small. Because it is an area of desperate poverty, even for the Delta, COFO has sponsored a food and clothing project in Ruleville for several months, with Mrs. Hamer and other local ladies in charge of the distribution.

For a Freedom School project in Ruleville, the local people have found a house which can serve 40 students, and have housing for 8 teachers. For the rent, and a few necessary supplies, we estimate that this Freedom School needs $200. Lunches for students would probably be another $500, but this is a service which is needed in the area.

Freedom School Curriculum Outline

Space constraints prevent us from including the entire curriculum package given to Freedom School teachers, but its table of contents provides a summary of what they taught.

TABLE OF CONTENTS

Because material trickled in until the very last moment, the actual contents of the curriculum do not correspond exactly with the "materials" listed at the beginning of each unit in the citizenship curriculum. The following Table of Contents describes what is actually in the curriculum. You can make corrections of the "materials" lists if you wish. Items marked (P) are included only in the coordinators' copies of the curriculum.

Two African American boys coloring at
an unidentified Freedom School.

Unit 6. Soul Things and Material Things.
   Case Studies: Statements of Discipline of non-violent movements
Unit 7. The Movement;
   Part I, Freedom rides and sit-ins;
   Part II, COFO's Political Program
   Case Studies: Readings on non-violence
                 Rifle Squads or the Beloved Community
                 Voter Registration Laws in Mississippi
                 Civil Rights Bill

Part III: Recreational and Artistic Curriculum

Curriculum Part II, Unit 1: Comparison of Students' Reality with Others

This and the following document are lesson plans used by Freedom School teachers. They were designed to counter the misinformation and deliberate omissions in the official curriculum that was provided to segregated public schools. Teachers used them to encourage young people to think critically about their lives.

Unit 1: Comparison of Students' Reality with Others
Purpose: To create an awareness that there are alternatives
Materials: Statistical data on education, housing, etc.; "The South as an Underdeveloped Country"

<u>Student, teacher each tell about themselves:</u>
Introduction: We are not here to teach you. We are here to help you learn and to learn together. We are going to talk about a lot of things: about Negro people and white people, about rich people and poor people, about the South and about the North, about you and what you think and feel and want, and about me.

And we're going to try to be honest with each other: and say what we believe.

We'll also ask some questions and try to find some answers.

<u>Schools—Conditions in Negro Schools:</u>
The first thing is to look around, right here, and see how we live in Mississippi.
1. What kind of a school is it? Sample questions: How many grades does it have? How many class rooms? What is it made of, wood or brick? Do you have textbooks, new or old? Do you have a library, movies, maps, charts, electric lights, a gymnasium? How many teachers, white or Negro? Laboratory space and equipment, desks, blackboards, etc.? Do you have history, geography, science, etc.?

2. What do you learn there? Sample questions: How many go to college? Are there trade or vocational schools? What kinds of jobs are you prepared for? What about current events—who do you learn is good, who do you

learn is bad, what do you learn about the South, about the North, about Negroes, about whites, about Kennedy, Johnson, Eastland, Castro, etc. What do you learn about voting and citizenship?

3. Where do you learn about these things? Radio, newspapers, TV, etc.

4. Is this bad or good? Can you think of anything that you would like to see changed? How could your school be made better?

Schools—Conditions in the white schools:
Where do the white children go to school? What are their schools like? Compare Negro schools to white schools.
Visual Aids (pictures of schools, laboratories, school libraries, school rooms, gymnasium):
Here are some pictures of other schools in other states besides Mississippi (or some in Mississippi, too).
Sample questions: Do you like these schools in the pictures? Are they like your schools? How are they different? Why would you like to have better schools?

What do you see in the pictures that is different from you and your school? Why do these differences exist?

Housing—Conditions for Negroes:
Visual Aids (pictures of both rural and suburban middle-class houses, modern bedrooms, bathrooms, kitchens, living rooms, etc.):
Sample questions: Where do you live? How many rooms are there? How many people live with you? How many beds do you have? Is your house made of wood or stone or bricks? What color is it? Is it painted, is there water, electricity, bathroom indoors, what kind of stove—wood, gas, kerosene, electric? Do you have heat in the winter? What kind? Furniture, what kind, how much?

Can you think of any kind of changes you'd like to see, any other kinds of houses you'd like to live in?

Questions: Where do white children live in this town? What kinds of houses—are their houses different? How? Better? How? Where does the Police Chief live? The banker? The store owner? etc.

Do you like these pictures? These houses? Are they like your house? How are they different? Would you like this kind of house? Why?

Note: discuss relationships between housing and schools (i.e., privacy, a place to study, quiet and books in the home, as related to studying) and housing and health (i.e., overcrowding, unheated housing as related to ease of sharing communicable diseases such as colds, TB, and infant mortality rates; bring in statistics on Negro-white life expectancy and mortality rates in Mississippi).

Question: Why do these differences exist?

Employment for Negroes:
Adult Employment (men and women):
Sample questions: Who works in your family? What kind of work does you father do? your mother? Do they work for white people or for Negroes? Who works most (mother or father)? Do they get paid a lot or a little? What do they do with the money they make? Pay rent, buy food, buy clothes, buy things for you? Do you think they could use more money? Why? Why don't they get more money?

Children's employment:
Sample questions: Do you ever work? What kind of work? After school? Or do you have to stay home from school to work sometimes? What happens when you stay home? Do you miss learning? If so, why do you have to do it?

Employment for whites:
In this town, what kind of jobs do white people do? Are there any Negro police or firemen, or store owners? Do Negroes work as clerks and cashiers in the store or the bank? Are there any Negroes that have tenant farmers, any Negro lawyers, doctors, Negroes who work at the textile mills?

What kind of jobs do people do? List responses and suggest areas through questions if necessary, i.e., who fixes cars, who makes our clothes, who sells them, who makes cars, airplanes, rockets, who builds houses, who invents machines (shoe last, air brake, telephone, etc.), who writes books, who fixes radios, plumbing, electricity, who drives tractors and mechanical cotton-pickers.

Break up into small groups and see which group can make up the largest list of jobs that people have, and what duties these jobs have.

Question: Can Negroes do these jobs? Are they smart enough? Do some Negroes do these jobs? If not, why not?

Material on Negroes in various fields, pictures, stories, etc. Poetry reading and discussion. Photos or drawings of Negroes and Negro history figures should be posted.
Questions:
Can anyone name:
1) a Negro inventor (George Washington Carver, Jan Matzeliger)
2) a Negro scientist (Dr. Charles Drews, Benjamin Banneker)
3) a Negro writer (Richard Wright, Phyllis Wheatley, Ralph Ellison, James Baldwin, Alexander Dumas, W. E. B. DuBois, Langston Hughes, M. L. King, Septima Clark, etc.)

Negro employment and white—salary comparison, etc. Review what has been discussed.

Medical facilities:
Is there any hospital here? Where do you (your parents) go if they are sick, have a baby, a car accident, etc.? Where is the nearest hospital? Is it for Negroes, whites, both? If there are different hospitals for Negroes and whites, compare facilities (how close are they? how many beds, doctors, operating rooms, etc.?).

Review Unit I (include schools, housing, employment, health):
Suggested approach: We've talked about jobs and health, in Mississippi and in other states, and we have seen that Negroes have to live one way and whites the other. Remember, we found out that your schools were (list) and we found that other schools were/had (list), etc.
Question: What can we do about this?

Re-introduce four [sic] basic questions:
1. Why are we (teachers and students) here in Freedom School?
2. What is the Freedom Movement?
3. What does the Freedom Movement have to offer you?

Curriculum Part II, Unit 6: Material Things and Soul Things

Unit VI: Material Things and Soul Things

Purpose:

    1. to develop insights about the inadequacies of pure materialism;

    2. to develop some elementary concepts of a new society.

Summary:

Starting with a questioning of whether the material things have given the "Power Structure" satisfaction, to raise the question of whether achievement will bring the Negro and/or poor white fulfillment. Then to explore whether the conditions of his oppression have given the Negro insights and values that contribute to the goal of a more humane society. And finally to develop this relevance into some insights into the characteristics of a new society.

Materials: Statement of discipline of non-violent movements.

Introduction: The last few days we have been exploring in another world—different than the one we live in everyday—the world of the "power structure" and we have made some interesting discoveries:

    1. That the "Power Structure" has a lot of power to make things just as they want them to be;

    2. That the "Power Structure" has a lot of money that buys big, luxurious houses, expensive cars, expensive clothing, trips, and all the other things we see on TV and in the movies. But we've also discovered that—

    3. The "Power Structure" is afraid of losing its power and its money; and

    4. The "Power Structure" is afraid of Negroes and poor whites finding out the "truth" and getting together.

Ideas to be developed:

    1. The possessions of men do not make them free. Negroes will not be freed by:

        a. taking what the whites have;

        b. a movement directed at materialistic ends only.

    2. The structure of society can be altered.

3. While a radically new social structure must be created in order to give man the room to grow in, it is not the changing of structure alone that produces a good life or a good world. It is also the ethical values of the individual.

4. There are many kinds of power we could use to build a new society.

Concept: That just taking the "Power Structure's" money and power would not make us happy either.

We have seen that having money and power does not make the "power structure" happy. We have seen that they have to pay a price for it.

Questions: Would just taking their money and power away and keeping it ourselves make us happy? Wouldn't we have to be afraid and distrust people too? Wouldn't we have to make up lies to convince ourselves that we were right? Wouldn't we have to make up lies to convince other people that we were right? Wouldn't we, too, have to keep other people down in order to keep ourselves up?

Suppose you had a million dollars. You could buy a boat, a big car, a house, clothes, food, and many good things. But could you buy a friend? Could you buy a spring morning? Could you buy health? And how could we be happy without friends, health, and spring?

This is a freedom movement: suppose this movement could get a good house and job for all Negroes. Suppose Negroes had everything the rest of the country has . . . everything that the middle class of America has . . . would it be enough? Why are there heart attacks and diseases and so much awful unhappiness in the middle class . . . which seems to be so free? Why the Bomb?

Concept: That the structure of society can be changed. Discussion of a possible new society.

1. Money—should a few people have a lot of money, should everybody have the same, should everybody have what they need? What could we do?

2. Jobs—should men be able to work at any job they can do and like, regardless of color, religion, nationality? Suppose a man were put out of a job by automation (like the mechanical picker?), what should happen to

him? Should he just sit around? Should he be trained for a new job? Who can train him? When he is old, should he have to depend on his family or be poor? Should he be helped when he is old? Why? Should all workers join together if they wish? Should they share in the profits? Why?

3. Housing—should every family be able to live where they wish to live, regardless of race or religion? Why? Should every family have a decent home? Should it have heat, a kitchen, a bathroom, hot water, nice furniture? Why does the kind of house a family has effect their family life? Suppose a family does not have enough money? Does a family have a basic right to good housing?

4. Health—should all people have a right to receive the same medical services regardless of religion or race or money? Should all people be able to receive whatever medical services they need regardless of how rich or poor they are? Why? Should people who need special care receive it? Why? From whom?

5. Education—should all children be able to go to the same schools regardless of their race or religion? Should all children have the right to get as much education as they are capable of? Suppose they can't afford to go to special high schools or to college? Should they still be able to go? How? Who should pay? What should be taught in schools? Do we teach myths and lies? Why? Should we? Should we train people for jobs in schools? To be good citizens? What else should we train people for? Culture, resourcefulness, world citizenship, respect for other people and cultures, peace. What about teaching adults? Should they have a chance too? Should it be free? Should they be able to go to special schools if necessary?

6. Legal—should the laws and the courts treat all people the same. Should the laws be more concerned with protecting the property a man has, or the man himself? Why?

7. Political system—should every man have the right to vote? What if he cannot read? Should he still have the right to vote and choose his representative? Should politicians have a right to give out favors? Can they be honest in this system? Suppose people can get good housing, jobs, health services, etc. in other ways . . . will they need political favors?

8. Mass media—should newspapers, TV, magazines tell the truth? Should that be their basic job? Should they have to support themselves by advertising? How else could they get enough money?

9. International relations—how should we want to treat other countries? Should we want them to be just like us? Should we help them if we have

more than they do? Should we work for peace? Can we have peace if we keep building bigger bombs and faster planes (what does fear do, threats? what about children fighting . . .)?

10. Cultural life—are artists, actors, musicians and writers important? Why? Should art and acting and music and writing be considered work? Should there be free concerts and free plays for everyone to see? Why?

Concept: It is not simply the changing of the structure that will make a good world, but the ethical values of the individual.

What if men were just naturally bad to each other—if they didn't care about each other? Would it matter about the structure of society? Are men good to each other because of laws? What is an ethical value?

Case Study: Statements of discipline of nonviolent movements
Discuss "do unto others as you would have them do unto you." Do you have a set of values? Are society's laws enough? Are your own personal "laws" important too? Are they ever more important than society's laws?

Is the movement the germ of a new society? How do people act toward each other in the movement? How do people act toward each other in Freedom School? How does this way of life differ from the way of life of the larger society? We must keep these good ethical and spiritual values in the new society which we build.

Concept: That there are many kinds of power we could use to build a better society. What is power? (Power is the ability to move things, or to make things happen or to change things.) What kinds of power are there?
Discuss. List on blackboard:

Mississippi	Physical Power	Freedom Movement
Police state	(Power to coerce or frighten)	Federal intervention
Intimidation		
	Political Power	
One party.	(Power to influence)	
No vote.		Vote.
Unjust laws.		Convention challenge.
		Negro candidates.

Economic Power

| Citizens Council | (Power to buy) | Boycott, |
| control, banks, jobs, etc. | | Strikes |

Do these "powers" balance each other? Do they succeed in bringing the two sides together or do they tend to pull apart? Are there any other kinds of power?

Truth Power

(Power to convince or persuade)

Does persuasion pull people apart? Is it a different kind of power? Can we use truth to reveal the lies and myths? What happens once they are revealed? Once someone is convinced or persuaded, can they join with us? Is the better world for them too?

Soul Power

(The power to love)

Can you love everyone like you love your family or your friends? What does compassion mean? Is that a kind of love? Is there something in other people that is like what is in you? Can soul power change things? How?

Dear Family and Friends

Cornelia Mack was a volunteer from Madison, Wisconsin, who taught in Palmer's Crossing, on the south side of Hattiesburg. Her excited letter home gives an excellent idea of the potential that Freedom Schools had to change students' lives.

Hattiesburg, Mississippi

August 26, 1964

Dear Family and Friends,

Many of you have asked for news of my experiences this summer; others, some of whom haven't heard of my summer plans, will, I think, be interested. To write each of you individually would tax my letter-writing capacity beyond its limit, so I write all of you at the same time.

Much of what you have read and heard of this summer's events has been grim. Tragic things have happened but I should like to focus on a few of the less-publicized and more hopeful aspects of the summer.

On August 7, 8, and 9 a Freedom School convention was held in Meridian, the city of about 50,000 from which Michael Schwerner, James Chaney, and Andrew Goodman set out in June to investigate a church burning.

I wish I could convey to you the excitement of the convention. Imagine a thousand or so high-school students, most of whom have been raised in poverty and have gone to poor schools, few of whose relatives have ever voted, who know policemen in general as people to avoid in time of trouble and white men as people who may have fathered their great grandparents and cheated their grandparents and parents. Next, give these young people a month in a freedom school, discussing, arguing, debating, learning about the Declaration of Independence and the Constitution and about Negroes who have struggled for better conditions for their people, and discussing, arguing, and debating. Finally, transport seventy-five of the brightest of them from many parts of the state to one room in Meridian and step aside. You, as one of some hundreds of freedom school teachers, gave them an initial nudge and they have taken off. Their enthusiasm is contagious, their determination thrilling and almost frightening. Some of the more cautious people of good will have said that much needs changing in Mississippi—as in many other places—but it should not be done by outsiders. Leadership should come from the Negro people themselves. From these young people it will come—if they will stay in Mississippi. Between 1950 and 1960 the number of Negroes in Mississippi between the ages of 20 and 44 decreased between a quarter and a third.

Along with several other teachers from Hattiesburg, I attended part of the convention. All teachers were observers; the meetings were run almost entirely by the students. Sometimes teachers disagreed with the stand taken by a student and occasionally a teacher would feel impelled to talk. On one such occasion the statewide director of the freedom schools asked that teachers not speak; he was thereupon squelched by a student, who said to the applause of other students, that the students welcomed comments by teachers as they didn't want to make fools of themselves. And so it went.

The schools in each community had sent resolutions to the convention. In committees the resolutions were discussed, argued, and combined (many similar ones naturally were brought in by several delegations). The resolutions adopted by the committees were presented to the convention and discussed again. Most were passed without change; some were altered and some discarded.

I watched at the meeting of the committee on voting. The delegates knew very well the rights denied to their relatives and friends. Their views can best be summarized by quoting the resolutions they passed, as adopted by the convention as a whole:

"VOTING

"1. The poll tax must be eliminated.

"2. Writing and interpreting of the Constitution is to be eliminated.

"3. We demand further that registration procedures be administered without discrimination, and that all intimidation of prospective voters be ended through federal supervision and investigation by the FBI and Justice Department.

"4. We want guards posted at ballot boxes during counting of votes.

"5. The minimum age for voting should be lowered to 18 years.

"6. We seek for legislation to require the county registrar or one of his deputies to keep the voter registration books open five days a week except during holidays, and open noon hours and early evening so that they would be accessible to day workers. Registrars should be required by law to treat all people seeking to register equally."

Five pages of resolutions were passed dealing with public accommodations, housing, education, health, foreign affairs, federal aid, job discrimination, the plantation system, civil liberties, law enforcement, city maintenance, voting, and direct action, I'll quote some which especially struck me:

> "We . . . demand . . . that the school year consist of nine consecutive months (in some areas the Negro school year is interrupted in late spring so that the children can chop cotton and in the late summer so that they can pick it; school is then in session in July and August, at which time the children learn virtually nothing), that taxpayers' money not be used to provide private schools . . . , that all schools be integrated and equal throughout the country . . . , academic freedom for teachers and students . . . , that teachers be able to join any political organization to fight for Civil Rights without fear of being fired . . . , that teacher brutality be eliminated. . . . All doctors should be paid by skill, not by race. . . . All patients should be addressed properly. . . . The United States should stop supporting dictatorships in other countries, and should support that government which the majority of the people want . . . that the federal minimum wage law be extended to include all workers, especially agricultural and domestic workers. . . . The federal government should force plantation owners to build and maintain fair tenant housing. . . . Section Two of the Fourteenth Amendment should be enforced, specifically in Mississippi and other Southern States, until voter registration practices are changed. . . . A national committee should be set up to check police procedures, to insure the safety of people in jail. . . . Law enforcement officials should provide protection against such hate groups as the KKK. . . . Police and public officials should not belong to any group that encourages or practices violence . . ."

Other things went on at the convention. There were speakers. James Forman said, "Young Negroes have to begin to decide to stay in Mississippi." Get the education you can get, he said, and then use it for other people. He left the young people with the question, "How do we translate the freedom school experience to those around us?" A. Philip Randolph, president of the Brotherhood of Sleeping Car Porters, is an impressive man. I wish I could put into words how it is that he is impressive; it's his whole bearing, and his speech. The main points of his talk were that freedom is never given; it must be won. Though a cause may be right, it will be won only if its supporters have power. The objective of the civil rights "revolution" is to effect a distribution of rights. A major problem, now that the civil rights act has been passed and is being implemented, is to gain full employment.

For me, the most exciting part of the convention was the discussion of the resolutions and the most moving part was the drama program. "In White America" [a play by Martin Duberman] tells of "what it has meant for two centuries to be a black man in white America." It was performed by the Free Southern Theater, which has played this summer in freedom schools and plans to tour the South performing for Negro and, where possible, integrated audiences. Another play, composed and performed by students of the Holly Springs freedom school, was about the life and death of Medgar Evers. There was no script; rather, the play was created each time it was performed, for the performers knew essentially what they wanted to say and made up their lines.

Perhaps you saw the article about the Mississippi Summer Project in the issue of *Newsweek* which had a picture of Robert Kennedy on the cover. In it the community center in Palmer's Crossing was described. I lived and worked in Palmer's Crossing and have been in the center many times. It has been wonderful to see it develop. Physically, it consists of a building with one large room complete with stage, two small rooms, and a tiny kitchen, and a large yard, in the center of this predominantly Negro community of perhaps 2,000, outside of Hattiesburg (about 40,000). Volunteers cleaned and painted the inside (white walls with black trimming—"black and white together") and built tables and shelves. There was a gala opening. Now each morning there is day care for small children, with games, art work, stories, and music, and each afternoon recreation for the older children, with the boys generally playing ball outside in the 90° to 100° heat! In the evening there are adult classes in sewing and health and a weekly dance for teenagers. Probably the summer's high point at the center was a visit by Pete Seeger, the folksinger, who charmed everyone in the packed house. On an individual basis, a volunteer is teaching literacy to adults. Her youngest pupil, 23, grew up away from any school and, since there is no compulsory school attendance law in Mississippi, never got around to going to school; her oldest is in his 80's. Moreover, she is teaching some local residents the art of teaching adults to read.

An important part of the summer's work has been the setting up of libraries. Next to the Hattiesburg COFO office are now shelved about 350 feet of books, sent from the North. Many are excellent; some should eventually be discarded. Most in demand, and in growing supply, are books by and about Negroes, especially history books. Now the main library is setting up others. In Palmer's Crossing an unused building belonging to a church is being transformed into a study center, which will be open several hours a day as a quiet place for high school pupils; classes may be held there, too. Some of the houses I have visited are so cramped, quite aside from their complete lack of books, that it must be virtually impossible to study in them. The libraries are being used eagerly, but by only a small portion of the Negro community. Perhaps in the more literate future more people, especially adults, will have a taste for reading.

What, you may be wondering, about the public library? Attached to the Hattiesburg community center for Negroes is the city library for Negroes. I visited it once. Uneven as the COFO library is in quality and made up as it is mostly of second-hand books, it is already better in most respects than the city library for Negroes. The city one has half as many books as COFO's and no catalog (nor has COFO's yet: circulate now, catalog later, is the idea). I was impressed by the paucity of children's books (COFO has lots and needs more). About ten days ago half a dozen freedom school teenagers went to the main (white) library downtown, which is many times as large, and asked for library cards in order to get books not available in their library. They were refused them and the library was hastily closed "for inventory." The (white) teacher who had accompanied them was arrested for vagrancy; she had in her purse some tens of dollars. A few days later, after a similar incident, it was closed again. It is still closed.

One important phase of the work conducted in Hattiesburg—as in other parts of the state—was voter registration. Since you have probably read more about that than the other phases, I'll not tell about voter registration, except to say that it is difficult for a Negro to register in Hattiesburg. My hostess (we lived with Negro families) has tried eight times to register to vote. Perhaps she passed the test she took this month (one doesn't learn the result for a month).

My own work was concerned primarily with the freedom schools. I taught in one of six schools conducted in churches in and near Hattiesburg, St. John Methodist Church in Palmer's Crossing. Since there were more teachers than rooms, we inevitably did team teaching. I had expected to teach math and English to high school students, but actually taught eight to twelve year olds. We concentrated on language arts (reading, writing, spelling), Negro history, and math. The most popular subject, I think, was history. We presented it in the form of biographies. The children loved acting out parts of the stories. The first time we did it, they all wanted to be dogs chasing a runaway slave (Harriet Tubman; she and Frederick Douglass were the favorite heroes). Sometimes we listened to music or drew. One eight-year-old is an extraordinarily gifted artist.

The teenagers and adults learned more about government, with less emphasis on English and math. The teenagers studied the Declaration of Independence and decided to write one for themselves. The beginning and end of theirs are, "In this course of human events, it has become necessary for the Negro people to break away from the customs which have made it very difficult for the Negro to get his God-given rights. We, as citizens of Mississippi, do hereby state all people should have the right to petition, to assemble, and to use public places. We also have the right to life, liberty, and to seek happiness. . . . We, therefore, the Negroes of Mississippi, assembled, appeal to the government of the State, that no man is free until all men are free. We do hereby declare independence from the unjust laws of Mississippi which conflict with the United States Constitution."

Members of all classes were encouraged to express themselves. The tales the adults told of treatment they had received at the hands of whites were almost incredible. Skeptics might say that some of them were fabricated to arouse our sympathy. If they had seen the depth of feeling with which the stories were told, and the response they evoked from the tellers' neighbors, I think the skeptics would have been convinced.

One of the purposes of the schools, as of all the things COFO did this summer, was to help give the Negroes in Mississippi a sense of dignity and a feeling of pride in being Negroes. The desire to learn Negro history must have come from a longing for a sense of identity and pride.

One day my class had a discussion on, "What is a free man?" The next day the children wrote on the same subject. Here are some excerpts from their papers, uncorrected: "a Free MaN have his rights Just as the white MaN have his rights . . . a Man Most have eQuaL rights to vote Pelpo Who Was Master Degree and Docter Degree Could Not Pass the test they therow Lind [the registrar] give to them. . . . Now they are trying to get a siMpLe test" (Clarence, age 9). "A free man is a man that has his rights. And a man that says he is a man. A free man feel like a real man" (Billy Ray, age 10). "A free man is a man that believe thats he's a man, and a free

Adult education class at the Priest Creek Baptist Church Freedom School, outside Hattiesburg. Freedom Schools often taught children during the day and their parents and grandparents in the evening. Adult subjects included basic literacy and voter education.

man who has his rights. Have the right to do the things that anybody do . . . he's a man that have the rights to drink out of a white water-fountain, and the rights to eat in the white folks restaurants Without the owners throwing you out, and we should have the rights to go to white folks movies, because our money is as good as anybody else money" (Jimmie, age 12).

Address after Sept. 1
3501 Sunset Drive
Madison 5, Wisconsin
Cornelia Mack

Freedom Schools in Mississippi, September 1964

> *This report by Liz Fusco, who succeeded Staughton Lynd as coordinator of Freedom Schools, was written as the summer came to an end. Like every good educator, she tries to assess the success of her program for students, teachers, and the community. She is better known today by her unmarried name, Elizabeth Aaronsohn.*

From the carbon copies of the spring's letters and reports, I see what real apprehensions, as well as hopes, the people who dreamed of Freedom Schools had. Out of Charlie Cobb's idea of a situation in which there would be questioning, release from rigid squelching of initiative and expression—from Charlie Cobb's bitterness about the way the Negro has had to be silent in order to survive in white America, and his vision of the kids' articulateness and reaching for change, meaningful change, in Mississippi—out of his seeing that the kids are ready to see "the link between a rotting shack and a rotting America"—came the original plan for Freedom Schools in Mississippi. That it could be an idea that people working desperately on voter registration and on keeping alive in the state could take seriously is perhaps evidence of the validity of Charlie Cobb's dream: Mississippi needed more, needs more, than that all Negroes 21 and over shall have the right to vote. The staff in Mississippi understood what Charlie was dreaming because they, too, were daring to dream that what could be done in Mississippi could be deeper, more fundamental, more far-reaching, more revolutionary than voter registration alone: more personal, and in a sense more transforming, than a political program.

The decision to have Freedom Schools in Mississippi, then, seems to have been a decision to enter into every phase of the lives of the people of Mississippi. It seems to have been a decision to set the people free for politics in the only way that people really can become free, and that is totally. It was an important decision for the staff to be making, and so it is not surprising that the curriculum for the proposed schools became everyone's concern. I understand that Lois Chaffee, Dona Moses, Mendy Samstein, and Casey Hayden as well as Noel Day, Jane Stembridge, and Jack Minnis worked on and argued about what should be taught, and what the realities of Mississippi are, and how these realities affect the kids, and how to get the kids to discover themselves as human beings. And then, I understand, Staughton Lynd came in to impose a kind of beautiful order on the torment that the curriculum was becoming—torment because it was not just curriculum: it was each person on the staff in Mississippi painfully analyzing what the realities of his world were, and asking himself, with what pain I can only sense, what right he had to let the kids of Mississippi know the truth, and what right he had had to keep it from them until now. And because of these sessions, the whole concept of what could be done in Mississippi must have changed.

In a way, the Freedom Schools began to operate in those planning sessions. A section of the curriculum called "Poor whites, poor Negroes and their fears," for example, considers the unity of experience between whites and Negroes, as well as the psychological and political barriers. And out of the discussions that produced this part of the curriculum came, perhaps, the idea of a "White Folks' Project," and the intense economic orientation of what was begun in Research, and Federal Programs, also new projects. And out of work with the people day after day in the Freedom Schools emerged medical concerns, and farm league ideas, and the community building of community centers. It was because the people trying to change Mississippi were asking themselves the real questions about what is wrong with Mississippi that the Summer Project in effect touched every aspect of the lives of the Negroes in Mississippi, and started to touch the lives of the whites.

It was the asking of questions, as I see it, that made the Mississippi Summer Project different from other voter registration projects and other civil rights activities everywhere else in the South. And so it is reasonable that the transformations that occurred—and transformations did occur—out of the Freedom School experience occurred because for the first time in their lives kids were asking questions.

The way the curriculum finally came out was that it was based on the asking of certain questions, questions which kept being asked through the summer, in connection with the kids' interest in their Freedom School teachers (mostly northern, mostly white, mostly still in college), in connection with Negro history, in connection with African culture, in connection even with the academic subjects, as well as in connection with the study of the realities of Mississippi 1964 in the light of Nazi Germany 1935. The so-called "Citizenship Curriculum" set up two sets of questions. The primary set was: 1. why are we (teachers and students) in Freedom schools? 2. what is the Freedom Movement? 3. what alternatives does the Freedom Movement offer us? What was called the secondary set of questions, but what seemed to me the more important, because more personal, set was: 1. what does the majority culture have that we want? 2. what does the majority culture have that we don't want? 3. what do we have that we want to keep?

The answering of these questions, and the continual raising of them in many contexts, may be said perhaps to be what the Freedom Schools were about. This was so because in order to answer anything out of what these questions suggest, it is necessary for the student to confront the question of who he is, and what his world is like, and how he fits into it or is alienated from it.

It was out of the experience of asking these questions that the transformations occurred. At the beginning of the summer, with rare amazing exceptions, the kids who were tentatively exploring us and the Freedom Schools were willing to express about themselves only one thing with honesty and passion, without the characteristic saying of the thing they think the white man wants to hear: that thing was that as soon as they could gather enough money for a ticket they were going off to Chicago, or to California! To leave the state was their ambition, and about it they were certain, even though they had not thought any further than that, even in terms of where the money was to come from, and certainly not in terms of what they would find there and what they would do there. Some sense of "go home to my Lord and be free"—some vague hope of a paradise beyond—seemed to inform their passion for the north, their programless passion.

But by the end of the summer almost all of these kids were planning to stay in Mississippi.

Within the flexible structure of the Freedom School it was natural that a confession of—an insistence on—the desire to race northward lead to a discussion of the condition of the Negro in the North, about which most of the teachers could tell specifically. And then came the news stories about Harlem, and Rochester, and Medford, Massachusetts, and the kids were interested, and worried. But it was not just because the truth about the North began to shatter their dream of it as paradise that the kids changed their minds. The yearning for the North was, of course, the expression of a need to escape the intolerability of the situation in Mississippi. But the nature of their need to escape was that they really did not know what it was about Mississippi that they hated—or, rather, they felt that what was intolerable for them had somehow to do with the white man, somehow to do with getting only $3.00 a day for 10 hours work chopping a white man's cotton, somehow to do with the police—but they had not yet articulated, if they knew, the connections among all these things. And they had not, as well, articulated the connections of those things with their experiences of repression at home and in school. And so the very amorphous nature of the enemy was threatening to them.

The experience in the Freedom School was that patterns began to be seen, and patterns were real and could be dealt with. So the kids began to see two things at once: that the North was no real escape, and that the South was not some vague white monster doomed irrationally to crush them. Simultaneously, they began to discover that they themselves could take action against the injustices—the specific injustices and the condition of injustice—which kept them unhappy and impotent.

Through the study of Negro History they began to have a sense of themselves as a people who could produce heroes. They saw in the story of Joseph Cinque of the *Amistad* a parallel to the kinds of revolts that the Movement, as they began to learn about it, represented. They saw that Joseph Cinque, in leading a mutiny on that slave ship instead of asserting his will to freedom by jumping off the ship into the shark-waiting waters, was saying that freedom is something that belongs to life, not to death, and that a man has responsibility for bringing all his people to freedom, not just for his own escaping. Connections between then and now kept being made—at first by the teachers, very soon by the students: who do you know that is like Joseph Cinque? How is Bob Moses like Moses in the Bible? How is he different? Why did Harriet Tubman go back into the South after she had gotten herself free into the North—and why so many times? And why doesn't Mrs. Hamer stay in the North once she gets there to speak, since she doesn't have a job on that man's plantation any more, and since her life is in so much danger? And what do you think about Fredrick Douglass's talking so straight to the President of the United States? And how does the picture of Jim Forman in the Emancipation Proclamation issue of *Ebony* suggest that same kind of straight talking? And who do you think the Movement is proving right—Booker T. Washington or W.E.B. DuBois? And what comment on your own upbringing is made by the fact that you all know about Booker T. Washington but most of you had never heard of W.E.B. DuBois? And why are the changes of gospel songs into Freedom Songs significant? What does "We Shall Overcome" really mean in terms of what we are doing, and what we can do?

Beginning to sense the real potency of organized Negroes in Mississippi, the kids in the Freedom Schools found an immediate area of concern in the Negro schools they attended or had dropped out of, the so-called "public" schools. They had grievances, but had, until drawn into the question-asking, only been able to whine, or to accept passively, or to lash out by dropping out of school or getting themselves expelled. Within the Freedom Schools, especially by comparing the Freedom Schools with the regular schools, they began to become articulate about what was wrong, and the way things should be instead: Why don't they do this at our school? Was the first question asked, and then there began to be answers, which led to further questions, such as why don't our teachers register to vote, if they presume to teach us about citizenship? And why can't our principal make his own decisions instead of having to follow the orders of the white super-intendent? And why do we have no student government, or why doesn't the administration take the existing student government seriously?

This was the main question, which came also out of why there are no art classes, no language classes, why there is no equipment in the science labs, why the library is inadequate and inaccessible, why the classes are overcrowd-ed. The main question was WHY ARE WE NOT TAKEN SERIOUSLY? which is of course the question that the adults were asking about the city and county and state, and the question the Freedom Democratic Party asked—and for which the Party demanded an answer—at the Convention.

The students were taken seriously in the Freedom Schools. They were encouraged to talk, and their talking was listened to. They were assigned to write, and their writing was read with attention to idea and style as well as grammar. They were encouraged to sing, to dance, to draw, to play, to laugh. They were encouraged to think. And all of this was painful as well as releasing because to be taken seriously requires that one take himself seriously, believe in himself, and that requires confrontation. And so Freedom School was painful for the kids who grew the most.

Tangibly, what was set in motion out of this experience of joy and pain was the thing the Mississippi staff had hoped could happen in Mississippi, but could not totally form. In the spring before the summer, SNCC in Mississippi had tried to organize a Mississippi Student Union, bringing together kids from all over the state. And there was good response, but not on the scale the MSU was soon to achieve out of the Freedom Schools. This summer the kids began to talk boycott of the schools, but to be able to discipline their thinking about boycott so that their action would not just be acting out their frustrations but careful, considered, programmed, revolutionary, meaningful action along the lines of the Montgomery bus boycott and African revolutionary action. The kids were able to come together in the middle of the summer, in Meridian, and draw up a series of resolutions which said with terrible clarity what they felt about their world: what a house should be, what a school should be, what a job should be, what a city should be—even what the federal government should be. And they were able to ask why it was that the people did not have a voice and to assert that their voices would be heard. The seriousness of their concern for a voice is reflected in the final statement of the list of grievances drawn up by the McComb Freedom School:

> We are 12 Pike County high school students. Until we are assured our parents will not suffer reprisals, until we are sure this list of grievances is met with serious consideration and good will, we will remain anonymous.

The McComb students are sending this list of grievances to the school officials, the city officials, the senators and the newspapers and the President of the United States. Out into the world: look at me—I am no longer an invisible man.

And back again into themselves. Whoever the Freedom Schools touched they activated into confrontation, with themselves and with the world and back again. On one level, it was the white teacher saying to the Negro girl that nappy hair vs. "good hair" is not a valid distinction: that it is a white man's distinction, and that the queens in Africa—in Songhai, Mali, Ghana, in Ethiopia—had nappy short hair! On another level, it was the northern Negro student-teacher saying to the kids yearning Northward that he himself had gone to an almost completely (or completely) segregated school, and that his home was in a ghetto. On another, it was a senior, suspended from the split-session summer school for participating in the movement and taking Freedom School academic courses (fully parallel) instead, saying of Robert Frost's "The Road Not Taken" that the man took the road that needed him more: "because it was grassy/and wanted wear. . . . and that has made all the difference." On another level, it was the white and Negro Freedom School teachers sitting with the adults in the evening classes talking about what kids want and what kids deserve, and hearing the adults express some of their concern for their kids in the forming of a parents' group to support the kids' action against the schools. On still another, it was the junior high school kids in the community coming over in the evening to sit with the adults who were learning their alphabets, one kid to one adult, and both, and the staffs, crying with awe for the beauty and strangeness and naturalness of it. And on all levels, it was the whites, the northerners, listening to the Mississippi Negroes, reading what they wrote, taking them seriously, and learning from them.

Visible results of the Freedom Summer include the kids' drawings on the walls of Freedom Schools and COFO offices all over the state, as well as kids' applications for scholarships (National Scholarship Service and Fund for Negro Students) and even more applications for the Tougaloo Work-Study program, which commits them to staying to work in Mississippi. In addition, there is the real probability that the Negro teachers in the regular schools—the teachers who have to sign an oath not to participate in civil rights activities or try to vote—have, this first week of school, begun to experience for the first time in their lives, the challenge from a student that is not adolescent testing or insolent acting out but serious demanding that in truth there is freedom and that he will have the truth!

Most significantly, the result of the summer's Freedom Schools is seen in the continuation of the Freedom Schools into the fall, winter, spring, summer plans of the Mississippi Project. Some project directors who had been in Mississippi since 1961 doing the slow sometimes depressing always dangerous serious tiring work of voter registration, first thought of the Freedom Schools as a frill, detrimental to the basic effort. At best, they were a front for the real activity. But Freedom Schools were not just, as the same project directors came to concede, a place where kids could be inducted into the Movement, a convenient source of canvassers. They were something else, and in realizing this the dubious project directors were themselves transformed by the Freedom Schools. They were, instead of anything superficial, and will go on to be, the experience—not the place—in which people, because we needed them, emerged as discussion leaders, as teachers, as organizers, as speakers, as friends, as people. I know that this is so because in leaving the Freedom School in Indianola, the county seat of Sunflower County where the Movement had been resisted for three years, and where, when we came in, the people did not know how to cross arm over arm to sing "We Shall Overcome," I learned for the first time in my life that with kids you love, to disconnect is to suffer. So the teachers were transformed, too.

The transformation of Mississippi is possible because the transformation of people has begun. And if it can happen in Mississippi, it can happen all over the South. The original hope of the Freedom School plan was that there would be about 1,000 students in the state coming to the informal discussion groups and other sessions. It turned out that by the end of the summer the number was closer to 3,000, and that the original age expectation of 16-17-18 year olds had to be revised to include pre-school children and all the way up to 70 year old people, all anxious to learn about how to be Free. The subjects ranged from the originally anticipated Negro History, Mississippi Now, and black-white relations to include typing, foreign languages, and other forms of tutoring. In fact, these aspects of the program were so successful that the continuation of the Freedom Schools into the regular academic year will involve a full-scale program of tutorials and independent study as well as exploration in greater intensity of the problems raised in the summer sessions, and longer range work with art, music, and drama.

To think of kids in Mississippi expressing emotion on paper with crayons and in abstract shapes rather than taking knives to each other; to think of their writing and performing plays about the Negro experience in America rather than just sitting in despairing lethargy within that experience; to think of their organizing and running all by themselves a Mississippi Student Union, whose program is not dances and fund-raising but direct action to alleviate serious grievances; to think, even, of their being willing to come to school <u>after school</u>, day after day, when their whole association with school had been at least uncomfortable and dull and at worst tragically crippling—to think of these things is to think that a total transformation of the young people in an underdeveloped country can take place, and to dare to dream that it can happen all over the South. There are programs now, as well as dreams, and materials, and results to learn from. And it may well be that the very staffs of the Freedom Schools in Louisiana and Georgia, etc. [for 1965], will be the kids who were just this past summer students in the Freedom Schools in Mississippi, and discovered themselves there.

Political posters for Mississippi Freedom Democratic Party
candidates Aaron Henry and Fannie Lou Hamer, fall 1964

THE MISSISSIPPI FREEDOM DEMOCRATIC PARTY

In 1964, Mississippi was effectively a one-party state. Republicans had never had significant support because they were historically the party of Abraham Lincoln and Northern invaders. The Democratic Party ruled all aspects of the state's political life. It was controlled by white supremacists who staunchly defended segregation. If black Mississippians were to get involved in electoral politics, they needed a new party in which to do it.

The Mississippi Freedom Democratic Party grew out of the Freedom Vote campaign for governor in autumn 1963, when more than 80,000 African Americans cast symbolic ballots in a mock election. The apparatus for that campaign led to the organization of the MFDP in April 1964 and the selection of candidates for the fall election.

Its long-term goal was to provide thousands of future voters with experience in electoral politics—canvassing for members, conducting meetings, writing platforms, formulating strategies, and running campaigns—so they would be ready to succeed when segregation was overturned. It had three short-term objectives for 1964: 1) to challenge the right of the all-white official Democrats to represent the state at the Democratic National Convention in Atlantic City in August; 2) to run a parallel election in November; and 3) to challenge the right of winners in the official election to occupy the state's seats in Congress.

The MFDP announced its program and candidates in the first document printed here, a long press release dated April 12. As expected, black Mississippians were excluded from the official Democratic caucuses and primaries that summer, so the MFDP sent their own delegates to the Democratic National Convention in August to challenge the official all-white delegation. The story of how the MFDP was betrayed by white liberals at the convention is told in the Reverend Charles Sherrod's brief account written shortly afterward.

The MFDP then regrouped in order to hold the "Freedom Election," October 31 through November 2, 1964. The next document in this chapter contains instructions from MFDP chairman Lawrence Guyot to party workers around the state detailing how the balloting was to be conducted. When the ballots were counted, more votes had been cast for MFDP candidates in the Freedom Election than for mainstream Democratic candidates in the official election almost everywhere that they ran head to head. Bob Moses commented, "They had the mock election. We had the real election."[1]

A month later, the MFDP filed a legal challenge to the winners of the official election. The final document in this chapter, a "fact sheet" on this congressional challenge, explains their reasons. Nine months later, the US House of Representatives rejected the MFDP challenge and allowed the segregationists to occupy Mississippi's seats.

---

1   Moses, Bob, "Speech at National Guardian Dinner, November 24, 1964," Alicia Kaplow Papers, 1964–1968 (Mss 507) Box 1, Folder 5.

Mississippi Freedom Candidates

> *This long April 12, 1964, press release was intended to inform Mississippi residents and the national media about the birth of the new party, its ideals, its candidates, and its plan of action during the 1964 election year.*

For the first time in this century, four Negroes are candidates for national office from Mississippi. One is a candidate for the Senate and three for the House of Representatives.

The four campaigns are being coordinated under the auspices of the Council of Federated Organizations (COFO), an umbrella civil rights organization in Mississippi comprising the Student Nonviolent Coordinating Committee (SNCC), CORE, the Southern Christian Leadership Conference (SCLC), and the NAACP.

All four candidates are entered in the regular Democratic primary in Mississippi to be held June 2. They are running on what is being called the FREEDOM DEMOCRATIC PARTY. If they are defeated in the Democratic party, they will be able to continue their campaigns as Independents in the General Election in November.

The candidacy of the Freedom Candidates is a direct challenge to the lily-white one-party political structure of the state. Only 28,000 or 6.6% of Mississippi's 422,000 Negroes of voting age have been registered to vote. 525,000 whites are registered voters.

All the Freedom Candidates will make Negro voting rights one of the basic issues of their campaigns. The campaigns themselves will serve as the focus for Voter Registration activities by COFO during the coming months.

For those not allowed to register on the official books, there will be a separate program: FREEDOM REGISTRATION. The Freedom Democratic Party has set up its own unofficial voter registration books for the purpose of registering as many as possible of Mississippi's 400,000 disenfranchised Negroes. These books, known as Freedom Registration Books, will be managed by Freedom Registrars appointed by COFO in every county. The Freedom Registrars will have the power to appoint deputy registrars to aid them in covering the county to provide every Negro with the opportunity to register to vote.

Freedom Registration has several purposes. First, it will serve as a mechanism through which Negroes can organize across the state. Secondly, it will be the focus of attempts to get Negroes registered on the official county books.

Thirdly, Freedom Registration will form the basis for FREEDOM ELECTIONS to be held at the same time as the official elections in June and November. In the Freedom Elections, the only qualifications will be that voters are 21 or over, residents of the state, and registered on the Freedom Registration Books before the election. Whites as well as Negroes will be allowed to vote. Democratic and Republican candidates will be listed together with Freedom Democratic Candidates.

Through Freedom Registration and the Freedom Elections, it will be made clear that thousands of Negroes who are denied the right to vote in the official elections would do so if they could. On this basis, the seating of successful Republican and Democratic candidates will be challenged in Congress and in the Federal Courts on the grounds that a significant portion of the voting-age population has been denied the right to vote because of color or race.

Thus, the Freedom Candidates will serve not only to bring the issues to the people of Mississippi, dramatize voter discrimination, and the atmosphere of harassment and resistance by the official state apparatus, but will serve as a basis for challenging the rights of the incumbents to assume their seats in Congress.

As a further part of its political program, the Freedom Democratic Party will send a FREEDOM DEMOCRATIC DELEGATION to the National Democratic Convention at Atlantic City in August.

The Freedom Candidates will serve as the titular heads of the Freedom Democratic Delegation. Other delegates will be chosen through a series of meetings on the precinct, county, district, and state levels just as in the regular Mississippi Democratic Party. Unlike the regular party machinery, however, which is all-white, exclusive, and often dominated by White Citizens Council members, Freedom Delegates will be chosen in open meetings in which all registered voters (whether official or Freedom registered), Negroes and whites alike, will be allowed to participate.

At the National Convention, the Freedom Democratic Delegation will attempt to have the Regular Democratic Delegation unseated and the Freedom Delegation seated in its place. It will do this on the grounds that the Regular Democratic Delegation was chosen by undemocratic means and that the Democratic Party of Mississippi has been disloyal to the National Democratic Party.

The Regular Mississippi Democratic Party split with the National Democratic Party in 1960. It did not support the National Democratic Ticket selected by the National Convention: John F. Kennedy and Lyndon B. Johnson. It also refused to support the platform adopted by the National Convention. The Regular Mississippi Democratic Party candidates in the gubernatorial race of 1963 told the voters that the Mississippi Democratic Party stands for white supremacy and against Negro voting power. The principles of the National Democratic Party make it clear that a State party which behaves in the manner of the Mississippi Democratic Party stands in violation of National Party policy. This is sufficient grounds, according to National Democratic Party rules, to withdraw recognition of the State party.

The Freedom Democratic Delegation will be pledged to support the National Democratic Ticket and the National Democratic Platform chosen at the National Democratic Convention—as well as being pledged to work for the full and equal rights of all Americans.

FREEDOM CANDIDATES: Below are brief biographical sketches and campaigning programs for the four Freedom Candidates.

MRS. FANNIE LOU HAMER—running in the 2nd Congressional district against Rep. Jamie Whitten, Chairman of the House Appropriations Subcommittee on Agriculture.

Mrs. Hamer, 47, comes from Sunflower County, the home of James Eastland, where Negroes are 69% of the population. She is the wife of Perry Hamer, a cotton gin worker in Ruleville. Until 1962, the Hamers had lived for 16 years on a plantation four miles from Ruleville. On August 31 of that year, the day Mrs. Hamer registered to vote, they were told they would have to leave the plantation immediately.

Mrs. Hamer began working with the Student Nonviolent Coordinating Committee in December 1962 and has been one of the most active workers in the state on Voter Registration. On June 9, 1963, while returning from a SNCC workshop, she was arrested in Winona, Miss., and brutally beaten with a blackjack while in jail. Mrs. Hamer opened her campaign in Ruleville on March 21. She hopes to use her campaign to articulate the grievances of Mississippi's Negroes, particularly in the cotton-rich Delta, the 2nd Congressional District, where Negroes are a clear majority (59%) of the population. Mrs. Hamer constantly tells her audiences that she is only saying "what you have been thinking all along."

But Mrs. Hamer plans to direct her campaign to whites as well as Negroes. It is her thesis that all Mississippians, white and Negro alike, are victims of the all-white, one-party power structure of the state. In her campaign, she explains how Jamie Whitten, from his position on the House Appropriations Sub-Committee on Agriculture, killed a bill to train 2400 tractor drivers. Six hundred of those to be trained were white.

Mrs. Hamer is presently ill in Ruleville (the nearest doctor is 10 miles away). Her condition is provoked and made more serious by after effects of the 1963 beating, from which she has never fully recovered.

JAMES MONROE HOUSTON—candidate from the 3rd Congressional District against Robert Bell Williams, second in command on the Interstate and Foreign Commerce Committee.

Mr. Houston, 74 years old, is a retired machinist from Vicksburg, member of the NAACP for over 20 years. He was arrested in 1934 for participation in a rural district meeting called to discuss the new Roosevelt programs. He was arrested again in Jackson in 1963 while attempting to march from a Methodist church to City Hall. In his opening campaign speech in Vicksburg on April 5, Mr. Houston told a crowd of 200–300 people that he would use his campaign to show what conditions for Negroes in Mississippi are really like. He claimed active support in all fourteen of the 3rd District's counties and said that he would represent all the people in the District if elected. For this reason, he said, his election would restore honor and dignity to the state of Mississippi.

REV. JOHN E. CAMERON—candidate for the seat of William Meyers Colmer, second in command of the House Rules Committee, from the 5th Congressional District.

Rev. Cameron, 31, opened his campaign in Hattiesburg on March 26, addressing an audience of approximately 200 from the back of an open truck. His campaign will stress jobs, education, and citizenship rights for Negroes. In Biloxi, on April 4, Rev. Cameron called on both state and federal governments to provide training for unskilled laborers so that they may qualify for full-time and rewarding employment. He stressed the importance of a candidate running in the 5th Congressional District who would represent the entire population of the district, rather than only one racial group.

Rev. Cameron is a former President of the National Baptist Student Union (1954–55), and holds a B.S. degree from Rust College and a Bachelor of Theology from American Baptist Theological Seminary. He is a member of the NAACP and a Friend of SNCC.

On April 4, Rev. Cameron was refused entrance to a public forum in Hattiesburg unless he agreed to sit in a section reserved for Negroes. A white minister with Rev. Cameron was threatened with arrest for attempting to discuss the matter with the Chairman of the forum. At present, Rev. Cameron is in jail, one of 66 people arrested, in Hattiesburg, April 9–10, under Mississippi's new anti-picketing law.

MRS. VICTORIA JACKSON GRAY—candidate for Senate against John Stennis. Mrs. Gray, 37, of Hattiesburg, is the mother of three children. She was one of the first Negroes to register in Forrest County, where Registrar Theron C. Lynn is under Federal indictment for refusing to register Negroes on an equal basis with whites.

In an opening campaign statement given to the press [in] April, Mrs. Gray stressed that "Unemployment, Automation, Inadequate Housing, Health Care, Education, and Rural Development are the real issues in Mississippi, not 'States Rights' or 'Federal Encroachment.'" Mrs. Gray's own emphasis during the campaign will be on the problems of education faced by Negroes in the state.

April 12, 1964

Notes on the Democratic National Convention Challenge

> *The Reverend Charles Sherrod was one of SNCC's earliest field secretaries in Alabama and was at the center of the 1962 Albany Movement and 1965 marches in Selma. His account of the proceedings at the Democratic National Convention in August 1964 explains how party regulars—afraid of losing Southern support—undermined the MFDP's challenge to the official racist Mississippi delegation.*

It was a cool day in August beside the ocean. Atlantic City, New Jersey, was waiting for the Democratic National Convention to begin. In that republican fortress history was about to be made. High on a billboard smiling out at the breakers was a picture of Barry Goldwater and an inscription, "In your heart you know he's right." Later someone had written underneath, "Yes, extreme right." Goldwater had had his "moment" two weeks before on the other ocean. This was to be LBJ's "moment," and we were to find out that this was also his convention.

The Mississippi Freedom Democratic Party had been working rather loosely all summer. Money was as scarce as prominent friends. A small band of dedicated persons forged out of the frustration and aspirations of an oppressed people a wedge; a moral wedge which brought the monstrous political machinery of the greatest power on earth to a screeching halt.

The Freedom Democratic Party was formed through precinct, county, district, and state conventions. An attempt to register with the state was frustrated. But the Party was opened to both black and white voters and non-voters, for the State of Mississippi had denied the right to vote to thousands. Ninety-three percent of the Negroes twenty-one years of age or older in Mississippi are denied the right to vote. To show to the Convention and to the country that people want to vote in Mississippi, we held a Freedom Registration campaign. In other words, a voter registration blank form from a northern state was used. Sixty-thousand persons signed up in less than three months. We presented our registration books to the Credentials Committee. Both the facts and the law were ably represented by our attorney, Joseph Rauh, Jr., who was also a member of the Credentials Committee.

No one could say that we were a renegade group. We had tried to work within the structure of the State Party. In fact, we were not only trying to be included in the State Party, but we also sought to insure that the State Party would remain loyal to the candidates of the National Democratic Party in November. We attended precinct meetings in several parts of Mississippi.

In eight precincts in six different counties, we went to polling stations before the time legally designated for the precinct meeting, 10:00 A.M., but were unable to find any evidence of a meeting. Some officials denied knowledge of any meeting; others claimed the meeting had already taken place. In these precincts we proceeded to hold our own meetings and elected our own delegates to the county conventions.

In six different counties where we found the white precinct meetings, we were excluded from the meetings. In Hattiesburg we were told that we could not participate without poll tax receipts, despite the recent Constitutional amendment outlawing such provisions.

In ten precincts in five different counties, we were allowed to attend the meetings but were restricted from exercising full rights: some were not allowed to vote; some were not allowed to nominate delegates from the floor; others were not allowed to choose who tallied the votes. No one could say that we had not tried. We had no alternative but to form a State party that would include everyone.

So sixty-eight delegates came from Mississippi—black, white, maids, ministers, carpenters, farmers, painters, mechanics, school teachers, the young, the old—they were ordinary people but each had an extraordinary story to tell. And they could tell the story! The Saturday before the convention began, they presented their case to the Credentials Committee, and, through television, to the nation and the world. No human being confronted with the truth of our testimony could remain indifferent to it. Many tears fell. Our position was valid and our case was just.

But the word had been given. The Freedom Party was to be seated without voting rights as honored guests of the Convention. The Party caucused and rejected the proposed "compromise." The slow and now frantic machinery of the administration was grinding against itself. President Johnson had given Senator Humphrey the specific task of dealing with us. They were desperately seeking ways to seat the regular Mississippi delegation without any show of disunity. The administration needed time!

Sunday evening, there was a somewhat secret meeting held at the Deauville Motel, for all Negro delegates. The M.F.D.P. was not invited but was there. In a small, crowded, dark room with a long table and a black board, some of the most prominent Negro politicians in the country gave the "word," one by one. Then, an old man seated in a soft chair struggled slowly to his feet. It was the black dean of politics, Congressman Charles Dawson of Chicago.

Unsteady in his voice, he said exactly what the other "leaders" had said: 1. We must nominate and elect Lyndon B. Johnson for President in November; 2. We must register thousands of Negroes to vote; and 3. We must follow leadership, adding "we must respect womanhood," and sat down. With that a little woman, dark and strong, Mrs. Annie Devine from Canton, Miss., standing near the front asked to be heard. The Congressman did not deny her. She began to speak. "We have been treated like beasts in Mississippi. They shot us down like animals." She began to rock back and forth and her voice quivered. "We risk our lives coming up here . . . politics must be corrupt if it don't care none about people down there . . . these politicians sit in positions and forget the people who put them there." She went on, crying between each sentence, but right after her witness the meeting was adjourned.

What nightmare were they having? Here we were in a life-death grip, wrestling with the best political strategists in the country. We needed only eleven votes for a minority report from the Credentials Committee. They had postponed their report three times; a sub-committee was working around the clock. If there had been a vote in the Credentials Committee Saturday we would have probably had four times as many votes as we needed, Sunday two times as many, and as late as Tuesday, we still had ten delegates committed to call for the minority report. We had ten state delegations on record as supporting us. We had at least six persons on the Credentials Committee itself who attended our caucus to help determine the best strategy. We had over half of the press at our disposal. We were the issue, the only issue, at that convention. But the bleak leadership at the convention went the way of the "black dean's" maxim: "Follow leadership"—the word had been given.

The Freedom Party had made its position clear, too. They had come to the Convention to be seated instead of the all-white party from Mississippi, but they were willing to compromise. A compromise was suggested by Congresswoman Edith Green (D.-Ore.), a member of the Credentials Committee. It was acceptable to the Freedom Party and could have become the minority report:

1. Everyone would be subjected to a loyalty oath, both the Freedom Party and the regular Party; 2. Each delegate who took the oath would be seated and the votes would be divided proportionately.

A nighttime rally outside the Atlantic City Convention Hall in support of the Mississippi Freedom Democratic Party at the 1964 Democratic National Convention, August 1964

It was minimal: the Freedom Party would accept no less.

The administration countered with another compromise. It had five points: 1. The all-white Party would take the oath and be seated; 2. The Freedom Democratic Party would be welcomed as honored guests of the Convention; 3. Dr. Aaron Henry and Rev. Edwin King, Chairman and National Committeeman of the Freedom Democratic Party respectively, would be given delegate status in a special category of "delegates-at-large"; 4. The Democratic National Committee would obligate states by 1968, to select and certify delegates through a process without regard to race, creed, color, or national origin; and 5. The Chairman of the National Democratic Committee would establish a special committee to aid the states in meeting standards set for the 1968 Convention and that a report would be made to the National Democratic Committee and be available for the next convention and its members.

The "word" had come down for the last time. We had begun to lose support in the Credentials Committee. This came mainly as a result of a squeeze play by the administration.

It was Tuesday morning when the Freedom Party delegation was hustled to its meeting place, the Union Temple Baptist Church. You could cut through the tension, it was so apparent. People were touchy and on edge. It had been a long fight; being up night and day, running after delegations, following leads, speaking, answering politely, always aggressive, always moving. Now, one of the most important decisions of the convention had to be made.

At about one o'clock, it was reported that a group from the MFDP had gone to talk with representatives of the administration and a report was given: it was the five point compromise. This was also the majority report from the Credentials Committee. There were now seven hours left for sixty-eight people to examine the compromise, think about it, accept or reject it, propose the appropriate action, and do what was necessary to implement it. The hot day dragged on; there were speeches and speeches and talk and talk—Dr. Martin Luther King, Bayard Rustin, Senator Wayne Morse, Congresswoman Edith Green, Jack Pratt, James Farmer, James Forman, Ella Baker, and Bob Moses. Some wanted to accept the compromise, and others did not. A few remained neutral and all voiced total support, whatever the ultimate decision. But time had made the decision. The day was fast spent when discussion was opened to the delegation.

The administration had succeeded in baiting us into extended discussion and this was the end. We had no time to sift through over five thousand delegates and alternates, through ninety-eight Credentials Committee members who could have been anywhere in the ocean for all we knew.

The proposal was rejected by the Freedom Party Delegation; we had come through another crisis with our minds depressed but our hearts and hands unstained. Again we had not bowed to "massa." We were asserting a moral declaration to this country that the political mind must be concerned with much more than the expedient; that there are real issues in this country's politics and "race" is one.

One can logically move from this point to others. First of all, the problem of "race" in this country cannot be solved without political adjustment. We must consider the masters of political power at this point and acknowledge that the blacks are not trusted with this kind of power for this is real power. This is how our meat making and money making and dress making and love making is regulated. A readjustment must be made. One hundred counties where blacks outnumber whites in the South need an example for the future. The real question is whether America is willing to pay its dues. We are not only demanding meat and bread and a job but we are also demanding power, a share in power! Will we share power in this country together in reconciliation or, out of frustration, take a share of power and show it, or the need for it, in rioting and blood?

The manipulation of power in our homeland is in white hands. The white majority controls the decision-making process here. At President Johnson's "Coronation" in Atlantic City there were no blacks with power to challenge the position of the administration. Moreover, there was opposition by blacks to any attempt to wield power against the administrative position. There was no black group supporting us; they had no power; they could show no power. But they had positions of power. One would support that it is part of the system to give positions meaningless labels and withhold the real power; this is the story of the bond between our country and its black children.

In the South and North, the black man is losing confidence in the intentions of the Federal Government. The case of Byron de la Beckwith is an example of what frustrates our people in this connection. The Klansmen freed in Georgia is another. Both can be explained, but the emotions which they arouse in the Negro in this country cannot be explained away. The seating of the Mississippi Freedom Delegation could have gone a long way toward restoring the faith in the intentions of our government for many who believe that the Federal Government is a white man. Many Negroes believe that the government has no intention of sharing the power with blacks. We can see through the "token." We have had a name for a white man's Negro ever since any white man named one. We want much more than "token" position or even representation. We want power for our people. We want it out of the country's respect for the ideals of America and love for its own people. We need to be trusted, each for his own worth; this is why we are not chanting everlasting praises for the civil rights bill. We remember all the bills before. In fact, we remember the Reconstruction period. This time, we will be our own watch dogs on progress. We will not trade one slavery for another.

Secondly, we refuse to accept the total responsibility for the conditions of race relations in this country. At the convention we were repeatedly told to be "responsible"; that Goldwater would benefit from our actions. We were told that riots in Harlem and Rochester and Jersey City and Philadelphia must stop. "Responsible" leaders have gotten up and called moratoriums in response to directives to be "responsible." The country is being hurt by the riots, we are told admonishingly.

Who can make jobs for people in our society? Who runs our society? Who plans the cities? Who regulates the tariff? Who makes the laws? Who interprets the law? Who holds the power? Let them be responsible! They are at fault who have not alleviated the causes which make men express their feelings of utter despair and hopelessness. Our society is famous for its white-washing, buck-passing tactics. That is one reason the Mississippi Freedom Democratic Party could not accept the administration's compromise. It was made to look like something and it was nothing. It was made to pacify the blacks in this country. It did not work. We refused to accept a "victory." We could have accepted the compromise, called it a victory and went back to Mississippi, carried on the shoulders of millions of Negroes across the country as their champions. But we love the ideals of our country; they mean more than a "moment" of victory. We are what we are—hungry, beaten, unvictorious, jobless, homeless, but thankful to have the strength to fight. This is honesty and we refuse to compromise here. It would have been a lie to accept that particular compromise. It would have said to blacks across the nation and the world that we share the power and that is a lie! The "liberals" would have felt great relief for a job well done. The Democrats would have laughed again at the segregationist Republicans and smiled that their own "Negroes" were satisfied. That is a lie! We are a country of racists with a racist heritage, a racist economy, a racist language, a racist religion, a racist philosophy of living, and we need a naked confrontation with ourselves. All the lies of television and radio and the press cannot save us from what we really are . . . black or white.

It is only now that a voice is being heard in our land. It is the voice of the poor; it is the tongue of the underprivileged; it is from the lips of the desperate. This is a voice of utter frankness: the white man knows that he has deceived himself for his own purposes yet he continues to organize his own humiliation and ours.

We have no political panaceas. We will not claim that responsibility either. But we do search for a way of truth.

Instructions for the Freedom Vote and Regular Election

To: All County Chairmen, FDP Executive Committee Members, and Project Director
From: Freedom Democratic Party
Re: Instructions for the Freedom Vote and Regular Election

The Freedom Vote will be held October 31 and November 1, 2. People will be allowed to vote at any time during those [three] days, up to 3:00 pm on the 2nd. They do not have to vote in their own precincts or immediate neighborhoods, they can vote at any Freedom Vote Polling Place. However, voting by precincts might well be a valuable parallel to precinct organization.

Anyone 21 years or older who is a resident of Mississippi can vote. You do not have to be Freedom Registered to vote. White people should certainly be encouraged to vote if they so desire. Keep a record of how many white people if any vote. Even a few votes from the white community will be valuable for future legal and political challenges.

Polling places should be established anywhere that is convenient. Homes, churches, restaurants, barber shops, stores are a few suggestions. If police and the weather permit, it would be good to have polling places out of doors as much as possible. Cars should be used as mobile units to work rural areas, if those are not convenient to other polling places.

Each polling place or mobile unit should have one person <u>at all times</u> who acts as Registrar to distribute and collect the ballots. Wherever possible, there should be another person who acts as a Poll Watcher, who does not administer ballots but watches for any irregularities regarding the vote.

Before a person votes they should be requested to sign their name and address in a notebook kept specifically for that purpose. They should also indicate whether they are Freedom Registered or not and whether they have attempted to register at the courthouse or not. The actual ballot should not be signed in any way. The purpose of this procedure is to have a record of people who have voted, both to check for multiple voting and to prove that people all over Mississippi actually cast the Freedom Votes.

If people are afraid to sign their names, they should be allowed to vote anyway but the Registrar or Poll Watcher should fill out an affidavit that such and such a number of people voted without signing because of fear of intimidation. The Registrars and Poll Watchers should also indicate in the notebook the times during which they were on duty.

If possible, ballot boxes should be made out of substantial material and should be sealed until the votes are counted. No campaigning should be allowed within fifty feet of the polling booths. Those voting are not to be encouraged to vote for the Freedom candidates while they are at the poll.

Ballots should not be counted before the polls close on the 2nd. However, totals of those voting should be made every day relying on the notebooks. All voting should end at 3:00 pm on the 2nd. Counting should begin immediately. We would like to announce totals on the evening of the 2nd, this being the eve of the Regular Election.

A Committee to count votes should be chosen in each area. If possible this should be local FDP people, aided by the COFO staff. They should sign a statement certifying the totals of the vote. Get these notarized if possible.

Polling places should be made as attractive as possible. Bunting and signs advertising the Freedom Vote should help attract attention. Where sound equipment is available, it might be used to call attention to the location of polling places.

Press should be contacted before the vote begins, and kept abreast of numbers voting, incidents, etc. Any major developments or things of special interest should be reported immediately to Jackson, so that we can direct press attention, send telegrams, etc.

Once the votes are counted, Jackson should be notified immediately of the totals. The ballots should then be forwarded to Jackson at the earliest possible date, together with the notebooks, any affidavits surrounding the Freedom Vote, and the statements of certification of the Counting Committees.

We understand that in many areas and many cases the fairly strict guidelines set down here cannot or will not be followed. However, we are also interested in using the Freedom Vote for challenges in the Courts and in the Congress. For this purpose, the strictest adherence to form will be advantageous. Our case was weakened with many delegates at Atlantic City because we did not seem "legal" enough either. The higher the percentage of polling places for which we have accurate records of Registrars and Poll Watchers, and the larger the number of Committees we can refer to in the counting of the vote, the better off we will all be in January.

We are also interested in obtaining votes from as many counties and communities as possible. If we could claim some votes from almost every county in the state, we would have made a considerable advance over our position in Atlantic City. Though Freedom Registration will not be required for the Freedom Vote, those who have not registered should be encouraged to do so. It would be good to have one person at each poll to work on Freedom Registration. During the Freedom Vote drive, registered voters should be encouraged to vote in the actual election on November 3. However, as it is unlikely that Dr. Henry, Mrs. Hamer, Mrs. Devine, and Mrs. Gray will be admitted to the ballot on November 3, registered voters should be encouraged to vote in the Freedom Vote as well. On the basis of the Freedom Vote and the exclusive character of the November 3 election, the FDP will file a suit asking the courts to nullify the Senatorial and Congressional elections in Mississippi. If this fails, an attempt will be made to have the Democratic caucus strip the Democratic candidates of their Congressional seniority.

Freedom Ballots will be distributed as early as possible. They will resemble the official ballots. However, no sample ballots will be available. A few ballots could be used for demonstration at mass meetings, etc. But projects will be expected to save the ballots until the Freedom Vote begins.

Please send Jackson a list of polling places by Oct. 20.

Lawrence Guyot

Congressional Challenge Fact Sheet

> *The MFDP offered abundant evidence that the official Democrats had been chosen and elected illegally in November 1964, since 42 percent of the electorate had not been allowed to vote.*
> *Their challenge (summarized below) went to the US House of Representatives, which decides such matters internally. After nine months of backroom deal brokering, the House voted in September 1965 to allow the segregationists to occupy Mississippi's seats.*

MISSISSIPPI FREEDOM DEMOCRATIC PARTY
1353 U Street, N.W.
Washington, D.C.

CONGRESSIONAL CHALLENGE - FACT SHEET

The Mississippi Freedom Democratic Party's decision to challenge the seating of five representatives-elect to the Congress came in the wake of the refusal by Herbert Ladner, Mississippi Secretary of State, to have the names of four FDP candidates placed on the state ballot for the November 3rd elections. Petitions bearing the 1,000 signatures from registered voters required by Mississippi law were ignored by the Secretary of State.

The MFDP will bring evidence to show that the political processes of the State violate the 14th amendment in that Negro citizens comprising some 42% of the voting age population are systematically disenfranchised and deprived of their political rights and that the MFDP has been subject to official intimidation and suppression from private and public sources within the state. We shall also base our challenge on Mississippi's violation of a federal law passed in 1870 which stipulated that the State of Mississippi be admitted to representation in Congress on the condition that the then existing constitutional qualifications to vote would "never be amended or changed so as to deprive any citizen of the right to vote."

In accordance with the process set forth in Title 2, U.S.C. 210 et. Seq., a notice of challenge has been served on the members-elect whose seats were obtained by violation of statutes and with the sub-committee on elections and privileges of the House Administration Committee. Lawrence Guyot, MFDP Chairman, calls the challenge, "A challenge to the entire political system of the state, not just to the congressmen-elect. The political structure of Mississippi is based, in the words of the Fifth Circuit Court of Appeals, 'on a system of steel hard segregation' which deprives over 400,000 voting age Negroes of their basic right to a ballot. We are challenging the right of this system to seat members in the U.S. Congress." Of Mississippi's 456,620 Negro citizens of voting age, only 28,000 are currently registered. Voter registration attempts by Negroes have been met with violent opposition and economic intimidation.

In support of the Challenge, there will be an effort by members of Congress to introduce a Fairness Resolution on the opening day of Congress. Prior to the swearing in of all congressmen-elect, a proposal will be made that in fairness no congressman from Mississippi will be seated until such time as the challenge is decided.

GENERAL BACKGROUND - THE FREEDOM ELECTIONS

Following the refusal of State officials to place the MFDP candidates on the ballot, the Freedom Democrats decided to run a parallel election in which all citizens old enough and desirous of voting would have an opportunity to vote. The ballot included the Presidential candidates of both major parties as well as the FDP candidates and their opponents. Ballots were cast from polling places in 53 of the State's 82 counties, while "underground ballots" were mailed in from those counties too dangerous for FDP workers to enter openly. In each race the number of freedom votes cast were sufficient to have significantly influenced the election. President Johnson received 63,839 votes in the Freedom Election as opposed to 52,538 votes he received in the "official elections." Aaron Henry received 61,044 votes as against 139 for Senate incumbent John Stennis.

2nd District: Mrs. Fannie Lou Hamer 33,009—Rep. Jamie Whitten 59
4th District: Mrs. Annie Devine 6,001—Rep. Winstead 4
5th District: Mrs. Victoria Gray 10,138

The figures for the candidates "winning" seats in the second and fifth districts and the senate race are not published since the candidates were "unopposed" on the ballot.

The Society Hill Baptist Church outside McComb, Mississippi, after it was bombed on September 20, 1964. A Freedom School had been held there over the summer. The Pike County sheriff told Rev. Taylor, pastor of the church, "You niggers is just bombing one another."

7

AFTER FREEDOM SUMMER

The Mississippi Summer Project officially lasted about nine weeks, from June 15 to August 21. Most Northern volunteers returned home when the MFDP delegates headed to Atlantic City.

The national media followed the Northern volunteers out of Mississippi, opening the door for reprisals against black residents. During September and October, black Mississippians who'd supported COFO suffered a new wave of harassment, assaults, and firebombings. The document that opens this chapter contains accounts of violence around the southwestern city of McComb that began as soon as the Northern press departed.

By fall, the organizers of Freedom Summer were exhausted, disappointed, and angry. Despite all they'd done, Mississippi's white-supremacist regime was as deeply entrenched as ever. Top-ranking officials in Washington and white liberals in the Democratic Party had both betrayed them. Many COFO staff turned their backs on nonviolence and electoral politics and put their energies into the emerging Black Power movement instead.

Local leaders in Mississippi tried to keep Freedom Summer initiatives alive despite renewed violence, and many Northern volunteers signed up to stay into the following year. The next piece in this chapter, COFO's short outline for winter 1964–spring 1965, provides details about their plans.

SNCC called a retreat at Waveland, Mississippi, from November 10 to 21, 1964, to consider its future. Executive secretary James Forman wrote a twenty-page document called "What Is SNCC?" to spark discussion. Half history and half speculation, it includes a section called "These Are the Questions" (given here) which reflects on what Freedom Summer's organizers should do next.

Nine months later, on August 6, 1965, after even more murders and televised violence in Alabama, President Johnson signed the Voting Rights Act. It outlawed literacy tests and other traditional ways of excluding black voters and authorized federal registrars to work in county courthouses wherever discrimination could be proved. Within a few weeks, more than forty thousand new black voters had registered in Mississippi. By the end of 1966, the majority of eligible African Americans in the South were reg- . istered. In the next elections, the century-old system of government-spon- sored racism crumbled.

Affidavits of Violence in August-September 1964

COPY OF AFFIDAVIT
STATE OF MISSISSIPPI
COUNTY OF PIKE
Mrs. Alyene Quin, Burgland

I am a Negro adult resident of McComb, Mississippi. I operate a cafe in McComb, Mississippi, and serve all customers there regardless of race. That during the summer, 1964, I served civil rights workers both Negro and white who were there, and many who are now in McComb working on voter registration of Negroes there. They have harassed me from time to time by getting phone calls from unknown callers; also molested by white persons in McComb.

On Sunday night, September 20, 1964, about 11:00 p.m., while my two children were asleep in the bedroom and a pregnant baby sitter was there, my home was bombed. The bomb tore up my whole house and all the furniture. My two children, luckily, were only slightly injured.

COPY OF AFFIDAVIT
STATE OF MISSISSIPPI
COUNTY OF PIKE
Rev. Ned Taylor, Baertown

I am a United States citizen, age sixty and am a minister at the Summit Baptist Church, Summit Mississippi, Society Hill Baptist Church, McComb, Mississippi, Mount Olive Baptist Church, McComb Mississippi, and New Home Baptist Church, Pike County, Mississippi.

During the past three years, the National Association for the Advancement of Colored People has been conducting voter registration classes in the Society Hill Baptist Church. Members of the Council of Federated Organizations, both white and Negro, have attended the Society Hill Baptist Church during the summer of 1964.

Sometime in the middle of July, 1964, I received an anonymous phone call. The speaker said, "Don't let no white folks come into your church." On September 20, 1964, the Society Hill Baptist Church was destroyed by a bomb.

On September 23, 1964, there was an explosion in the area of my home around 10:00 p.m. Shortly thereafter, Sheriff Warren of Pike County came to my home, because he said he thought my home had been bombed. Sherriff

Warren left but returned in about a half hour. In the course of the second conversation Sheriff Warren said, "You damn niggers won't tell the truth, and your a preacher too."

I was taken to the house of Mathew Jackson, whose home had been bombed, in my pajamas. Sheriff Warren told a uniformed officer, whose name I do not know, to stay in the car and watch me. The latter officer ordered me to put up my hands and placed handcuffs on me. I was then taken to the McComb jail where the handcuffs were removed and I was permitted to dress, after I agreed to take a lie detector test. Sheriff Warren left but returned in the course of the second conversation.

I was taken to Jackson and locked in a cell for the night. The following day around 8:30 a.m., I was taken to have the test, but the operator of the lie-detecting machine said his wife was sick so he left. The test was finally given around 4:30 p.m. I was then taken home. At no time was I ever put under arrest and I have heard nothing further from Sheriff Warren.

COPY OF AFFIDAVIT
STATE OF MISSISSIPPI
COUNTY OF PIKE
CITY OF McCOMB
Mrs. Willie Dillon, Whitestown

At about 12:55 a.m., Friday morning, August 28, 1964, there was a big explosion outside. It woke up everyone in the house who was asleep: Linda, age 14, Willie Jr., age 12, and myself. My husband, Willie, had been working on the car that belongs to C.O.F.O. and was in the bathroom shaving and getting ready for bed when the explosion occurred.

However, our neighbors heard a car pull away fast, though we heard nothing. We did not call the police ourselves. They were called from Burgland by someone. They arrived at about 1:45 a.m. They were Highway Patrolman Bobby Felder, who had seen me attempt to register and who asked most of the questions, F.B.I. agent Ford, Sheriff Warren, Chief Guy, and Deputy Sheriff Beardon, who had also seen me try to register down at the Magnolia Courthouse.

For a little while, they seemed interested in the bombing. They looked at the scorched hole in the lawn, and Patrolman Felder took away the unexploded sticks. I think there were about nine sticks that did not go off. I believe only the cap went off. If all of them had gone off, there would have been a tremendous damage to the house. Our children could have been badly hurt or killed. But they weren't interested in the bombing for long, about twenty minutes, I'd say. They all dropped it as soon as they found out the car belonged to C.O.F.O.

Either Chief Guy or Sheriff Warren asked what had my husband been doing before the bombing. He said he had been working on the green Buick near the house. Felder asked, "Who's car is that?" My husband said it belonged to C.O.F.O. Then Felder and Agent Ford and Warren all started in on him real fast. They wanted to know who owned the car. My husband said he didn't know exactly who it was that owned it. All of them said he was lying, trying to protect us. My husband repeated that he didn't honestly know. Warren and Agent Ford asked us both if we would take a lie detector test. We said we would not. "Why not?" they asked. We said, because we have not done anything. I think it was the F.B.I. Agent, Ford, who said, "If you haven't done anything, why are you afraid to take it?" All the time they were referring back to the car and how there wasn't any dew on it, how the tires were warm, and all. I think that my husband tried it out after working on it.

They were all looking inside the car, everywhere. They didn't ask our permission to search the car and they didn't have a search warrant. They took a letter out of it from the owner and took it off. There was some C.O.F.O. literature on a chair by the porch which one of them read.

Sheriff Warren said to us, "If you don't cooperate with us more than C.O.F.O., more than that is going to happen to you." He meant more than the bombing.

Either Warren or Felder said, "The C.O.F.O.'s might have thrown it." Then Sheriff Warren, Chief Guy, Felder, and Agent Ford got together and talked among themselves. They saw we weren't going to take the lie detector test. So Warren came up and said, "You are under arrest for opening a garage without a license and tampering with the electricity and then you'll have to take the test."

Then they took my husband off and left me alone with the children. We had been seeing cars stopping out front with white people in them practically every night, so my husband had fixed up a light on the porch and attached it onto the electricity line going to the house. It gave us a little protection to have our lawn lighted up. He hadn't rigged it up in an illegal way. I know because that very same night, they were there. They called an electricity man to come out and check the light, and he said it wasn't doing any harm. Frank Watson heard him say it.

When it comes to the car, about a month ago, a policeman asked my husband to repair his private car, a Rambler station wagon. My husband did the work. He was never paid. The policeman didn't ask about any license to operate a garage then.

The next day, still Friday, August 28, I had a lot of trouble seeing my husband. They said the trial was at 3:00 p.m. down at the Magnolia Courthouse. But then they moved it up to 2:30 p.m. and had it here in McComb. We were driving back and forth, and it was all over when we got there; I never could get to see him. He tried everything to get to my husband, but they kept him out. By him, I mean the C.O.F.O. lawyer from Jackson, Frank Jones.

When I saw him, finally, in the Pike County jail, it was all over. He had been tried without a lawyer and had pleaded guilty. They sentenced him to nine months in jail, six for the garage and three for the electricity, and they had fined him $600.00, $500 for the garage and $100.00 for the electricity. I asked him why he pleaded guilty, and he said he couldn't think of anything else to do.

On my way in to see my husband, I saw Lawyer Reeves. I think his first name is Bob. I asked him if my husband could get a suspended sentence. He said to ask him if he's ready to talk. He wanted to get him to say that C.O.F.O. did the bombing.

Sometime after 5:00 p.m. I went by McComb Scrap Iron Company to tell Mr. Virgil Hickman what happened. Mr. Hickman is my husband's boss. He said yes, that he had heard about it, that the police had come by. He said he was going to have to replace my husband and there was a man coming tomorrow. We talked about it and he said it was because my husband had been taking part in C.O.F.O. Then he said, "Now you get a lawyer and try to do something."

On Sunday, August 28, I spoke with the F.B.I. agent, the same one who was here the night of the bombing. He talked the same way, like we did it.

Then I called the F.B.I. office in Jackson from the C.O.F.O. office and told them everything. They said they would get someone on it. Then I called Mr. Doar in the Justice Department in Washington, D.C., but he wasn't in, so I spoke with Mr. MacIntyre and told him everything. He seemed interested and said he would look into it.

My children could have been killed by that bomb. Now they have my husband in jail for nine months and fixed it so he won't have a job.

COFO Program, Winter 1964-Spring 1965

The Council of Federated Organizations (COFO) is extending its Mississippi Summer Project into a year round project. Both volunteers and paid staff will be used to implement the programs. The following programs are planned as part of the project:

1. Freedom Democratic Party and voter registration. Suits filed by the Justice Department have opened up several counties in the state to the possibility of registering large numbers of Negroes. Emphasis will be placed on these areas, but voter registration will continue to form the basis for much of the community organization throughout the state. The Freedom Democratic Party experience of the summer has provided a basis for extensive voter education. This work will be carried on by local voter groups in different parts of the state. The Freedom Democratic Party operations may be worked out of offices distinct from the COFO offices, but there will be close connections in both staff and planning between the offices.

2. Freedom Schools. The Freedom Schools will be continued in all areas where possible, but their scope will be somewhat limited as the majority of students will be in regular school full time. Freedom schools will concentrate on late afternoon and evening courses. Content will be Negro history, political education, modern languages—all not available in the regular schools—as well as remedial math and reading and writing. In some areas freedom schools will serve to intensify regular studies. In some areas freedom schools may serve in place of regular schools in the event of trouble in the regular school system.

3. Pre-school education. Plans are underway for pre-school day care centers in several areas of the state. This program will attempt to provide nursery school enrichment programs to better prepare children for school. The program will provide working mothers with a place to leave their children under supervision during the day.

4. White Community Project. Contacts in the upper middle class and power structure will be continued, but these will be on a limited basis. Emphasis will be placed on trying to organize in the lowest classes, attempting to bridge the gap between the white and Negro communities.

5. Federal Programs. The project will attempt to implement various federal programs that are available for the Mississippi rural poor. Emphasis

is being placed on programs for farmers, cooperatives—both housing and consumer—public health programs, and implementing the anti-poverty bill.

6. Community Centers. During the summer community center programs began in many areas of the state. Lack of buildings and trained staff delayed implementation of a permanent program. During the year the National Council of Churches will take on increased responsibility for some of the community centers. Emphasis in programs will be on day care, citizenship, library, literacy, health program, and specialized programs arising out of skills of a particular applicant.

7. Literacy Program. The state-wide literacy program will be continued. Several different systems (each one/teach one, classes, self-help, etc.) are being used.

8. Medical Programs. The Medical Committee on Human Rights, a cooperating group, will expand its work. The programs will be partly connected with the freedom schools and the community centers. The actual content of the programs will depend, on local need and available personnel, but the minimum desired program will include public health, dietary guidance, first aid, pre-natal care, and instruction in available federal, state, and local aid.

9. Legal Programs. Legal assistance under the Lawyer's Constitutional Defense Committee and the Lawyer's Guild will be continued. Lawyers will be permanently stationed in the state and will work with visiting lawyers here on a short term basis.

10. Audio-visual Program. A variety of movies and slides will be shown in different parts of the state.

11. Food & Clothing Distribution. Food and clothing is being distributed to people who have suffered harassment for movement activities or who are economically destitute for other reasons. The food and clothing is collected in other parts of the country and sent here. This distribution is done in cooperation with other interested agencies.

12. Mississippi Student Union (High School Student Organization). Chapters of this state-wide movement organization are established in many areas. Other chapters will be added. The organization serves as a focus for all civil rights-connected activities on the high school level.

13. Libraries. Usually libraries will be a part of a community center program. In some areas there may be buildings only large enough to house a library. In other places mobile libraries may be used. The libraries are simple and are only sketchily catalogued. Emphasis is placed on training local people to run the libraries.

"These Are the Questions"

The Student Nonviolent Coordinating Committee exists primarily because racial segregation is rampant in the United States and the people within the Student Nonviolent Coordinating Committee feel that these problems of racial discrimination and segregation should be eliminated.

There exist within SNCC at this present time some 210 staff people, some 200 other people working as volunteers, many people across the United States working in the Friends of SNCC groups. Undoubtedly these many people associated with SNCC have become involved in the movement for a variety of reasons. And, therefore, lacking this general consensus on what we are about, it seems only appropriate that each individual speak from his own conviction as to why he feels we should organize. Therefore I shall not attempt to project my ideas as universal within SNCC. I speak only for myself.

Whenever we are asked what is the difference between SNCC and other civil rights organizations we are essentially being asked, "why do we organize, who, where, when, how and what?"

<u>Why Do We Organize?</u>

Obviously we are organizing because we feel that racial segregation is wrong. We are organizing because we ourselves have within us so many drives to end racial segregation that we feel that the best expression of these drives is to get other people to act in accordance with what we believe.

I believe we also organize because people who suffer from discrimination and segregation are denied a sense of dignity. In June, as you will recall, we had a long discussion on why we are organizing, and there was much discussion around the question of dignity. We were trying to find some umbrella, some over-all objective, around which we could close, or gather around, or form some type of consensus. It was then we projected the concept that a person working in Mississippi, a person earning $2–$3 a day, was being denied a sense of dignity, was being exploited economically and that this exploitation made it very difficult for him to hold his head high, to say to his family, "I am a man," in whatever full sense of the term we usually use it. Also a man without a job has a very difficult time holding his head high. He is a man being deprived of his dignity.

A student going into a lunch counter, knowing that he can buy coffee pots in the five and ten cents store, but unable to buy coffee at that lunch counter, is being denied a sense of dignity.

Freedom Summer director Bob Moses speaking,
with SNCC executive secretary James Forman (center)
and field secretary Bob Zellner (left) in the background

It is almost four years now since the student movement started. Many of us forget that the students who sat in, who were the historical forerunners to whatever we are doing now and will do in the future, were basically concerned about the caste system. The caste system in the United States denied them a sense of dignity. It was an affront to their existence, to their education and, one may say, to their sense of being an American. But, stripped of all this, it was undignified to say to a college-trained student, "come into the five and ten cent store, buy a coffee pot, but don't buy a cup of coffee." And also, the caste system had to be destroyed. In destroying bits and pieces of segregation, including the sitting at a lunch counter, forcing the owner to recognize that lunch counter discrimination was wrong, the students were helping to break down the larger area of the caste system. For the caste system re-enforces basic attitudes, and these attitudes obviously will not be changed unless people chip away bit by bit, step by step.

Let us take this concept of dignity and look at what we have organized. Let us begin with the Albany Movement in 1961. Charles Sherrod, Cordell Reagon went into Southwest Georgia and they were attempting to organize a movement in Albany. First of all they were interested in voter-registration in the surrounding counties. But they believed at that moment there was too much fear in Terrell and Lee, in Dawson, in Baker County, too much fear for the people to attempt to go down to register to vote, and that this fear had to be overcome. One of the ways that it could be overcome was by showing in Albany, Georgia, the largest metropolis in that area, that people were not afraid. In order to displace the fear of Albany, people had to be organized into some form of movement. There were many civil rights groups in Albany, Georgia in 1961. The Student Nonviolent Coordinating Committee was another. It came with the voter-registration project; its organizers assisted in the formation of the Albany Movement, trying to constantly project the local people as the people who should lead in that area. We were organizing basically to break down the fear in Albany and the surrounding counties, and once the fear disappeared and once the people felt that they could move on their own, then going to the voter-registration booth in Albany and the surrounding counties would not be that difficult. Time has proven this theory correct. Just last month, the King-for-Congress campaign was a justification of that rationale.

In Mississippi we were concerned about voter-registration in the underprivileged areas, in the bayous, in the small cities. We started in McComb, gathered a few forces, went into the Delta, said COFO could be a viable entity. We are now organizing around political objectives, trying to force the nation to see what is wrong in the state of Mississippi.

I contend we are also trying to bring hope, we are trying to give a sense of dignity to the people, wherever we work, be it Arkansas, Mississippi, Alabama or Georgia. Underlying all of our actions, we believe if the people themselves can feel a new spirit, a new sense of dignity, that they would easily gather together in some organizational form and begin to take certain steps of their own in order to help alleviate the suffering and the depraved human conditions in which we and they find ourselves. I am simply advancing dignity as a concept around which we can operate, around which we can give some definition to our work and some meaning to the lives of the people with whom we are working and around which we can also relate to them what it is that we are doing.

We have said we want to change the system, the system of segregation, the system of discrimination. We have said that it is not the people, it is not the segregationists, it is not the discriminator who is to blame, but rather it is the system. Now we did not carry the analysis of the system perhaps to other conclusions. We did not say, except in a few instances, that the system of segregation is wrapped up in the American system of political and economic exploitation, and this is a fact. But, when we spoke of changing the system of segregation we did not completely speak of an overhaul in the economic and political institutions of this country.

<u>Who Do We Organize?</u>

We are going to organize people. What types of people? We are going to organize old people and young people, people without jobs, people with jobs. We have been concerned with organizing two groups of people: the students and the adults in the community. We should organize the young people in grammar schools. We should organize high-school students. We should organize those groups of students or ex-students who have dropped out of high-school, who have not gone to college. We should organize the college students. These are four categories of young people that we should attempt to organize.

On the level of the adults, we should organize the women. We must be aware that both within and without SNCC subtle and blatant forms of discrimination against women exist. We should consciously endeavor to correct this situation. We should organize the old people, people 50, 60, 70 years old. These are the people who have never had very much, who understand what we are talking about. We should organize the unemployed, young and old. SNCC as an entity has not been concerned with organizing unemployed people. We simply have not done that. We could organize the maids in the towns where we work and we could organize the men who are working in certain factories. Or we can work conjointly with some unions to help organize these people.

Where Do We Organize?

Every city in the United States has people that can be organized. Every major city, every small village, North, South, East, West. Therefore we have to say: we only have so much time in our lives; we have limited resources, we have limited people, limited money, limited time, limited paper on which to write and to propagandize, and therefore we have got to consciously define an area for ourselves where we can organize.

Where have we organized in the past? On the college campuses and in the communities. During 1960 and the early part of 1961 the student movements on the campuses organized people, young people, who then motivated and forced into motion a lot of the community forces, primarily in the big cities. In 1961 it became quite apparent that the student movement had to go beyond the large communities because many of these problems were in the process of being solved. But the cities of 50,000 or less were unorganized and there was very little motion in these places. A degree of complacency was setting in in the United States. We went into Albany, Georgia. We went into McComb and some of the cities of the Delta. One of the greatest features of Albany was that we demonstrated to the country that there were significant numbers of people in the Black Belt, in the hard-core areas of the South, in the smaller cities, that also wanted to be free.

The Black Belt area in the United States is basically unorganized. It's in the rural areas. We can predict that not many of the civil rights organizations, if any, are going to be willing to go and work in these areas where we have been working: Southwest Alabama, where we have not succeeded to any appreciable degree, Southwest Georgia, Black Belts in Mississippi and Arkansas. The Black Belt is an area that we can properly stake out as a territorial entity for ourselves.

There is a danger, however, in this form of organization and we must be aware of this. The population statistics show that there is a move from the rural areas to the cities. Therefore in the major cities, in a lot of the ghettoes, in a lot of the pockets of black people there will be found many people who have come from these rural areas. The decision that we then have to make for ourselves is whether or not it is best to go into these rural areas or better to come into the cities. Given the resources that we have, given the way in which we have been working in these rural areas, I say that we should continue to work in the Black Belt. We must begin to find some way to transplant what we are doing to certain areas of the major cities in the South also.

There are other reasons why we should concentrate on the Black Belt at this particular moment. The significance of the Mississippi Freedom Democratic Party was not so much in what it immediately accomplished in Atlantic City, but in what it accomplished for the future. In the Call to the Convention in 1968 there is a stipulation that the National Democratic Party shall set up a committee to review State Parties and that no State Democratic machine can come to the Convention and be represented if it is denying people the right to participate in that machinery. We know, as [*New York Times* reporter] Claude Sitton has aptly pointed out, that the greatest problem, the greatest inequities in the electoral process, the greatest difficulty in people participating in the political machinery are going to occur in the Black Belt across the South. From now until 1968 we should establish a four-year plan. A plan for four years of activity in the Black Belt areas of the South so that we can go into every county, at least in the Black Belt area, and begin to document some of the inequalities in the electoral process, or rather in the political machinery, and be able to present this kind of a unified claim to the Democratic Convention in 1968. To do that we cannot wait until the year 1968 because it means getting our roots into those fertile areas now so that by 1967 the people have confidence in us and are willing to work with us on this program.

That's organizing in the communities in the Black Belt. It does not seem that we have to give up the other area of organization in the major cities. Most of the college campuses do exist in and around certain cities. We can set up two types of organizers, those on the college campuses or youth organizers in cities, and those in the communities. The college campus organizers can attempt to get people in the major cities to translate some of our programs into those areas. Let's make it concrete. Why can't the Nashville student movement be revitalized and people begin to set up Freedom Schools in some of the ghettoes of Nashville? Why can't we here in Atlanta, for instance, even those of us who work in the Atlanta office, set up a Freedom School in Buttermilk Bottom and begin to teach one or two hours a week in the Freedom School?

We know that we cannot organize everything. We cannot work in every city. Therefore I would say let us forget the Northern cities. There are many people up there who can work on it. We just can't do everything. SNCC cannot save the world.

When Do We Organize? We organize now. Where Do We Organize? We organize in the Black Belt areas of this country and in the poor sections of the cities. How Do We Organize? We organize people in Freedom Schools, in Community Centers, in voter-registration programs, in federal research programs. We organize people into maids' unions, we organize them in student groups, college groups, unemployed, drop-out groups, high-school groups, grammar school groups. We organize the old people. And Why Do We Organize? We organize in order to give people a new sense of dignity, to give them the machinery, the tools with which to fight their particular battles.

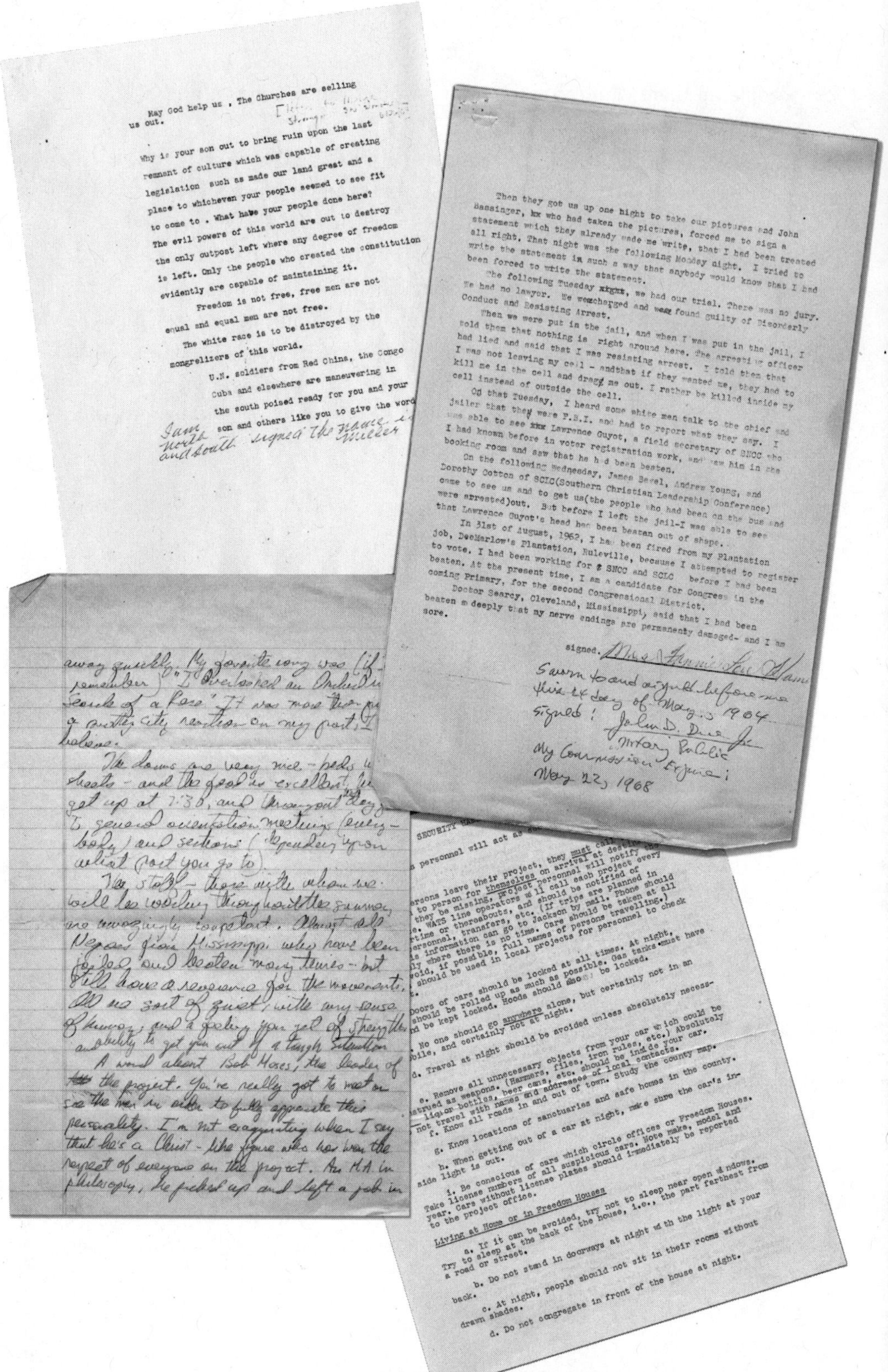

[Fragment 1 — top left typed letter]

May God help us . The Churches are selling us out.

Why is your son out to bring ruin upon the last remnant of culture which was capable of creating legislation such as made our land great and a place to whichever your people seemed to see fit to come to . What have your people done here? The evil powers of this world are out to destroy the only outpost left where any degree of freedom is left. Only the people who created the constitution evidently are capable of maintaining it.

Freedom is not free, free men are not equal and equal men are not free.

The white race is to be distroyed by the mongrelizers of this world.

U.S. soldiers from Red China, the Congo Cuba and elsewhere are maneuvering in the south poised ready for you and your son and others like you to give the word. *[handwritten]* I am north and south signed the name Mueller...

[Fragment 2 — right typed affidavit]

Then they got us up one night to take our pictures and John Bassinger, he who had taken the pictures, forced me to sign a statement which they already made me write, that I had been treated all right. That night was the following Monday night. I tried to write the statement in such a way that anybody would know that I had been forced to write the statement.

The following Tuesday night, we had our trial. There was no jury. We had no lawyer. We wercharged and were found guilty of Disorderly Conduct and Resisting Arrest.

When we were put in the jail, and when I was put in the jail, I told them that nothing is right around here. One arresting officer had lied and said that I was resisting arrest. I told them that I was not leaving my cell - andthat if they wanted me, they had to kill me in the cell and drag me out. I rather be killed inside my cell instead of outside the cell.

On that Tuesday, I heard some white men talk to the chief and jailer that they were F.B.I. and had to report what they say. I was able to see Mr Lawrence Guyot, a field secretary of SNCC who I had known before in voter registration work, and saw him in the booking room and saw that he had been beaten.

On the following Wednesday, James Bevel, Andrew Young, and Dorothy Cotton of SCLC(Southern Christian Leadership Conference) come to see us and to get us(the people who had been on the bus and were arrested)out. But before I left the jail-I was able to see that Lawrence Guyot's head had been beaten out of shape.

In 31st of August, 1962, I has been fired from my Plantation job, DeeMarlow's Plantation, Ruleville, because I attempted to register to vote. I had been working for SNCC and SCLC before I had been beaten. At the present time, I am a candidate for Congress in the coming Primary, for the second Congressional District.

Doctor Searcy, Cleveland, Mississippi, said that I had been beaten so deeply that my nerve endings are permanently damaged- and I am sore.

signed- Mrs Fannie Lou Hamer

Sworn to and signed before me this 24 day of May in 1964. signed: John D. Due Jr. Notary Public My Commission Expire: May 22, 1968

[Fragment 3 — bottom left handwritten letter]

away quickly. My favorite song was (if I remember) "I overlooked an Orchid..." Sounds of a fiddle? It was most too ... city reaction on my part, I believe.

The dorms are very nice - beds and sheets - and the good no excellent. We get up at 7:30, and the most days to general orientation meetings (everybody) and sections (depending upon what poet you go to)

Yes, still - there will when we will be working they had the summer no one quite important. Almost all Negros from Mississippi who have been in jail and beaten many times - but still have a reverence for the movement. All so sort of quiet, with any sense of humor, and a feeling you get of strength and ability to get you out of a tough situation.

A word about Bob Moses, the leader of the project. You're really got to meet him to see the man in order to fully appreciate this personality. I'm not exaggerating when I say that he's a Christ - like figure who has won the respect of everyone on the project. An M.A. in philosophy, he picked up and left a job in

[Fragment 4 — bottom right typed security memo]

SECURITY

...personnel will not a...

...persons leave their project, they must notify... to person for themselves on arrival at destination. If they be missing, project personnel will notify every... the WATS line operators and should each project every... line or thereabouts, etc., if trips are planned in... time or transfers, etc. Cars by mail. Phone there should personal information can go to Jackson by mail. Care should be taken at all is where there is no time. Care should be taken at all void, if possible, the full names of persons travelling... should be used in local projects for personnel to check.

3. Doors of cars should be locked at all times. At night, should be rolled up as much as possible. Gas tanks must have be kept locked. Hoods should also be locked.

4. No one should go anywhere alone, but certainly not in an bile, and certainly not at night.

5. Travel at night should be avoided unless absolutely necessary.

6. Remove all unnecessary objects from your car wich could be as weapons.(Hammers, files, iron rules, etc.) Absolutely liquor bottles, beer cans, etc. should be inside your car. If travel with named and addresses of local contacts car. not Know all roads in and out of town. Study the county map.

7. Know locations of sanctuaries and safe homes in the county.
a. When getting out of a car at night, make sure the car's in...
b. ...light is out.

8. Be conscious of cars which circle offices or Freedom Houses. Take license numbers of all suspicious cars. Note make, model and year. Cars without license plates should be immediately be reported to the project office.

Living at Home or in Freedom Houses

a. If it can be avoided, try not to sleep near open windows. Try to sleep at the back of the house, i.e., the part farthest from a road or street.

b. Do not stand in doorways at night. People should not sit in their rooms without drawn shades.

c. At night, people should not sit in front of the house at night.

d. Do not congregate in front of the house at night.

AFTERWORD:
FREEDOM SUMMER DOCUMENTS

By September 1, nearly all of the 1,500 volunteer students, lawyers, doctors, nurses, and clergy had gone home. In their luggage were hundreds of manila envelopes and file folders stuffed with handouts, diaries, newsletters, snapshots, and similar papers they'd accumulated. These scattered across the country like leaves on the wind, dropped into file drawers, tucked away in shoeboxes, slipped under beds, and jammed into closets from New York to Los Angeles.

Most of Freedom Summer's leaders and office staff left Mississippi, too. After the betrayal in Atlantic City, the project's directors went to Africa at the invitation of entertainer Harry Belafonte. Most of the paid staff gradually spread out among other CORE and SNCC projects in Louisiana, Georgia, and Alabama. In the Jackson COFO headquarters, discipline gave way to dissension in the fall of 1964; in small cities and towns, black residents struggled to keep local offices alive; all across the state, the communications and organizing infrastructure shut down. The office files that documented Freedom Summer were boxed up and pushed aside.

The survival of the project's records had always seemed precarious.

Instructions to local projects had required that every written record of importance should have at least four copies: the original and carbon copies were to be sent to COFO, CORE, and SNCC staff in Jackson, Greenwood, and Atlanta. But that rule was often ignored because there was no culture of record keeping. Members were suspicious of paper trails and documentation, which they associated with the dominant power structure. "I want you to know that I am not making a carbon copy of this letter," SNCC's Jane Stembridge wrote to her colleague Mary King, "because when one makes carbon copies, one is either assuming one has something to say, or is assuming that we are involved in a business that keeps records. We do not keep records like that. If you want the record, it's inside of me. . . ."[1]

It was also hard to document events because they unfolded so quickly. "Many things which are happening now and should be preserved are not being recorded," reflected SNCC supporter Lucile Montgomery. "Of course, the people who know most about what is going on are so busy making it happen that they can't stop long enough to write it down. . . ." And when thorough records were kept, they were vulnerable to theft, vandalism, and arson. After the Tupelo and Indianola COFO offices were firebombed in 1964 and 1965, police and firefighters swooped in immediately to carry off all the files that could identify local civil rights workers.[2]

Records in local homes and freedom houses were often discarded by their creators. Southern black communities had safeguarded their memories for generations with oral traditions. Denied formal schooling and exploited by legal forms and documents, they didn't necessarily value records kept on paper. People who could accurately recite their history out loud often assumed that nobody would ever want their old letters, memos, and clippings.

So it was with a sense of urgency that a handful of history students who had volunteered in the South approached Wisconsin Historical Society director Les Fishel in December 1964 with a proposal to collect civil rights manuscripts.

Mimi Feingold had arrived in Madison as a history graduate student at the end of August. While an undergrad at Swarthmore, she'd been arrested during one of the first Freedom Rides. She'd postponed graduate school for a year to organize residents in Louisiana with CORE before coming to the University of Wisconsin. She soon connected with Bob and Vicki Gabriner, who'd also arrived that fall. They'd spent the previous summer in West Tennessee working with the local black community. "Our minds were

---

1   "Security Handbook," in "Civil Rights miscellaneous files 1964–1966," Robert Gabriner Papers, 1961–1981 (Mss 575) Box 9, Folder 9. Jane Stembridge to Mary King, November 15, 1963, quoted in King, Mary E. *Freedom Song: A Personal Story of the 1960s Civil Rights Movement* (New York: William Morrow and Co., 1987): 123.

2   Lucile Montgomery to Vicki Gabriner, WHS Field Reports (Series 678), Wisconsin Historical Society Archives, Box 10, Folder 6. "Reports from Madison, Miss., 1964, January 1965, November," Congress of Racial Equality. Southern Regional Office Records, 1954–1966 (Mss 85) Box 8, Folder 7. "August, 1964 WATS Line Calls," Mary E. King Papers, 1962–1999 (M82-445) Box 1, Folder 9. "Incident summary, March 1965," in "Freedom School mimeo materials 1963–64," Pamela P. Allen Papers, 1967–1974 (M85-013) Folder 1.

blown by this experience we had had," Vicki recalled. "We were very full of it and carried it with us when we came to Madison."[3]

The Wisconsin Historical Society was a second home for history students. Several, including Feingold, found part-time jobs there that fall. Other student workers in the Society archives included sophomore Chris Hexter, who'd been a Freedom School teacher in Ruleville, Mississippi, that summer; grad student Danny Beagle, who'd volunteered in West Tennessee with the Gabriners; and Alicia Kaplow, another sophomore, who'd spent the summer of 1964 raising money for the Mississippi Freedom Democratic Party.

Although they studied hard, Bob recalls, "We didn't see ourselves in academic careers." They saw themselves as political activists making a temporary detour through academia. Vicki remembers, "We were always trying to figure out ways to bring those two pieces of our lives together." One way to integrate politics and academia was collecting records of the civil rights movement, especially those created at the grassroots level.[4]

From their work in the South, they knew that the struggle was being waged by common people who had everything to lose. "We do not believe that people can really understand the civil rights movement," Vicki wrote at the time, "if they just look at the papers of some national air-conditioned office." As historians, they were most interested in the stories of local people who were seizing control over their own destiny. Bob was worried "that all of those stories would evaporate and it would be the story of the most visible leadership only."[5]

So on December 17, 1964, he approached Society director Les Fishel on behalf of the others. "The thrust of what we proposed," he recalls,

> was to collect the stuff that wasn't easily collectible; but we could [do it] because we had cachet, we had knowledge, we had people we knew, we were part of the movement. And we believed that that would be a great way to ensure that all of this stuff was kept and taken care of. . . . Fishel

---

3   Email, December 27, 2012, from Mimi Feingold Real. Telephone interviews, January 16 and 29, 2013, with Vicki and Bob Gabriner.

4   Telephone interview, January 16, 2013, with Vicki and Bob Gabriner. Robert S. Gabriner Papers, 1961–1981 (Mss 575) at the Wisconsin Historical Society, Box 9, Folder 8.

5   Vicki Gabriner, letter to Gould (AR) Citizens for Progress, August 10, 1966, Gabriner Papers (Mss 575) Box 9, Folder 8. Telephone interview, January 16, 2013, with Vicki and Bob Gabriner.

didn't blink an eye. He said, this is great. I mean, he said, we'll *pay* you for it, we'll pay your way. And it was like, Holy Moly, this guy really understands what we're talking about.

Feingold adds, "I think it was amazingly forward-thinking and out-of-the-box for the director of an august research library to open his doors to a bunch of upstart grad students; but of course at the time we didn't stand on ceremony, especially having just come from leading protest activities of all sorts in the South."[6]

Fishel didn't usually stand on ceremony either. His field was black history, and he'd spent years trying to research African Americans who were hard to find in the conventional historical record. He also appreciated the Society's century-old tradition of collecting the evidence of current events and saving them for posterity. Within a few weeks, the students had been put on the payroll and organized into a collecting team.[7]

Fishel assigned them to work with Russell Gilmore in the Society's Field Services (collecting) division. Gilmore was not politically left-wing like the others (he would write his dissertation on the National Rifle Association and spend his career running military museums), but as a historian he immediately grasped the importance of the project. "He was our guy on the ground," Vicki recalled. "We would be in some out of the way place in Mississippi or Alabama or Georgia and we could call Russell and he would be extremely responsive to anything we needed. . . . Les giving the OK on it was great, but we couldn't have pulled it off without Russ Gilmore."[8]

They began by gathering papers from people they knew. "Don't be intimidated by the letterhead," Bob wrote to friends in Tennessee, "I am now in the employ of the Wisconsin Historical Society collecting material on the civil rights movement." The first manuscripts arrived in February 1965 and by April the Society's staff newsletter could report that "since January of this year, the Manuscripts Division has received more than two dozen collections sent in by civil rights volunteers. . . ." On their first trip

6   Telephone interview, January 16, 2013, with Vicki and Bob Gabriner. Email, December 27, 2012, from Mimi Feingold Real. Vicki, Bob, Alicia, and Chris Hexter suspect the idea began with Bob; Feingold does not recall who first proposed it.

7   WHS Field Reports (Series 678) Box 14, Folder 3.

8   *Wisconsin Magazine of History* 50, number 1 (autumn 1966): 99. Telephone interview, January 16, 2013, with Vicki and Bob Gabriner.

South, the Gabriners had stopped in Louisville to consult veteran activists Anne and Carl Braden. When Bob called them in November 1965 to solicit their papers, they not only promised their own files but suggested dozens of potential donors from New Orleans to New York.[9]

Another breakthrough came early in 1966 when, after two years of cultivation by Fishel, CORE's national office decided to donate its noncurrent files to the Society. When Gilmore went to New York in March 1966 to pack their twenty-eight cartons, he also called on Elizabeth Sutherland (better known today as Betita Martinez). She had collected hundreds of letters from Freedom Summer volunteers, most of which could not fit in her 1965 book *Letters from Mississippi*. She let Gilmore have all her files for the Society's collection.[10]

As the summer of 1966 approached, Feingold and the Gabriners outlined a road trip through the South. They gave Fishel a three-page "Immodest Proposal for Civil Rights Collection at WHS" that suggested collecting papers and taping interviews wherever civil rights struggles had taken place. Feingold would circulate through Louisiana and southwestern Mississippi while Bob and Vicki Gabriner drove through the Mississippi Delta and then into Alabama and Georgia. Fishel approved the idea on April 3, 1966, with a budget of $4,200 that included $1,500 for bail in case they were arrested. He also consulted Wisconsin's attorney general about the Society's liability if they were injured or killed.[11]

Fishel's concern for their safety was well founded. In the previous three years, more than thirty civil rights workers were murdered in the South. Mickey Schwerner, one of three workers killed on Freedom Summer's first day, was a fraternity brother of Bob's. When he disappeared, the Gabriners knew the same thing could happen to them. The local Klan had called for Bob's assassination in Tennessee during their first summer working there.[12]

---

9   Gabriner Papers (Mss 575) Box 9, Folder 8. Staff newsletter, April–May 1965: 2. Miriam Feingold Papers (Micro 845) reel 2, frame 94. Michael Lipsky and David J. Olson Papers, 1935–1981 (Mss 851) Box 1, Folder 13. Lead file, Archives Division, Wisconsin Historical Society (Braden).

10 Lead file (CORE and Sutherland); Gabriner Papers (Mss 575) Box 8, Folder 12.

11 SHSW Divisional Files: Field Services (Series 678) Box 29, Folder 10.

12 "Partial List of Racial Murders in the South in the Last 2 Years, April 1963 through February 1965," Poor People's Corporation Records, 1960–1967 (Mss 172) Box 1, Folder 6. Telephone interview, January 29, 2013, with Vicki and Bob Gabriner. *Step By Step; Evolution and Operation of the Cornell Students' Civil-rights Project in Tennessee, Summer, 1964* (New York: Published for the Fayette County Fund by W. W. Norton, 1965): 77.

"Guns were everywhere," Vicki recalls. "Every pickup truck had a rifle rack in the cab, and you could see them as they drove by. We felt unsafe all the time, constantly. . . . If we had really thought about how dangerous it was, if we had let that rise to the surface and be the first thing we thought about—well, that would not have been a good strategy." Bob added, "We were also very aware that any black person we talked to could be lynched afterwards, just for talking to us."[13]

On July 21, 1966, the Gabriners and Feingold rendezvoused at the Memphis airport to discuss itineraries. After agreeing to meet in Jackson, Mississippi, three weeks later, they set off in opposite directions to hunt for manuscripts.[14]

The Gabriners drove east to Fayette County, Tennessee, and on July 31 went down to Holly Springs, Mississippi, to make a pitch to the local SNCC office. By 1966, SNCC had been spied upon by the FBI and infiltrated by white supremacists, so it had good reason to mistrust outsiders. Holly Springs staff told the Gabriners that COFO's headquarters files from Jackson had been transferred there in early 1965 but had since been burned. (They were later discovered in 1969 in an abandoned office outside Holly Springs but subsequently disappeared. In August 2013, a visiting scholar told Society staff that the files were still in private hands in Jackson.) Bob and Vicki left Holly Springs empty-handed.[15]

A week later they headed to Arkansas to call on Daisy Bates, former president of the local NAACP and leader of the 1957 Little Rock school desegregation fight. She and her husband enthusiastically supported the Society's plan and immediately promised their files. When Gilmore picked up their collection a few weeks later, it included not only papers but also a rock thrown through Bates's living room window. Attached was a note reading, "Next time will be dynamite."[16]

The approval of Daisy Bates opened all movement doors in Arkansas. Staff at the state's SNCC headquarters happily gave the Gabriners boxes of records dating back to 1962, and local offices around the state followed

13 Telephone interviews, January 16 and 29, 2013, with Vicki and Bob Gabriner.

14 Field Reports (Series 678) Box 10, Folder 6. Gabriner Papers (Mss 575) Box 9, Folder 8.

15 Lead file (SNCC Project Office, Holly Springs).

16 Lead file (Arkansas–Bates).

suit. By the time Bob and Vicki crossed the Mississippi River, they had shipped five cartons to Madison.[17]

Mississippi, however, was a different story. Without local references or the sanction of a leader like Bates, the Gabriners were cold-shouldered by local activists. After a fruitless visit to Jackson, they headed north into the Delta. "We turned off the paved highways when we reached the towns we were looking for," they later wrote in the staff newsletter,

> and traveled the dirt roads which run through the Negro communities. In some instances we had the addresses of Freedom Houses to look for, in others we would look for Negroes, ask directions to the homes of the local civil rights leaders, directions which sometimes led us out into the rural hinterlands. Once having found the people for whom we were searching, it became necessary for us to prove that we were not interlopers, not FBI agents, but civil rights workers doing work related to the movement. . . . We met with people in wooden shacks, under trees, and in cars, from early in the morning until late at night.[18]

In Batesville, they discovered that all the files from the former Freedom House had been burned. In Clarksdale, MFDP leader Aaron Henry refused to speak with them because he suspected they were infiltrators. "Really, this is one hell of a way to make a living," they wrote to Gilmore from the village of Marks, near the Mississippi River:

> Working 12–18 hours a day, being greeted in a manner ranging from frank hostility to having papers thrust at us without even a satisfactory explanation of what we're doing (the latter having happened only once, and unlikely to re-occur), not having eaten before we get involved somewhere and unable to be nice Historical Society people because our stomachs are convulsed. . . .[19]

They headed back to Madison about August 21. In two weeks, they'd met with more than twenty donors in three states and shipped

---

17 Gabriner Papers (Mss 575) Box 9, Folder 8.

18 Field Reports (Series 678) Box 10, Folder 6. Staff newsletter, December 1966: 3.

19 Field Reports (Series 678) Box 10, Folder 6.

seven cartons of papers back to the Society. They never connected with Feingold, though, because she found more to do in Louisiana than she'd anticipated.[20]

Feingold had gone straight to New Orleans, where she found CORE's Southern Regional Office shutting down and was told she could have all the records more than a year old. "Beginning with the filing cabinets," she wrote,

> I systematically went through the files, leaving behind everything after June 1, 1965, and taking everything else.... I attacked a pile of file folders gathering dust on a shelf over the filing cabinet . . . then I took all the files from cartons labeled "State Office, Baton Rouge, La., Ronnie Moore, CORE field secretary." . . . Under a table in a small room in the front of the office, which was filled mostly with garbage, I found piles of loose papers and cartons labeled "Louisiana Reports." . . . Just as I thought I was through, someone pointed out a small file cabinet hiding in the corner which contained more material from the Research Department.

She shipped eight cartons of Southern Regional Office papers to Madison documenting CORE's activities across the South from 1959 to 1965.[21]

For the next three weeks, Feingold drove a Volkswagen beetle around Louisiana and southwestern Mississippi collecting papers, taping interviews, and recording promises to donate in the future. She was ticketed by local police in Mandeville for changing clothes on a beach, rescued records in Clinton from "a ramshackle hut which was on the verge of collapsing and in which the CORE papers were slowly rotting," and was guarded by shotguns while sleeping in an African American home in Ferriday.[22]

"Driving around in black rural Louisiana," she says today, "was like going back in time a century or so. The roads were often dirt or gravel, and wind would blow dust in your face. It's hot and humid in Louisiana in the summer—uncomfortably so, especially to a Northern girl who'd just come off a Madison winter. . . ." Her directions often read like this: "when speed limit drops to c. 20mph @ bridge (c. 1 mi from center of town)—cross bridge—1st street on left (4th St.), 1st building on left is

20 Field Reports (Series 678) Box 10, Folder 6.

21 Field Reports (Series 678) Box 10, Folder 6. Feingold reel 2, frame 218.

22 Field Reports (Series 678) Box 10, Folder 6.

McGee's Café. Across from Café—2d or 3rd house down from corner—are Movement people."[23]

She recalls that, "most of my 'donors' were ordinary, local blacks [who had fought for civil rights] in small Louisiana towns like Clinton or Plaquemine. They had no idea that anything they might still have hanging around their modest homes (shacks, really) would be considered valuable records. Their concern was not so much any reluctance in parting with the stuff, but with why in the world I or anyone else might want it." On August 21 she headed for Madison. During her month on the road she'd visited thirty-eight people, taped fourteen interviews, received thirteen promises of papers, and shipped nine collections to Madison.[24]

Despite their best efforts, sometimes success depended on simple luck. Vicki Gabriner remembers

> pulling into some town and meeting the people we were supposed to meet who told us they'd just burned their papers, and we flew out to the backyard and went through the cinders to see what we could find. I can't remember if we saved anything or if it was all burned by the time we got there. Those were the unlucky days. Then there were lucky days when somebody would say to us, "You know, I've been wondering what to do with this stuff. I'm so glad you came because I've been thinking I should throw it out." And they would bring out a box. . . . [25]

The 1966 collecting tours yielded a total of twenty-four cartons of records, including some of the Society's richest civil rights manuscripts. Nearly all donors took advantage of the Society's offer to restrict access for five years so the identities of local movement leaders wouldn't fall into the wrong hands.

Meanwhile, the staff back in Madison had been hard at work. Elizabeth Sutherland's files were a gold mine since they contained hundreds of addresses of Freedom Summer volunteers. "Alicia Kaplow and Chris Hexter," the staff newsletter announced, "with the aid of the Society's typing pool, sent 800 letters to volunteers of the Freedom Summer and 800 more

---

23 Field Reports (Series 678) Box 10, Folder 6. Feingold reel 2, frame 218.

24 Email, December 27, 2012, from Mimi Feingold Real. Feingold Papers, reel 2, frame 195. Email December 27, 2012. Field Reports (Series 678) Box 10, Folder 6.

25 Telephone interview, January 16, 2013, with Vicki and Bob Gabriner.

letters to their parents, inviting them to donate their materials, letters home, anything they had relating to civil rights."[26]

In September 1966, Feingold earned her master's degree and moved to New Jersey, so Vicki Gabriner was hired to work in the office. Between September 1966 and June 1967, the staff brought in nearly forty new civil rights collections. "This winter," Vicki wrote in the December staff newsletter, "we are closing leads we developed last summer, writing to people we met who indicated they might send us their papers, and opening new leads to people and organizations in both the North and South." By the end of January 1967, the list of donors ran to ten pages and contained 131 individuals and organizations.[27]

Vicki pulled off a major coup in February 1967 by saving the extraordinarily rich collection of Chicago millionaire Lucile Montgomery. "Mrs. M. has supported many aspects of the CR movement for the past few years," she noted, "to the tune of thousands upon thousands of dollars. Much of her material is correspondence thanking her or requesting large donations. Because she has so much money, and has contributed so much of it to the movement, people keep in constant touch with her." Montgomery's files were microfilmed, returned to her, and subsequently disappeared. If Vicki had not secured them for microfilming, thousands of unpublished documents about civil rights activities during the height of the movement would have vanished forever.[28]

As the summer of 1967 approached, Alicia Kaplow announced her intention to leave Madison, so, in April, Gilmore hired recent history grad Leah Johnson to follow up on existing leads and travel around the South. Johnson remembers being paid $3.50 per hour, $1.00 more than the standard rate for students, since she had to act with more independent judgment.[29]

The team searched for someone with Mississippi credentials to accompany Johnson. They found the perfect person in undergraduate Gwen Gillon, who had dropped out of Tougaloo College in 1963 to work full-time

---

26 Staff newsletter, December 1966: 2.

27 Staff newsletter, December 1966: 4. Lead file analysis. Lipsky Papers (Mss 851) Box 1, Folder 13.

28 Lead file. Field Reports (Series 678) Box 10, Folder 6. Searches of the University of Georgia's comprehensive digital civil rights archives database and WorldCat. Most of Montgomery's surviving papers are now online in the Society's Freedom Summer collection.

29 Telephone interview, January 30, 2013, with Alicia Kaplow. Telephone interview, March 15, 2013, with Leah Johnson Wise.

for SNCC. At seventeen, she'd been SNCC's youngest staff member. This didn't stop her from risking her life in June 1964 in the back country of Neshoba County searching for Chaney, Goodman, and Schwerner. While the FBI dragged its heels, she reconnoitered white farms at night looking for the missing men with Stokely Carmichael, who remembered her as "a gutsy little sister" in his autobiography. Society staff hoped that Gillon's friendships would open doors in Mississippi that had been shut to the Gabriners.[30]

The Gabriners, who are white, and Johnson and Gillon, who are black, always traveled as separate teams since integrated cars were sure to attract the attention of police. Johnson and Gillon met on July 7 in Atlanta with SNCC's steering committee and came away with an agreement that, "We were not to take organizational records, but personal records of SNCC activists were okay, and it was approved that we could take papers from COFO offices in Mississippi, since it was a coalition of groups, not solely SNCC." SNCC even gave them the names and phone numbers of its members to approach.[31]

About July 15 they arrived in Jackson, Mississippi, where they acquired the very rich papers of attorney R. Hunter Morey, COFO's legal coordinator during Freedom Summer. His five cartons contained meticulous documentation of voting rights, police harassment, the MFDP challenges, and internal COFO discussions. Then they headed north for the Delta, hoping to gather papers scattered across its rural communities.[32]

Their three-day "Delta escapade," as Johnson called it, began on July 18 in Greenwood, where she and Gillon enlisted SNCC veteran Hollis Watkins to help. Watkins, an early SNCC field secretary, had survived arrests, assaults, and bombings since 1961 and was admired by everyone in the movement. He was also a former boyfriend of Gillon, and he was happy to guide her and Johnson through the Delta to people who might have preserved papers.[33]

---

30 Gwen Gillon Ozanne Papers (M73-288) Box 1, Folder 2. Ture, Kwame (Stokely Carmichael). *Ready for Revolution* (New York: Charles Scribner's Sons, 2003): 277. Interview, July 3, 2013, with Gwen Gillon Ozanne.

31 Emails, July 2, 2013, from Leah Johnson Wise and Gwen Gillon Ozanne.

32 Field Reports (Series 678) Box 10, Folder 6. Lead file (Morey). Telephone interview, March 15, 2013, with Leah Johnson Wise.

33 Interview, July 3, 2013, with Gwen Gillon Ozanne. Telephone interview, March 15, 2013, with Leah Johnson Wise.

Johnson did all the driving, following Watkins's leads. By day, they discovered records in boarded-up storefronts, abandoned farm buildings, and vacant offices; at night, they slept on friends' floors or couches. Johnson doesn't think Watkins was ever paid by the Society. He appreciated the importance of saving history and just pitched in.[34]

On July 19, they drove to Sunflower County to visit Fannie Lou Hamer, a civil rights icon. She had survived beatings by police, dodged gunfire from the Klan, helped launch the Freedom Summer project, and run for Congress on the MFDP ticket. She knew every movement leader in the South, and Johnson and Gillon assumed that she'd have a large, important cache of manuscripts. When they pulled up in front of her two-room home in Ruleville, though, Hamer was outside in the yard burning all her old papers. "She said there were so many that she didn't know what to do with them all," Johnson recalled, "and had no idea they might interest anybody else." She promised to look around for more if they would come back the next day.[35]

In nearby Cleveland, they got in touch with the Reverend Bob Beech, a Minnesota minister who ran the Hattiesburg office of the Delta Ministry, and the Reverend Harry Bowie, who was in charge of its McComb operation. They willingly contributed more than ten boxes that closely documented hundreds of Northern clergy who volunteered to work for justice in the South. A side trip to Canton brought them to Annie Devine who, like Hamer, had run for Congress on the MFDP ticket in 1964. She arranged for the Fourth Congressional District CORE files to be sent to Madison. When microfilmed, these filled five reels with several thousand pages on the struggle in central Mississippi between 1961 and 1966, including CORE's role in Freedom Summer.[36]

The trio got up early the next morning, July 20, and called again on Hamer, but she'd been able to find only a single folder. They then drove to Cleveland and called on Amzie Moore, who had braved white supremacy in Mississippi since the 1940s. He claimed to have nothing of value; though when he donated his papers three years later, they filled a dozen boxes. As

---

34 Telephone interview, March 15, 2013, with Leah Johnson Wise.

35 Telephone interview, March 15, 2013, with Leah Johnson Wise. Mott, Ronni, "Hollis Watkins," *Jackson (Miss.) Free Press*, December 3, 2012. DeMuth, Jerry, "Tired of Being Sick and Tired," *The Nation* (June 1, 1964). Field Reports (Series 678) Box 10, Folder 6. Lead file (Hamer).

36 Lead file (Beech, Bowie). Field Reports (Series 678) Box 10, Folder 6. Interview, July 3, 2013, with Gwen Gillon Ozanne.

the sun set, they dropped Watkins in Greenwood and stopped making calls. Johnson wrote in her field report, "it was about 10:30 p.m. and since Hollis wasn't with us, we decided against it (ain't too safe to go driving through the Delta at night, at least not for us, pickup trucks with rifles hung up in the back window throughout the area)." Instead, they hit the highway and arrived back in Jackson past midnight after what Johnson called, "a successful three days, in our estimation."[37]

Bob and Vicki Gabriner, meanwhile, had started in Atlanta by calling on Sam Shirah, a SNCC member from its earliest days who had been instrumental in recruiting volunteers for Freedom Summer. On July 10 they shipped three boxes of his papers from Atlanta containing personal records of the group's activities since the early 1960s. The next day they headed into southwestern Georgia searching for records from the Albany Movement, in which hundreds of people had been arrested in 1961 and 1962. They met with its leader, the Reverend Charles Sherrod, who donated two boxes weighing fifty-six pounds when they were shipped from Albany on July 14.[38]

From there they drove northwest to Montgomery, Alabama, where for two days they tried unsuccessfully to cultivate leaders of the Montgomery bus boycott of 1956. Despite face-to-face appeals and written proposals, they came away only with the archives of the local civil rights newspaper, *The Southern Courier.*[39]

They arrived in Jackson, Mississippi, at 2:00 a.m. on July 20, which turned out to be the most successful day of their trip. In the morning they called on the Freedom Information Service and the Poor People's Corporation; both agreed to donate their substantial archives. That afternoon Lawrence Guyot promised the central files of the Mississippi Freedom Democratic Party, totaling thousands of pages, and the next day they shipped the records of the Meridian COFO office, the one from which Chaney, Goodman, and Schwerner had disappeared three years earlier.[40]

Both teams were back in Madison by the end of July 1967. They had brought in twenty-two new collections, including large and important files

---

37 Field Reports (Series 678) Box 10, Folder 6. Lead file (Hamer, Moore).

38 Gabriner Papers (Mss 575) Box 8, Folder 12. Lead file (Sherrod, Shirah).

39 Gabriner Papers (Mss 575) Box 8, Folder 12.

40 Lead file (MFDP). Gabriner Papers (Mss 575) Box 8, Folder 12. Field Reports (Series 678) Box 10, Folder 6.

from the MFDP, R. Hunter Morey, the Fourth Congressional District CORE office, and the Delta Ministry.

Kaplow left Madison that fall, followed by Johnson in January 1968 and Vicki Gabriner the next April. Russ Gilmore also resigned from the Society in 1968 to concentrate on his studies. In January 1969, having completed everything for his PhD except the dissertation, Bob Gabriner moved to San Francisco. Society director Les Fishel departed in June 1969 to become the president of Heidelberg College. Of the original team formed in the spring of 1965, no one was left at the Society four years later.[41]

Between 1965 and 1968, they'd brought in 232 shipments of civil rights manuscripts. Over the next fifteen years, 343 more would arrive, mostly from leads generated in the mid-1960s (for example, another 65 accessions of Braden papers were processed after 1968). As the 1960s unfolded, their successors spent most of their time and energy collecting papers from antiwar, draft resistance, women's movement, and leftist political groups, often from the same donors who had been civil rights workers a decade earlier. About a dozen civil rights–related donations continued to arrive at the Society each year through 1990. The most important ones were microfilmed and made available to other libraries in the 1980s.

The Society's collection of civil rights manuscripts is neither the largest nor the richest in the nation. That honor probably belongs to the King Center in Atlanta (where Leah Johnson was the founding archivist, after leaving the Society). Other superb collections have been built at the University of Southern Mississippi, Tougaloo College, and the major East Coast institutions. The University of Georgia collates descriptions of several hundred manuscript collections housed in more than 150 institutions at its Civil Rights Digital Library (http://crdl.usg.edu). The group Civil Rights Movement Veterans has gathered documents and recollections from hundreds of movement workers and published them online (http://crmvet.org).

The Wisconsin Historical Society's civil rights manuscript collections are distinguished by two features. First is their emphasis on papers of local activists and grassroots organizations rather than on large institutional archives. Second is their age: they were collected in the mid-1960s, when

---

41 Telephone interviews with Bob and Vicki Gabriner, January 16, 2013, and Leah Johnson Wise, March 15, 2013. *Wisconsin Magazine of History* 52, number 3 (Spring 1969): 204. Interview, July 3, 2013, with Gwen Gillon Ozanne.

few other institutions were interested in saving the stories of common people in McComb, Mississippi, or Clinton, Louisiana. For half a century, every serious researcher on the history of the civil rights movement has used the Society's manuscripts.

The readings in this book are all from the Society's collection. Most of these documents have never been published before. These forty-four documents have been selected from more than thirty thousand pages of archival records accessible online at www.wisconsinhistory.org/freedomsummer. All royalties from the sale of this book will go toward publishing more of the Society's civil rights records on the web, so the next generation of Americans can discover other people who dared to risk everything.

ACKNOWLEDGMENTS

The civil rights workers who created these documents deserve not just our thanks but that of the entire nation. We are especially grateful to those who allowed us to print writings from fifty years ago that are still protected by copyright: Elizabeth Aaronsohn, Joel Bernard, Charles E. Cobb Jr., Jerry DeMuth, Robert Feinglass, Walter Kaufmann, Ellen Lake, Charles McLaurin, the Reverend Charles Sherrod, and the Reverend David Steffenson. We also thank Matt Herron, the Newseum, and Harvey Richards for letting us use their images.

We owe another debt of gratitude to the activists-turned-archivists who collected most of these manuscripts in the South in 1966 and 1967: Bob and Vicki Gabriner, Alicia Kaplow, Gwen Gillon Ozanne, Mimi Feingold Real, and Leah Johnson Wise. Without their foresight and dedication, many of these documents would not have survived at all.

Movement veterans Bruce Hartford, Mary Elizabeth King, Lisa Anderson Todd, and Leah Johnson Wise critiqued early drafts of chapters or the Society's Freedom Summer 50th anniversary exhibit text. Their tactful criticisms saved me from misconstruing important aspects of the Mississippi Summer Project. Errors that survived despite their generosity are entirely my own.

For digitizing, indexing, editing, and interpreting archival documents, thanks are due to Jonathan Cooper, Diane Drexler, Laura Gottlieb, Laura Kearney, Chris Lay, Steve Nonte, and Antonia Rath. Dave Deprey and Sarah McDole performed essential image research.

Finally, this book would never have been begun without the vision and support of Matt Blessing and Kathy Borkowski.

SOURCES

Documents

Unless otherwise noted below, all documents are printed from manuscripts at the Wisconsin Historical Society with minimal editing, such as minor punctuation changes made for clarity. We have allowed idiosyncratic spellings and grammar to stand uncorrected. The originals can be viewed online at the Web addresses listed below.

Chapter 1. Before Freedom Summer

"A Guide to Mississippi," Spring 1964: Jerry DeMuth Papers, 1962–1987 (SC3065).
http://cdm15932.contentdm.oclc.org/cdm/ref/collection/p15932coll2/id/15142

"Rugged, Ragged 'Snick': What It Is and What It Does": Hank Werner Papers (M65-066) Box 1, Folder 5. First published in *Chicago Daily News,* July 20, 1963. This text is from a SNCC offprint of the article.
http://cdm15932.contentdm.oclc.org/cdm/ref/collection/p15932coll2/id/21028

Fannie Lou Hamer Deposition: In "Legal Documents re: COFO v. Rainey, 1964: Brief, 1964." Arthur Kinoy Papers, circa 1930–2003 (M2007-010) Box 8, Folder 22.
http://cdm15932.contentdm.oclc.org/cdm/ref/collection/p15932coll2/id/393

SNCC Biography: Bob Moses: In "SNCC Staff Biographies, 1964." Mary E. King Papers, 1962–1999 (M82-445) Box 1, Folder 13.
http://cdm15932.contentdm.oclc.org/cdm/ref/collection/p15932coll2/id/24300

Notes on Biography of Dave Dennis: In "CORE Southern Regional Office—Personnel information, May 1964–January 21, 1965." Congress of Racial Equality. Southern Regional Office Records, 1954–1966 (Mss 85) Box 9, Folder 7. These notes have been reformatted slightly to improve legibility.
http://cdm15932.contentdm.oclc.org/cdm/ref/collection/p15932coll2/id/16225

Chapter 2. Debates, Preparations, Training

Memo to SNCC Executive Committee, September 1963: In "Documents Relating to Bob Moses." William Heath Research Papers, 1963–1997 (M2009-045) Box 5, Folder 17.
http://content.wisconsinhistory.org/cdm/ref/collection/p15932coll2/id/1812

Notes on Mississippi: Mendy Samstein Papers, 1963–1966 (SC3093).
http://cdm15932.contentdm.oclc.org/cdm/ref/collection/p15932coll2/id/17673

Dear Friend: In "Mississippi Summer Project Material (SNCC COFO), 1964." Jerry Tecklin Papers, 1964 (Mss 538) Box 1, Folder 5.
http://content.wisconsinhistory.org/cdm/ref/collection/p15932coll2/id/9559

Application to Work on the Freedom Summer Project: In "Freedom Summer Volunteers – Missing volunteers, 1964." William Heath Research Papers, 1963–1997 (M2009-045) Box 3, Folder 10.
http://content.wisconsinhistory.org/cdm/ref/collection/p15932coll2/id/1894

Mississippi Summer Project Launched: In "Chronology, 1963–1964." Howard Zinn Papers, 1956–1994 (Mss 588) Box 1, Folder 22.
http://content.wisconsinhistory.org/cdm/ref/collection/p15932coll2/id/11412

Letter from Volunteer Training in Oxford, Ohio: In "Joel Bernard Correspondence, 1964–1966." Jacqueline Bernard Papers, 1964–1967 (Mss 230) Box 1, Folder 1.
http://cdm15932.contentdm.oclc.org/cdm/ref/collection/p15932coll2/id/3612

Possible Role-Playing Situations: Two documents: "Possible Role Playing Situations." Sandra Hard Papers, 1964–1965 (SC 642).
http://cdm15932.contentdm.oclc.org/cdm/ref/collection/p15932coll2/id/17954
And a different document with the same title in Jerry Tecklin Papers, 1964 (Mss 538) Box 1, Folder 5.
http://cdm15932.contentdm.oclc.org/cdm/ref/collection/p15932coll2/id/9547

Security Handbook: In "Mississippi Summer Project Material (SNCC, COFO), 1964." Jerry Tecklin Papers, 1964 (Mss 538) Box 1, Folder 5.
http://cdm15932.contentdm.oclc.org/cdm/ref/collection/p15932coll2/id/9589

Nonviolence: Two Training Documents: "Non-violence" in "Friends of SNCC— General, 1964–1967, undated." Alicia Kaplow Papers, 1964–1968 (Mss 507) Box 1, Folder 4
http://content.wisconsinhistory.org/cdm/ref/collection/p15932coll2/id/6140

And "Case Study: Statements of Discipline of Non-violent Movements" in "Freedom School mimeo materials 1963–64." Pamela P. Allen Papers, 1967–1974 (M85-013) Folder 1.
http://content.wisconsinhistory.org/cdm/ref/collection/p15932coll2/id/2133

Chapter 3. Opposition and Violence

Mississippi Readies Laws for Freedom Summer: In "The Mississippi Legislature, 1964." CORE Southern Regional Office: Legal Matters, 1964, February–September (Congress of Racial Equality. Southern Regional Office Records, 1954–1966 (Mss 85) Box 8, Folder 10.
http://cdm15932.contentdm.oclc.org/cdm/ref/collection/p15932coll2/id/16089

The Klan Ledger: Candy Brown Papers, 1964 (SC 3045).
http://cdm15932.contentdm.oclc.org/cdm/ref/collection/p15932coll2/id/34728

The Citizens' Council: A History: In "Miscellany, 1964, undated." Jerry Tecklin Papers, 1961–1963 (Mss 538) Box 1, Folder 4.
http://cdm15932.contentdm.oclc.org/cdm/ref/collection/p15932coll2/id/20536

Summary of Major Points in Testimony by Citizens of Mississippi to Panel of June 8, 1964: In "Mississippi Summer Project, miscellaneous files." Mary E. King Papers, 1962–1999 (M82-445) Box 1, Folder 21.
http://content.wisconsinhistory.org/cdm/ref/collection/p15932coll2/id/24827

"Road to Mississippi": From special issue of *Ramparts Magazine: Mississippi Eyewitness* (excerpt: pages 14–19) in "News releases, newsletters, and miscellaneous publications, 1964–1965." Carolyn Goodman Papers, 1964–2000 (Mss 192) Box 1, Folder 1. First published in *Mississippi Eyewitness . . . a Special Issue of Ramparts Magazine* (Menlo Park: *Ramparts Magazine*, 1964), from which the text here is taken.
http://cdm15932.contentdm.oclc.org/cdm/ref/collection/p15932coll2/id/27860

Memo to Parents of Mississippi Summer Volunteers, Late June 1964: In "Mississippi Freedom Project background information, 1964." Shelton Stromquist Papers, 1963–1978 (Mss 641) Box 1, Folder 3.
http://cdm15932.contentdm.oclc.org/cdm/ref/collection/p15932coll2/id/30329

Selected Hate Mail: Letter to John Lewis, in "Mississippi Freedom Project background information, 1964." Shelton Stromquist Papers, 1963–1978 (Mss 641) Box 1, Folder 3.
http://cdm15932.contentdm.oclc.org/cdm/ref/collection/p15932coll2/id/30351

    Letters to parents of Shelton Stromquist in "Mississippi Freedom Project correspondence and writings, 1964." Shelton Stromquist Papers, 1963–1978 (Mss 641) Box 1, Folder 4.
http://cdm15932.contentdm.oclc.org/cdm/ref/collection/p15932coll2/id/34654

    Letters to the Goodmans in "Hate Letters, 1964." Carolyn Goodman Papers, 1964–2000 (Micro 482) Reel 3, Segment 5.
http://cdm15932.contentdm.oclc.org/cdm/ref/collection/p15932coll2/id/36656

Notes and Letter from Neshoba County, August 15–22, 1964: In "Mississippi Project daily log; August 15–20, 1964." Walter Kaufmann Papers, 1964–1965 (SC 1210).
http://cdm15932.contentdm.oclc.org/cdm/ref/collection/p15932coll2/id/21839

Chapter 4. Voter Registration

Negro Voters by District and County, 1963: In "Atlantic City DNC Challenge, August, 1964." Howard Zinn Papers, 1956–1994 (Mss 588) Box 1, Folder 23. Originally appeared in *Congressional Quarterly*, July 5, 1963, pp. 1091–3.
http://cdm15932.contentdm.oclc.org/cdm/ref/collection/p15932coll2/id/18401

Voter Registration Summer Prospects: In "General COFO Records and Printed Matter, 1963–1965." R. Hunter Morey Papers, 1962–1967 (Mss 522) Box 3, Folder 7.
http://content.wisconsinhistory.org/cdm/ref/collection/p15932coll2/id/9863

Techniques for Field Work: Voter Registration: In "General COFO Records and Printed Matter, 1963–1965." R. Hunter Morey Papers, 1962–1967 (Mss 522) Box 3, Folder 7.
http://content.wisconsinhistory.org/cdm/ref/collection/p15932coll2/id/9869

Sworn Written Application for Registration: In "Friends of SNCC—General, 1964–1967, undated." Alicia Kaplow Papers, 1964–1968 (Mss 507) Box 1, Folder 5. This is a mimeographed facsimile produced by COFO from the form used in Mississippi courthouses. It was used in voter education classes.
http://cdm15932.contentdm.oclc.org/cdm/ref/collection/p15932coll2/id/6265

What Were We There To Do?: From a longer mimeographed report entitled, "How Shall We Sing the Lord's Song in a Strange Land? (Psalm 137:4): a Report on Hattiesburg." In "Ministerial projects and organizations, February–August 1964." Robert Beech Papers, 1963–1972 (Mss 945) Box 6, Folder 6.
http://cdm15932.contentdm.oclc.org/cdm/ref/collection/p15932coll2/id/16851

Dear Dad: In "Rust College, Holly Springs, Miss.: Dear Dad." Robert Feinglass Papers, 1964 (SC3066).
http://cdm15932.contentdm.oclc.org/cdm/ref/collection/p15932coll2/id/17027

Dear Mom and Dad: In "July 4, 1964; Letter from Ellen Lake to Mom and Dad." Ellen Lake Papers, 1964 (SC 3057).
http://cdm15932.contentdm.oclc.org/cdm/ref/collection/p15932coll2/id/14630

To Overcome Fear: From "By Charles McLaurin; To overcome fear" in "SNCC & COFO Papers." Samuel Walker Papers, 1964–1966 (Mss 655) Box 1, Folder 1.
http://cdm15932.contentdm.oclc.org/cdm/ref/collection/p15932coll2/id/12141

Chapter 5. Freedom Schools

Some Notes on Education: From "Overview of the Freedom Schools" in "Freedom Schools, 1964." Mary E. King Papers, 1962–1999 (M82-445) Box 1, Folder 16.
http://cdm15932.contentdm.oclc.org/cdm/compoundobject/collection/p15932coll2/id/24532/rec/9

Profiles of Typical Freedom Schools: Hattiesburg, Meridian, Holly Springs, and Ruleville, Spring 1964: In "Freedom Schools, 1964, Jan. 14–Dec. 2." Harry J. Bowie Papers, 1964–1967 (Mss 31) Box 1, Folder 4.
http://cdm15932.contentdm.oclc.org/cdm/ref/collection/p15932coll2/id/3833

Freedom School Curriculum Outline: In "Freedom School mimeo materials 1963–64."
Pamela P. Allen Papers, 1967–1974 (M85-013) Folder 1.
http://cdm15932.contentdm.oclc.org/cdm/ref/collection/p15932coll2/id/2132

Curriculum Part II, Unit 1: Comparison of Students' Reality with Others:
In "Freedom School mimeo materials 1963–64." Pamela P. Allen Papers, 1967–1974
(M85-013) Folder 1. The formatting and layout have been edited from the
mimeographed original.
http://cdm15932.contentdm.oclc.org/cdm/ref/collection/p15932coll2/id/2152

Curriculum Part II, Unit 6: Material Things and Soul Things: In "Freedom School
mimeo materials 1963–64." Pamela P. Allen Papers, 1967–1974 (M85-013) Folder 1.
The formatting and layout have been edited from the mimeographed original.
http://cdm15932.contentdm.oclc.org/cdm/ref/collection/p15932coll2/id/2175

Dear Family and Friends: In "Letter to Family from Cornelia Mack; August 26, 1964."
Robert W. Park Papers, 1964–1966 (SC658).
http://content.wisconsinhistory.org/cdm/ref/collection/p15932coll2/id/21079

Freedom Schools in Mississippi, September 1964: In "COFO and Mississippi Freedom
Schools." James N. Mays Papers, 1960–1967 (Mss 404) Box 1, Folder 7.
http://cdm15932.contentdm.oclc.org/cdm/ref/collection/p15932coll2/id/5091

Chapter 6. The Mississippi Freedom Democratic Party

Mississippi Freedom Candidates: In "CORE Southern Regional Office—Mississippi
Freedom Summer, 1962, August; 1964, March; 1965, October." Congress of Racial
Equality Southern Regional Office Records, 1954–1966 (Mss 85) Box 17, Folder 2.
http://content.wisconsinhistory.org/cdm/ref/collection/p15932coll2/id/16515

Notes on the Democratic National Convention Challenge: From "Statement by Charles
M. Sherrod" in "Mississippi Freedom Democratic Party and Election Challenges,
1964–1965." R. Hunter Morey Papers, 1962–1967 (Mss 522) Box 4, Folder 4.
http://content.wisconsinhistory.org/cdm/ref/collection/p15932coll2/id/8626

Instructions for the Freedom Vote and Regular Election: In "Freedom Schools—
Memos and Staff Documents, 1964." Council of Federated Organizations
Panola County Office Records, 1963–1965 (Mss 521) Box 1, Folder 8.
http://content.wisconsinhistory.org/cdm/ref/collection/p15932coll2/id/7987

Congressional Challenge Fact Sheet: In "Mississippi Freedom Democratic Party
and Election Challenges, 1964–1965." R. Hunter Morey Papers, 1962–1967
(Mss 522) Box 4, Folder 4.
http://content.wisconsinhistory.org/cdm/ref/collection/p15932coll2/id/8649

Chapter 7. After Freedom Summer

Affidavits of Violence in August–September 1964: In "Bombings and Burnings." Candy Brown Papers, 1964 (SC 3045). Quin: pp. 15–16; Taylor: p. 19; Dillon: pp. 10–12. http://content.wisconsinhistory.org/cdm/ref/collection/p15932coll2/id/34717

COFO Program, Winter 1964–Spring 1965: In "Summer Project, 1964." Howard Zinn Papers, 1956–1994 (Mss 588) Box 2, Folder 7. http://content.wisconsinhistory.org/cdm/ref/collection/p15932coll2/id/11800

"These Are the Questions": Part of a longer report entitled, "What Is SNCC?," prepared for the November 1964 SNCC retreat at Waveland, Mississippi. In "SNCC proposals, programs, workshops, 1964." Stuart Ewen Papers, 1961–1965 (Mss 531) Box 1, Folder 4. http://content.wisconsinhistory.org/cdm/ref/collection/p15932coll2/id/19595

Images

Most of the illustrations were selected from a filmstrip produced by the Mississippi Freedom Democratic Party in the winter of 1964–1965. It contains seventy-nine images depicting all aspects of the Mississippi Summer Project and can be seen online at www.wisconsinhistory.org/whi/feature/mfdp.

Illustration credits:

Page ii, WHS Image fsTecklinB1F3056; p. x, WHi Image ID 98097; p. xviii, WHS Image fsCOREsroB8f1001238; p. xx, WHi Image ID 97741; p. 34, WHi Image ID 97877; p. 64, WHi Image ID 97709; p. 110, WHi Image ID 97866; p. 134, WHi Image ID 97888; p. 146, WHi Image ID 97882; p. 172, WHi Image ID 97975; p. 183, WHi Image ID 97966; p. 192, WHi Image ID 97712: unidentified photographers; images from the archives of the Mississippi Freedom Democratic Party.

Page xv, WHi Image ID 97870; p. 129, WHi Image ID 97868: photographs by Ted Polumbaum; used by permission of the Newseum.

Page 39, WHi Image ID 32236: photograph by Harvey Richards; used by permission of his estate, www.estuarypress.com.

Page 47, WHS Image fsHeathB3F10016.

Page 119, WHS Image fsTecklinB1F3055: used by permission of photographer Matt Herron.

Page 162, WHi Image ID 97441: unidentified photographer; image from the papers of Freedom Summer volunteer Sandra Adickes.

Page 202, WHi Image ID 99501: unidentified photographer; image from the papers of Amzie Moore.

Page 208 (clockwise, from top left): Selected Hate Mail (page 102), Fannie Lou Hamer Deposition (pp. 27–28), Security Handbook (pp. 56–57), and Letter from Volunteer Training in Oxford, Ohio (pp. 50–51).

INDEX

Page numbers in *italics* refer to illustrations.

Brady, Tom, 13

Brannan, Paul J., 3–4

Brewer brothers, 139

Brown v. Board of Education (1954)

    Citizens' Councils' opposition to, 80–81

    Mississippi's refusal to enforce, 4, 11

Cameron, Benjamin F. "Ben," 13–14

Cameron, John E., 48, 178–179

Campbell, L. F., 11

Carmichael, Stokely, 65, 219

Carter, Hodding, 11, 16

Castle, Doris, 31, 33

Castle, Oretha, 31

Chaffee, Lois, 163

Chaney, James, *x*, xiv, 66, 91–95, 105, 156, 219, 221

Chatfield, Jack, 23

children, African American

    departure from Mississippi as goal of, 157, 165

    racist conditioning of, 137–140

        undoing of in Freedom Schools, 135, 140

churches in Mississippi

    African American, bombing of, 91, 99, 105, 108, *192*, 195

    white

        opposition to Freedom Summer, 65

        support for segregation, 2–4

Cinque, Joseph, 166

Citizens' Councils

    associated organizations, 12–13

    on Communist/Socialist incitement of racial tension, 81, 83, 84

    and discriminatory laws, 10

    Freedom School lessons on, 155

    functions of, xiv, 80, 82–83

    handbook of, 13, 14–15

    history of, 11, 80–84

    on integration, 84–85

    police cooperation with, 91

    pressure from civil rights activists and, 22

    prominent members and supporters of, 2, 3, 13, 14–15, 16

    school materials prepared by, 5

    state support of, 11–12, 138

    states with, 83

Civil Rights Act of 1957, Mississippi's efforts to circumvent, 69

Civil Rights Act of 1960, Mississippi's efforts to circumvent, 69

civil rights activists. *See also* violence against activists

    African Americans' fear of abandonment by, 29–30

    fired or evicted, xii, 27, 86, 137, 144, 158, 177, 198

        aid to, as part of Freedom Summer campaign, 32, 48–49

    frustration with nonviolent tactics, xv, 193

    Mississippi legislation hostile to, 67–71

    Mississippi's plans to harass, 12

    sacrifices of, xvii

civil rights documents

    acquisition by Wisconsin Historical Society, 209–223

    activists' lack of record keeping culture and, 209–210

    destroyed records, 210, 214, 215, 217, 220

    large collections of, 222

    police-confiscated records, 210

civil rights movement. *See also* Freedom Movement

    Freedom Schools' awakening of impulse toward, 165–170

    public's sanitized understanding of, xi, xvi–xvii, 66

Cobb, Charles E. "Charlie," Jr., 137–140, 163

ABOUT THE AUTHOR

Photo by Joel Heiman

Michael Edmonds is Deputy Director of the Library–Archives at the Wisconsin Historical Society and curator of its online collection of more than 30,000 pages documenting Freedom Summer. A 1976 graduate of Harvard University, he earned an MS degree at Simmons College in 1979 and taught part-time at the University of Wisconsin–Madison from 1986 to 2010. For the last decade he has led the teams that share the Society's manuscripts, photographs, and rare books on the web. The author of several articles and books, Edmonds has won national awards from the American Folklore Society and the American Association for State and Local History.